THE PROBLEM OF MARKAN GENRE

Society of Biblical Literature

Academia Biblica

Saul M. Olyan,
Old Testament Editor

Mark Allan Powell,
New Testament Editor

Number 3

The Problem of Markan Genre
The Gospel of Mark and the Jewish Novel

The Problem of Markan Genre
The Gospel of Mark and the Jewish Novel

Michael E. Vines

Society of Biblical Literature
Atlanta

The Problem of Markan Genre
The Gospel of Mark and the Jewish Novel

Library of Congress Cataloging-in-Publication Data

Vines, Michael E.
   The problem of Markan genre : the Gospel of Mark and the Jewish novel / Michael E. Vines.
      p. cm. — (Academia biblica series ; no. 3)
Includes bibliographical references.
   ISBN 1-58983-030-X (paper : alk. paper)
   1. Bible. N.T. Mark—Criticism, interpretation, etc. 2. Classical fiction—History and criticism. 3. Jewish fiction—History and criticism. I. Title. II. Academia Biblica (Series : Society of Biblical Literature) ; no. 3.
   BS2585.52 .V56 2002b
   226.3'066—dc21

                                    2002006305

07 06 05 04 03 02   5 4 3 2 1

Printed in the United States of America
on acid-free paper

"The character of the evidence depends on the shape of the examination."

C. S. Lewis (*The Discarded Image*, 223)

TABLE OF CONTENTS

ACKNOWLEDGMENTS

In the process of completing any project of this scope, one quite naturally incurs a great many debts. Although words alone will not suffice to repay them, I will nevertheless take this opportunity to offer words of thanks and gratitude.

I owe my ongoing interest in the Gospel of Mark, in the first place, to Paul Beyer, who taught me how to ask questions and look for answers. These rough skills were honed by my teachers at Fuller Theological Seminary, especially Donald Hagner and Marianne Meye Thompson. While at Fuller Seminary, it was also a special privilege to work with Robert Guelich, who further contributed to my interest in the Gospel of Mark and initiated my interest in Markan genre.

The generous financial support of Union Theological Seminary—PSCE allowed me to pursue my interest in Mark, and the marvelous resources of the William Smith Morton Library at Union Seminary enriched my research. Among the able staff of the Morton Library, I owe a special debt of gratitude to Patsy Verreault. My thoughts on the Gospel of Mark and its literary genre benefited greatly from many conversations with my doctoral colleagues Blake Grangaard, William Malas, and James Miller. I forged the thesis of the dissertation in conversation with my advisor Jack Dean Kingsbury, and his many helpful suggestions, along with those of the other members of my dissertation committee, John Carroll and James Brashler, greatly improved the final project.

I completed this dissertation while filling a temporary vacancy at George Fox Evangelical Seminary. For the past two years, George Fox University has provided additional financial support for my research, and my faculty colleagues at the seminary have faithfully supported me with their friendship and words of encouragement.

To all of these people and the many and diverse ways they contributed to this project I am deeply grateful. On a more personal note, my parents, Howard and Dorothy Vines, have been steadfast in their support for me throughout this project. I owe my most profound debt of gratitude, however, to my children, David and Jeanette, and my wife Alice. This work is dedicated to them for the many sacrifices they have made over the years to see this project to its completion.

ABBREVIATIONS

Abbreviations follow those of Patrick H. Alexander, et al., *The SBL Handbook of Style: For Ancient Near Eastern, Biblical, and Early Christian Studies* (Peabody, Mass.: Hendrickson, 1999), and the *Oxford Classical Dictionary*. Additional abbreviations are as follows:

A&A	*Art and Answerability*
ALC	*Ancient Literary Criticism*
CAGN	*Collected Ancient Greek Novels*
DI	*The Dialogic Imagination*
FM	*The Formal Method in Literary Scholarship*
PDP	*Problems of Dostoevsky's Poetics*
SpG	*Speech Genres and Other Late Essays*
THL	Theory and History of Literature
TPA	*Toward a Philosophy of the Act*
MPL	*Marxism and the Philosophy of Language*
UTPSS	University of Texas Press Slavic Series

Chapter One

THE GOSPEL OF MARK AND
THE GENRE OF THE GOSPELS

Alastair Fowler claims that genre is the most important code of literary *langue*, since "genre primarily has to do with communication." For Fowler, genre is "an instrument not of classification or prescription, but of meaning."[1] Similarly, C. S. Lewis reminds us that: "The first qualification for judging any piece of workmanship . . . is to know what it is—what it was intended to do and how it is meant to be used."[2] If we fail to identify the genre of a literary work correctly, it is very likely that we will misconstrue the function of both its individual parts and the aesthetic unity of the work as a whole. Its importance notwithstanding, the genre of the gospels has shown itself to be a perplexing problem for New Testament scholars. Simply stated, the problem is that, without significant qualification, the gospels do not resemble any of the standard genres of antiquity.

New Testament scholars have long tried to explain the generic relationship between the gospels and the literature of the Hellenistic period. In spite of numerous attempts to clarify this relationship, no single hypothesis has carried the field. The gospels resist a facile classification

---

[1] Alastair Fowler, *Kinds of Literature: An Introduction to the Theory of Genres and Modes* (Cambridge: Harvard University Press, 1982), 22.

[2] C. S. Lewis, *A Preface to Paradise Lost*, rev. and enlarged ed. (Oxford: Oxford University Press, 1942), 1. I owe this quote to Christopher Bryan, *A Preface to Mark: Notes on the Gospel in Its Literary and Cultural Settings* (Oxford: Oxford University Press, 1993), 9.

among the genres of antiquity. If we assume, with the majority of New Testament scholars, that the Gospel of Mark was the first narrative account of Jesus' life the problem of its genre takes on increased importance.[3] Nevertheless, the literary antecedents of Mark's Gospel remain obscure. In fact, one scholar recently referred to Mark's genre as "the elusive Holy Grail of gospel studies."[4] What literary genre (or genres) influenced the Markan author's arrangement, selection, and presentation of the oral and written materials at his disposal? A convincing answer to this question would presumably offer further insight into the purpose of Mark's Gospel. Unfortunately, contemporary research into the genre of the gospel has reached a stalemate: either Mark belongs to a subspecies of Greco-Roman biography, or it is *sui generis*. As we shall see, neither of these suggestions is satisfactory because each in its own way fails to account for the inherent complexity of genre.

A Brief History of the Problem of Gospel Genre[5]

The investigation of gospel genre has tended to oscillate between two opposing positions. On the one hand, there is the analogical approach, which claims that an existing genre can account for the written form of the gospels. On the other hand, there is the evolutionary approach, which claims that the gospels are a unique creation of the church. The choice of an analogical or evolutionary approach to the

---

[3] William R. Telford identifies the determination of Mark's literary genre as one of the persistent problems of Markan research. See William R. Telford, "The Pre-Markan Tradition in Recent Research (1980–1990)," in *The Four Gospels 1992: Festschrift Frans Neirynck*, ed. F. Van Segbroeck et al., BETL, 100 (Leuven: Leuven University Press/Peeters, 1992), 2:696, 711; idem, "Introduction: The Interpretation of Mark: A History of Developments and Issues," in *The Interpretation of Mark*, 2d ed., ed. William Telford, Studies in New Testament Interpretation, ed. Robert Morgan (Edinburgh: T&T Clark, 1995), 15–17.

[4] Dennis R. MacDonald, *The Homeric Epics and the Gospel of Mark* (New Haven: Yale University Press, 2000), 3.

[5] For more detailed surveys of the debate surrounding the genre of the gospels see David E. Aune, *The New Testament in Its Literary Environment*, Library of Early Christianity, ed. Wayne A. Meeks, vol. 8 (Philadelphia: Westminster, 1987), 17–76; Richard A. Burridge, *What Are the Gospels? A Comparison with Graeco-Roman Biography*, SNTSMS, ed. G. N. Stanton, 70 (Cambridge: Cambridge University Press, 1992), 3–25; and Detlev Dormeyer, *Evangelium als literarische und theologische Gattung*, ErFor, Bd. 263 (Darmstadt: Wissenschaftliche Buchgesellschaft, 1989).

problem of gospel genre dictates in part which aspect of the text is stressed. The evolutionary approach, which finds the origins of the "gospel genre" in the early Christian kerygma, stresses the content of the gospels. The analogical approach highlights features the gospels share in common with other ancient literature and thereby stresses formal aspects of the gospels.

Scholars who accent formal similarities between Mark and the literature of the Hellenistic period have proposed a number of different genres. Among the more prominent genres proposed are aretalogy,[6] encomium,[7] memorabilia,[8] Socratic dialogue,[9] Greek tragedy,[10] and most recently Homeric epic.[11] Few of these proposals have gained broad support among Markan scholars. The genre that generally elicits the most attention is Greco-Roman biography. An examination of the ebb and flow of scholarly opinion concerning the relationship between the gospels and Greco-Roman biography will provide a useful point of de-

---

[6] Morton Smith, "Prolegomena to a Discussion of Aretalogies, Divine Men, the Gospels and Jesus," *JBL* 90 (1971): 174–99; Dieter Georgi, "The Records of Jesus in the Light of Ancient Accounts of Revered Men," in *SBLSP*, vol. 2, ed. Lane C. McGaughy (n.p.: Society of Biblical Literature, 1972), 527–42; and Jonathan Z. Smith, "Good News Is No News: Aretalogy and Gospel," in *Christianity, Judaism and Other Greco-Roman Cults: Studies for Morton Smith at Sixty*, Part 1, *New Testament*, ed. Jacob Neusner, Studies in Judaism and Late Antiquity, ed. Jacob Neusner, vol. 12 (Leiden: E. J. Brill, 1975), 21–38.

[7] Philip L. Shuler, *A Genre for the Gospels: The Biographical Character of Matthew* (Philadelphia: Fortress, 1982). Shuler argued that Mark belongs to the genre of encomium biography in "The Synoptic Gospels and the Problem of Genre" (Ph.D. diss., McMaster University, 1975), 225–59.

[8] Vernon K. Robbins, *Jesus the Teacher: A Socio-Rhetorical Interpretation of Mark* (Philadelphia: Fortress, 1984), 60–69.

[9] David Lawrence Barr, "Toward a Definition of the Gospel Genre: A Generic Analysis and Comparison of the Synoptic Gospels and the Socratic Dialogues by Means of Aristotle's Theory of Tragedy" (Ph.D. diss., Florida State University, 1974).

[10] Gilbert G. Bilezikian, *The Liberated Gospel: A Comparison of the Gospel of Mark and Greek Tragedy*, Baker Biblical Monograph (Grand Rapids: Baker, 1977); Bascom Wallis, *Mark's Memory of the Future: A Study in the Art of Theology* (North Richland Hills, Tex.: Bibla, 1995); Friedrich Gustav Lang, "Kompositionsanalyse des Markusevangeliums," *ZTK* 74 (1977): 1–24; Curtis Beach, *The Gospel of Mark: Its Making and Meaning* (New York: Harper & Brothers, 1959), 48–51; and Ernest W. Burch, "Tragic Action in the Second Gospel: A Study in the Narrative of Mark," *JR* 11 (1931): 346–58.

[11] MacDonald, *Homeric Epics and the Gospel of Mark*.

parture for our own inquiry into the literary heritage of Mark's Gospel. The history of this debate will show what is at stake in the debate over gospel genre, and why the issue has not yet been satisfactorily resolved.

Analogies with Greco-Roman Biography

Clyde Weber Votaw first suggested that the gospels are a subset of Greco-Roman biography in 1915.[12] In retrospect, it is clear that Votaw's interests were primarily historical rather than literary. His main concern was to explain how the gospels, which present "portraits" of Jesus rather than precise "photographs," could nevertheless convey historically reliable information about Jesus.[13] By comparing the gospels with other ancient writings, he hoped to demonstrate that the gospels were at least as reliable as documents that record the life and activity of other famous teachers like Epictetus, Socrates, and Apollonius of Tyana. In making this comparison, Votaw emphasized that ancient biography was, strictly speaking, not a historical enterprise. Ancient biographers did not conduct careful scientific research into the life of their subject in order to preserve their memory accurately for posterity. Instead, their biographies were of a more "popular" nature. According to Votaw, ancient biographies were "generally written to eulogize their subjects, or to affect political opinion and action, or to teach uprightness and usefulness by example."[14] Thus, Votaw believed the purpose of the gospels was

> to restore the reputation of a great and good man who had been publicly executed and defamed by the state; to re-establish his influence as a supreme teacher in respect to right living and thinking; and to render available to all the message of truth and duty to which each had made it his life-work to promulgate.[15]

To make his case, Votaw pointed to parallels between the life and activity of Jesus and the lives of Epictetus, Socrates and Apollonius. Furthermore, he noted that the gospels are similar to the biographies of these three figures in purpose, method, and the type of material

---

[12] Clyde Weber Votaw, "The Gospels and Contemporary Biographies," *AJT* 19 (1915): 45–73 and 217–49; reprinted as *The Gospels and Contemporary Biographies in the Greco-Roman World*, FBBS 27 (Philadelphia: Fortress, 1970).

[13] Ibid., 4, 35, 61.

[14] Ibid., 7.

[15] Ibid., 58.

they preserve. The difficulty with Votaw's approach is that it never directly addressed the literary question of genre. Similarities between Jesus and the figures of ancient biography are an inadequate basis upon which to compare the literary products that record those lives. Authors can compose very different literary works about the same figure, let alone about similar figures. Votaw's observations on similarities of method, purpose, and content are also too general to establish a generic connection between the gospels and Greco-Roman biography. As we shall see, a general "parallelism" between literary works is not sufficient to establish a generic connection.[16]

Form Critical Reactions to the Comparison with Greco-Roman Biography

Votaw's thesis fell into disfavor under the influence of form criticism.[17] Critics, like Karl Ludwig Schmidt, pointed to the superficiality of the parallels adduced by Votaw. In many ways, the gospels are quite unlike Greco-Roman biographies. Although Votaw was aware of these dissimilarities, according to Schmidt, he failed to appreciate their importance. Schmidt emphasized the unliterary quality of the gospel writings in contrast to the sophisticated literary style of the biographies. In contrast to the *Hochliteratur* of sophisticated Greek culture, the gospels are *Kleinliteratur*. The gospels are folk literature, an unsophisticated creation of the early Christian community.[18] For Schmidt, Mark is

---

[16] Ibid., 27.

[17] Rudolf Bultmann, *The History of the Synoptic Tradition*, trans. John Marsh, rev. ed. (New York: Harper & Row, 1963), 369–72; idem, "The Gospels (Form)," in *Twentieth Century Theology in the Making*, vol. 1, *Themes of Biblical Theology*, ed. J. Pelikan, trans. R. A. Wilson, Fontana Library Theology and Philosophy, 12/6, 86–92 (New York: Harper & Row, 1969); Karl Ludwig Schmidt, "Die Stellung der Evangelien in der allgemeinen Literaturgeschichte," in *EYXAPIΣTHPION: Studien zur Religion und Literatur des Alten und Neuen Testaments*, hrsg. Hermann Gunkel and Hans Schmidt, FRLANT (Göttingen: Vandenhoeck und Ruprecht, 1923), vol. 2, 50–134, reprinted in *Neues Testament Judentum Kirche: Kleine Schriften*, hrsg. Gerhard Sauter (Munich: Chr. Kaiser, 1981), 37–130. References to Schmidt refer to the reprint.

[18] Martin Dibelius also applied the distinction between *Hochliteratur* and *Kleinliteratur* to the gospels, *From Tradition to Gospel*, trans. Bertram Lee Woolf (Greenwood, S.C.: Attic, 1982), 2. The description of the gospels as *Kleinliteratur* was only a moderate improvement over Franz Overbeck's earlier description of them as *Urliteratur*. See Hubert Cancik, "Die Gattung Evangelium: Markus im Rahmen der antiken Historiographie," in *Markus-Philologie: Historische,*

not a self-conscious author with literary aspirations, but a naïve teller of folk stories.[19]

Schmidt also finds another indication of the unliterary quality of the gospels in the relative absence of the author's personality. In Greco-Roman biography, the personality of the author is a ubiquitous guiding presence. In addition to recording important events and sayings, the author of the Greco-Roman biography tells his reader how to evaluate the hero. The gospel narratives, however, lack this kind of authorial presence. The evangelists tend to retreat behind their narratives, and rely more heavily on direct speech and dialogue.[20]

Rudolf Bultmann followed the main lines of Schmidt's argument against comparing the gospels with the literature of antiquity. Since the gospels "show no interest in historical or biographical matters" and "contain no account of Jesus' human personality, his origin, education or development, or his appearance and character," Bultmann concluded that they could not be favorably compared to Greco-Roman biography.[21] Even a cursory sampling of Greco-Roman biography suggests that most examples of the genre would fail to meet Bultmann's standards. Ancient biography had little interest in psychological development. Nor does historical accuracy appear to be its main concern. Nevertheless, Bultmann's description of the gospels as "expanded cult legends" does indeed place them beyond the scope of Greco-Roman biography.[22] For Bultmann, the gospels constitute a unique literary class, of which Mark was the progenitor, precisely because of their unique func-

---

literargeschichtliche und stilistische Untersuchungen zum zweiten Evangelium, hrsg. Hubert Cancik, WUNT, hrsg. Martin Hengel und Otfried Hofius, 33 (Tübingen: J. C. B. Mohr [Paul Siebeck], 1984), 87–90. Erhardt Güttgemanns has subjected the distinction between *Hochliteratur* and *Kleinliteratur* to critical scrutiny in his *Candid Questions concerning Gospel Form Criticism: A Methodological Sketch of the Fundamental Problematics of Form and Redaction Criticism,* trans. William G. Doty, PTMS, ed. Dikran Y. Hadidian, no. 26 (Pittsburgh: Pickwick, 1979), 66–67, 136–39.

[19] "Der Evangelist berichtet eben wie ein naiver Volkserzähler, er bringt Einzel-Erzählungen (Anekdoten) oder Gruppen von solchen, wobei es auf Zeit und Ort der Geschehnisse nicht ankommt," W. Heitmüller, "Jesus Christus: I Quellen des Lebens Jesu," *RGG¹* 3. 354. Quoted with approval by Schmidt, "Die Stellung," 65.

[20] Marius Reiser, "Die Stellung der Evangelien in der antiken Literaturgeschichte," *ZNW* 90 (1999): 18.

[21] Bultmann, "Gospels (Form)," 87.

[22] Bultmann, *History,* 371–72; "Gospels (Form)," 88.

tion within the early Christian community.[23] Even close analogies with "popular oriental books" such as *Ahiqar* fail because they lack the mythic and cultic orientation of the gospels.[24] Bultmann believed that the unique experience of the early Christian community led to the spontaneous creation of a new literary form essentially discontinuous with past forms. It was the kerygma, rather than literary antecedents, that dictated the shape of this new genre.[25]

Of course, the kerygma itself never constituted a genre of literature. Instead, it presented in summary fashion the most significant aspects of the Church's claims about Jesus (e.g., Acts 2:14–39; 3:13–26; 10:36–43; I Cor 15:1–7).[26] Mark's Gospel certainly coincides with the main outlines of the primitive Christian kerygma. This correspondence, however, pertains only to its content and not to its literary form. There is nothing in the kerygma that requires the creation of a previously unknown form of literature. The Church adapted other literary genres such as epistle, sermon, and apocalypse to convey its kerygmatic message, so there is no compelling reason to assert the need for the creation of a *sui generis* literary form to accommodate the kerygma. It seems unlikely, therefore, that the kerygma alone dictated the literary form of Mark's Gospel.

In the past, literary scholarship often assumed that genres evolved in a deliberate manner.[27] According to this theory, new genres were the necessary product of the incremental mixing and perfecting of old genres. Recent literary scholarship offers a more nuanced approach.

---

[23] Bultmann, *History*, 371.

[24] Ibid., 372.

[25] Others, perhaps under the influence of the form critics, have also advanced this thesis: Norman Perrin, *What is Redaction Criticism?* GBS, ed. Dan O. Via, Jr. (Philadelphia: Fortress, 1969), 75; Amos Niven Wilder, *Early Christian Rhetoric: The Language of the Gospels* (Cambridge: Harvard University Press, 1971), 28; G. N. Stanton, "The Gospels and Ancient Biographical Writing," in *Jesus of Nazareth in New Testament Preaching*, SNTSMS, ed. Matthew Black, 27 (Cambridge: Cambridge University Press, 1974), 117–36; Howard Clark Kee, *Community of the New Age: Studies in Mark's Gospel* (Philadelphia: Westminster, 1977; reprinted with corrections, ROSE 6, Macon, Ga.: Mercer University Press, 1983), 30; and Robert Guelich, "The Gospel Genre," in *The Gospel and the Gospels*, ed. P. Stuhlmacher (Grand Rapids: Eerdmans, 1991), 205.

[26] See C. H. Dodd's description of the kerygma in *The Apostolic Preaching and Its Developments* (New York: Harper & Brothers, 1962), 21–23.

[27] For a notable critique of this assumption, see R. K. Hack, "The Doctrine of Literary Forms," *Harv. Stud.* 27 (1916): 1–65.

New genres do not evolve naturally. Authors intentionally create new genres to meet the specific needs of a community of readers.[28] These new genres are, however, never *sui generis* but are fashioned out of old literary forms and traditional topics. New genres, therefore, do not emerge through spontaneous evolution but instead have a necessary relation to antecedent genres. To understand this transformation we must identify a literary work's antecedent genres and investigate the cultural conditions that brought the new form to life.

The limitations of the description of the gospels as *sui generis* notwithstanding, there is perhaps some merit to the suggestion the kerygma placed unusual demands on written communication. The power of the Christian message may have been difficult to convey using established literary genres. Nevertheless, today scholars maintain that it is virtually impossible for a genre to emerge apart from some connection to antecedent literature.[29] Indeed, it is nearly inconceivable that an author could create a literary genre with no connection to pre-existing literary forms. Even if we appeal to divine inspiration, a new genre would be a problematic vehicle for proclamation. Genre functions as a conventional bridge between author and reader, therefore an utterly new genre would be either incomprehensible, or at least seriously prone to misinterpretation. A new genre cannot emerge *ex nihilo*. Instead, authors create new genres by modifying existing literary forms. The needs of the community animate this creative process and therefore, to some extent, the special demands of the kerygma may have provided the impetus for the composition of the gospels. Nevertheless, the kerygma alone cannot account for the gospels' *literary form*.[30] The notion of a *sui generis* gospel genre therefore fails to resolve the question of the gospels' generic relationship to the literature of antiquity.

---

[28] Frank Kermode, *The Genesis of Secrecy: On the Interpretation of Narrative* (Cambridge: Harvard University Press, 1979), 162–63; Fowler, *Kinds of Literature*, 147–69; Francis Cairns, *Generic Conceptions in Greek and Roman Poetry* (Edinburgh: Edinburgh University Press, 1972), 129.

[29] Kermode, *Genesis of Secrecy*, 162–63; E. D. Hirsch, Jr., *Validity in Interpretation* (New Haven: Yale University Press, 1967), 76; and Fowler, *Kinds of Literature*, 20–24.

[30] Guelich, "Gospel Genre," 202.

The Recent Revival of Votaw's Thesis

The recent revival of a generic connection between the gospels and Greco-Roman biography represents dissatisfaction with the form critic's suggestion that the gospels were *sui generis* and a return to the main lines of Votaw's thesis. In the late seventies, Charles Talbert challenged Bultmann's claim that the gospels constituted a unique literary class wholly unrelated to Greco-Roman biography.[31] Talbert's dismantling of Bultmann's objections against such a comparison, however, did not constitute proof of such a connection. David Aune, whose thorough examination of Talbert's thesis exposed its many deficiencies, nevertheless has also come to advocate a connection between the gospels and Greco-Roman biography.[32] However, the most significant attempt to defend the connection between the gospels and Greco-Roman biography is that of Richard Burridge.[33]

Burridge addresses the objections customarily raised against the biographical description of the gospels in hopes of establishing more firmly their biographical qualities. He contends that Greco-Roman biography, or βίος, exhibits enough flexibility to account for any perceived differences with the gospels. Having accounted for these differences, Burridge is confident that the gospels fit comfortably within the genre of Greco-Roman biography, broadly conceived, and concludes that first century readers would have recognized them as such.

Although Burridge does not deny that differences exist between the canonical gospels and examples of Greco-Roman biography, he contends that, in both number and importance, the similarities far outweigh the differences.[34] In support of this claim, Burridge appeals to the sustained focus on the protagonist in both the gospels and the

---

[31] Charles H. Talbert, *What is a Gospel? The Genre of the Canonical Gospels* (Philadelphia: Fortress, 1977; reprint, Macon, Ga.: Mercer University Press, 1985). References refer to the reprint edition.

[32] David E. Aune, "The Problem of the Genre of the Gospels: A Critique of C. H. Talbert's *What is a Gospel?*" in *Gospel Perspectives: Studies of History and Tradition in the Four Gospels*, ed. R. T. France and D. Wenham, vol. 2 (Sheffield: JSOT, 1981), 9–60. For Aune's advocacy of a connection with biography, see *The New Testament in Its Literary Environment*, 46–76; "The Gospels as Hellenistic Biography," *Mosaic* vol. 20, no. 4 (1987): 1–10; and "The Gospels: Biography or Theology?" *Bible Review* 6, no. 1 (1990): 14.

[33] Burridge, *What Are the Gospels?* Christopher Bryan follows the main lines of Burridge's argument in *A Preface to Mark*.

[34] Burridge, *What are the Gospels?* 258.

Greco-Roman biographies. This focus is evident first in the tendency of both the gospels and the biographies to name their protagonist at the outset. It is also apparent in the frequency with which the protagonist appears as the subject of verbs. Moreover, Burridge contends that in both the gospels and the biographies the length, mode, and scale of the presentation are similar.[35] For Burridge, therefore, the conclusion is inescapable: the canonical gospels belong to a subset of the Greco-Roman genre of biography.

The breadth and flexibility of Burridge's definition of Greco-Roman biography limit somewhat the hermeneutical implications of his analysis—a limitation that Burridge himself acknowledges.[36] He defines Greco-Roman biography as works that "concentrate on one individual" and share a "similar appearance, length and structure, mode of representation and units of composition."[37] Such a definition is broad enough to include a wide array of literary works. Furthermore, some of the formal similarities adduced by Burridge, such as the use of *chreia* and anecdote, are general enough that they might simply reflect instruction in the *progymnasmata* rather than familiarity with Greco-Roman biography.

Nor does Burridge claim that the biographical qualities of Mark's Gospel necessarily depend on a direct connection with Greco-Roman models. He suggests instead that the biographical features of Mark may simply be a natural, even unconscious, consequence of Mark's decision to present his Christian message with an emphasis on the life, deeds, and words of Jesus.[38] Despite these concessions, however, Burridge still insists on the importance of a generic connection with Greco-Roman biography. Burridge's determination to relate Mark to Greco-Roman biography derives in part from his conviction that the gospels themselves form a discrete (sub-)class of literature. Burridge

---

[35] Ibid., 218.

[36] Ibid., 255–56. Several reviewers underscored the significance of this defect. See Adela Yarbro Collins, *JR* 75 (1995): 245–46; Charles H. Talbert, *JBL* 112 (1993): 715; Loveday Alexander, *EvQ* 66 (1994): 75; Christopher Tuckett, *Theology* 96 (1993): 75. For criticism of Burridge's thesis from a different quarter see Mark Edwards, "Biography and the Biographic," in *Portraits: Biographical Representation in the Greek and Latin Literature of the Roman Empire*, ed. M. J. Edwards and Simon Swain (Oxford: Clarendon, 1997), 228–31.

[37] Burridge, *What are the Gospels?* 189.

[38] Ibid., 253, 248–49.

may be correct when he postulates a generic relationship between Matthew and Luke and the Greco-Roman biographies. Matthew and Luke do exhibit more of the characteristic features of Greco-Roman biography. Concerning Mark, however, he appears to have overstated his case.

Burridge claims that the identification of the synoptic gospels as a subspecies of Greco-Roman biography underscores the thematic importance of Jesus as their main character. He claims that if the gospels are biography, "then the key to their interpretation must be the person of their subject, Jesus of Nazareth."[39] Furthermore, if the gospels are biographies, Burridge suggests that we might expect to find in them the same "didactic, apologetic, and polemical purposes" that are characteristic of Greco-Roman biography. Although Burridge never states it explicitly, his analysis suggests that the purpose of Mark's Gospel is therefore the same as that of Greco-Roman biography: to provide a moral paradigm for readers to emulate.[40] Ultimately, the plausibility of this suggestion rests on the strength of the connection with Greco-Roman biography. If Mark shares only a weak connection with Greco-Roman biography, then its purposes may be quite different. Thus, if we define biography as a work that focuses on the actions of a single individual, then Mark may be such a work. If, however, the connection between Mark and specific examples of Greco-Roman biography is indeterminate, we may look elsewhere for a generic model that is more hermeneutically useful.

Burridge may overstate the formal continuity of the Gospel of Mark with Greco-Roman biography, but even if the formal similarities were stronger, other reasons exist for questioning his analysis. A formal analysis, such as Burridge's, is unable to account for significant aspects of the content of Mark. There are major motifs in Mark that cannot be subsumed under the rubric of a biographical account of Jesus. For example, in Mark, Jesus' activity is significant primarily as an earthly manifestation of divine presence and action. Jesus receives a divine commission from God to act as God's agent (1:11; 9:7). Some of the characters in the gospel recognize this. The crowds are amazed and glorify God when Jesus heals the paralytic (2:12). The demons recognize in Jesus the power and authority of God (1:24; 3:11; 5:7). Even the cen-

---

[39] Ibid., 256.
[40] Ibid., 252.

turion at the foot of the cross recognizes Jesus' special relationship to God (15:39). In these passages, the central concern is not a biographical interest in the earthly deeds of Jesus per se, but a soteriological interest in the way Jesus manifests God's presence through his earthly activity.

A biographical account of the earthly Jesus is also unable to account for the predictions concerning the eschatological Son of Man (8:38; 13:26; 14:62). The classical scholar Arnaldo Momigliano defines ancient biography as "an account of the life of a man from birth to death."[41] The Markan narrative, however, cannot be so conceived. Mark enigmatically connects Jesus' future role with that of the Son of Man. In his capacity as Son of Man, Jesus will return under the aegis of divine power to judge the world. Jesus' future role as eschatological Son of Man explodes the normal boundaries of biographical time. Not only does Jesus' role as Son of Man extend beyond the story-world of Mark; it also transcends the limits of historical time altogether. Thus, in his description of Jesus, Mark's story extends beyond the biographical boundary of death to Jesus' role as the future eschatological judge.

Therefore, the content of Mark, with its themes of Jesus' divine commission and his role as the eschatological Son of Man, exceeds the generic limitations of Greco-Roman biography. Burridge tries to account for the content of Mark by claiming that both Mark and the biographies focus on a single individual. Nevertheless, his description of such similarity in content is too general to be persuasive. Because the formal connection between Mark and Greco-Roman biography is tenuous, and their content is dissimilar in important respects, the attempt to classify Mark as a sub-set of biography is inadequate.[42]

David Aune defends the biographical qualities of the gospel along lines similar to those of Burridge. He is more cognizant, however, of differences between the gospels and Greco-Roman biography. He observes that ancient biography was primarily interested in individuals as "representative types," and it was, therefore, "more *idealistic* than *realistic*."[43] These idealistic presentations displayed the hero as a

---

[41] Arnaldo Momigliano, *The Development of Greek Biography*, expanded ed. (Cambridge: Harvard University Press, 1993), 11.

[42] Some of those who reviewed the book have also expressed skepticism concerning the usefulness of Burridge's conclusions. See Charles H. Talbert, *JBL* 112 (1993): 715; Christopher Tuckett, *Theology* 96 (1993): 75; and Loveday Alexander, *The Evangelical Quarterly* 66 (1994): 75.

[43] Aune, "Greco-Roman Biography," in *Greco-Roman Literature and the*

model of traditional virtues, or, conversely, as a cautionary example against common vices. Aune admits that the gospels do not share this type of content with Greco-Roman biography. He writes,

> Unlike Hellenistic biography . . . Jesus is *not* presented as a paradigm of virtue, at least not in the Hellenistic understanding of the term. Nor is there a great deal of explicit information suggesting that lives of Jesus were intended to serve as models for early Christian readers.[44]

Instead, Aune bases his comparison of the gospels with Greco-Roman biography on formal similarities. The main points of comparison are the stereotypical presentation of the main character, a static notion of personality, and an anachronistic approach to a historical figure. A comparison along these lines would be stronger if these similarities were unique to Greco-Roman biography. Unfortunately, in the ancient world, other genres, such as Greek romance, shared these three features. What is distinctive of Greco-Roman biography is the presentation of the hero as an ethical model, and yet it is precisely here that the gospels are different.

Aune's separation of form from content further weakens his argument. He maintains that the content of the gospels is clearly Jewish and Christian, while their form is Greco-Roman. He writes that "the message is Christian; the background of the message, the soil in which it grew, is Jewish; but the form is Hellenistic biography."[45] This suggests that literary form is merely a container that an author can fill indiscriminately with content. This is a weak premise upon which to build a successful theory of literature. As René Wellek and Austin Warren note:

> Instead of dichotomizing 'form-content', we should think of matter and then of 'form', that which aesthetically organizes its 'matter'. In a successful work of art, the materials are completely assimilated into the form. . . . All of these [materials] . . . exist outside the work of art, in other modes; but in a successful poem or novel they are pulled into polyphonic relations by the dynamic of aesthetic purpose.[46]

New Testament: Selected Forms and Genres, ed. David E. Aune, SBLSBS, ed. Bernard Brandon Scott, no. 21 (Atlanta: Scholars, 1988), 109–10.

[44] Aune, "The Gospels as Hellenistic Biography," 7.

[45] Aune, "The Gospels: Biography or Theology?" 37.

[46] René Wellek and Austin Warren, *Theory of Literature*, 3rd ed. (New York: Harcourt Brace Jovanovich, 1956), 241. On the unity of form and content see

Of course, some might quarrel over the description of the gospels as "successful works of art," but, in general, Wellek and Warren's point is still valid. Products of human creativity achieve a unity of form and content through the creative intention of their creator. We would expect then, according to Aune's scheme, to find some overlap of form and content. Thus, the "Hellenistic" aspect of the gospel's form should also be detectable in its content, and "Jewish" or "Christian" content should likewise influence its form. Aune, however, leaves the aesthetic unity of the gospels unexamined.

One of Aune's more interesting suggestions is that the gospels might be favorably compared to the late second century C.E. biography of Secundus the silent philosopher. The *Life of Secundus* is an unpretentious biography aimed at a popular audience. In that respect, it is a somewhat unusual work. There are few examples of "popular, novelistic type" biographies in Greco-Roman literature.[47] In addition to *Secundus*, surviving examples include Xenophon's *Cyropaedia* and the *Life of Aesop*. These examples of popular biography may indeed compare more favorably with the gospels, but not for the formalistic reasons adduced by Aune.

A more recent attempt to compare the gospels with the "popular, novelistic type" of Greco-Roman biography is that of Lawrence Wills.[48] Wills proposes that at an early stage, an *Urgospel* took shape under the influence of a biographical tradition similar to that found in the *Life of Aesop*. According to Wills, this *Urgospel* is detectable in both Mark and John, who made use of it independently from one another. Wills successfully argues that "popular" biographies, like those of Secundus and Aesop, are more comparable to the gospels than sophisticated biographies like those of Plutarch and Suetonius. However, such comparisons are nevertheless inadequate. They are largely dependent on the comparison of formal similarities and fail to account for

---

also Seymour Chatman, "On Defining 'Form'," *New Literary History* 2 (1971): 217–28; and Wilder, *Early Christian Rhetoric*, xxii, 4, 25.

[47] As Aune notes ("Greco-Roman Literature," 109), this is one of Klaus Berger's four classes of ancient biography. See Klaus Berger, "Hellenistische Gattungen im Neuen Testament, Erster Teil: Methodische Vorfragen," in *ANRW* 2.25.2, hrsg. H. Temporini und W. Haase (Berlin und New York: Walter de Gruyter, 1984), 1236.

[48] Lawrence M. Wills, *The Quest of the Historical Gospel: Mark, John, and the Origins of the Gospel Genre* (London: Routledge, 1997).

important differences between "popular" biographies and the gospels. We will examine more closely the nature of these "popular" biographies, as well as their possible relation to Markan genre, in chapters three and four.

Lingering Doubts about Biography and the Genre of Mark

In spite of its persistence as an explanation of the gospel's genre, many scholars continue to express dissatisfaction with the connection with Greco-Roman biography.[49] These dissenting voices come from a number of different quarters, but they are especially common among those who employ a literary approach to the gospel narratives. While these critics do not agree on a solution to the problem of gospel genre, their dissatisfaction is instructive, since it draws attention to problems that continue to plague the comparison to Greco-Roman biography.

One of the earliest dissenting voices among literary critics belonged to Eric Auerbach, who stressed the inadequacy of Greco-Roman forms to account for the dialogical quality of the gospels. For Auerbach, the striking realism of the gospels makes any connection with the standard Greco-Roman genres impossible. Commenting on the depiction of Peter's denial, he observes that it could not possibly fit within any of the ancient genres: "It is too serious for comedy, too contemporary and everyday for tragedy, politically too insignificant for history—and the form which was given it is one of such immediacy that its like does not exist in the literature of antiquity."[50] The most important symptom of this difference, which, as Auerbach remarks, "may seem insignificant," is the pronounced use of direct discourse in the gospels. Auerbach claims that there is no similar use of direct discourse in classical literature.[51] Biographies often contain anecdotal dialogues, but their function is quite different from that of the gospels. In biography, these dialogues only serve to buttress the controlling rhetorical and ethical interests of the author. The use of dialogue in the gospels, however, has a dramatic tension and immediacy that is "rare in antique lit-

---

[49] Guelich, "The Gospel Genre," 181; Dihle, "The Gospels and Greek Biography," 379, 381, 383; Wilder, *Early Christian Rhetoric*, 28; and M. Eugene Boring, "Mark 1:1–15 and the Beginning of the Gospel," *Semeia* 52 (1990): 46, 64.

[50] Eric Auerbach, *Mimesis: The Representation of Reality in Western Literature*, trans. Willard R. Trask (Princeton: Princeton University Press, 1953), 45.

[51] Ibid., 46.

erature."[52] For Auerbach, then, the realism of the gospel narratives makes them distinct from the classical genres and from biography in particular.

Dissatisfaction with the comparison to Greco-Roman biography has led Norman Petersen to question the validity of the genre quest itself. He urges scholars to "cease talking about the four canonical gospels as belonging to the same genre or sub-type of genre . . . simply because their common denominator is that they are stories about Jesus."[53] The gospels may stem from different generic antecedents, and therefore we should first investigate them separately. His disdain for Burridge's conclusion is apparent in his remark that "the very triviality of this conclusion empties the generic classification of the gospels as biographies of any hermeneutical significance whatsoever."[54] Petersen sees Mark as a parodistic narrative. Thus, whatever generic models Mark may be using, he is subverting them in the process. His contention that the Markan narrative is really about the foibles of the disciples is less convincing.[55] The central character of Mark's Gospel is clearly Jesus. Nor is it necessary to despair of the generic enterprise altogether as Petersen suggests. Genre is a sociological and linguistic necessity, even when its precise dimensions are vague and obscure.[56]

Willem Vorster is critical of both evolutionary and analogical approaches to gospel genre. He finds that each in its own way is too preoccupied with the history behind the text to attend to the text as a meaningful "autosemantic unit."[57] Rather than compare the Gospel of Mark with various types of ancient literature, Vorster prefers to read Mark simply as a self-contained narrative. Although Vorster's emphasis on the literary activity of the Markan author is helpful, narrative is too broad a category to qualify as a genre.

Roland Frye also emphasizes the literary quality of the gospel texts. Like Vorster, he underscores the importance of reading the gos-

---

[52] Ibid.

[53] Norman Petersen, "Can One Speak of a Gospel Genre?" *Neot* 28, no. 3 (1994): 139.

[54] Ibid., 146.

[55] Ibid., 153.

[56] A point that Petersen himself makes elsewhere in the same article, ibid., 145.

[57] W. S. Vorster, "Mark: Collector, Redactor, Author, Narrator?" *Journal of Theology for Southern Africa* 31 (1980): 57.

pels as unified narratives and rejects atomistic and reductionistic approaches that try to analyze the gospels piecemeal. Frye observes that the evangelists "construct a literary universe of experience and of value," and in doing so they "bring us into contact with the living personality of Jesus."[58] In evaluating the message of the gospels, the integrity of their "literary universe" is of utmost importance. Frye describes the gospels as "dramatic history," without trying to find analogous literary forms in the ancient world. Although Frye is reluctant to do so, it would nevertheless be instructive to compare the way the gospels create their "literary universe" with similar ancient literary works.

A recent work that treats Mark as a unified narrative within the conventions of first century literature is Mary Ann Tolbert's *Sowing the Gospel*. Tolbert rejects biography as a helpful model. Biography is an unsuitable genre for Mark because the gospel lacks the proper scope. The biographies are accounts of a person's life from birth to death, while Mark clearly is not. Furthermore, the prominent role played by the disciples and the crowds is quite different from the sustained focus on the individual in biography. Tolbert also notes that the Gospel of Mark lacks the linguistic, technical, and philosophical refinement of the Greco-Roman biographies.[59] Thus, Tolbert finds that in spite of much scholarly activity, the Gospel of Mark still "lacks a convincing explanation of the unity of its overall plan."[60]

Unlike some contemporary literary critics, who eschew historical research in favor of a reader-actualized interpretation of the text, Tolbert chooses to read Mark against the backdrop of its cultural environment. In modern literary critical terms, Tolbert tries to approximate a native reading of Mark from the perspective of its implied reader. This is a difficult task. We know little about the conditions specific to the composition of Mark's Gospel, and the Markan narrative supplies

---

[58] Roland Mushat Frye, "The Jesus of the Gospels: Approaches through Narrative Structure," in *From Faith to Faith: Essays in Honor of Donald G. Miller on his Seventieth Birthday*, ed. Dikran Y. Hadidian, PTMS, 31 (Pittsburgh: Pickwick, 1979), 77. Compare William A. Beardslee's similar observations on the importance of the gospel's narrative world, *Literary Criticism of the New Testament*, GBS, ed. Dan O. Via, Jr. (Philadelphia: Fortress, 1969), 13.

[59] Mary Ann Tolbert, *Sowing the Gospel: Mark's World in Literary-Historical Perspective* (Minneapolis: Fortress, 1989), 58–59.

[60] Ibid., 2.

only an incomplete picture of its intended readers.[61] Tolbert compensates for the lack of precise information about the gospel's intended readers by resorting to the wider social and literary environment of the first century. By situating Mark within this environment, Tolbert hopes to augment her understanding of Mark's implied reader and thereby approximate a native reading of the gospel. She proposes to widen her field of view in two ways: first, by examining the broad social conditions of the first century, and second, by comparing the gospel to similar popular literature.

First, Tolbert sets Mark within the broad social conditions of the early Roman Empire. Increased mobility throughout the Mediterranean region characterized this period. The presence of a common language (Koine Greek), and a standardized approach to education (rhetoric), made travel to remote parts of the empire much more feasible. This element of minimally shared culture facilitated the free exchange of ideas and beliefs. While the *pax romana* made freedom to travel possible, imperial government intruded upon regional identity and local practices of self-government. The result was a destabilization of traditional social structures. Governed by a foreign power and increasingly under the influence of alien ideas and practices, the identity of the individual, traditionally rooted in clan and polis, began to erode. The cumulative effect was a heightened sense of alienation and anxiety among the inhabitants of the Roman Empire.

Second, Tolbert hopes to expand our understanding of Mark's implied reader by comparing the gospel with narrative literature contemporary with it.[62] Tolbert proposes that Mark is best understood as popular narrative.[63] The chief examples of the popular stratum of first century literature are the Greco-Roman novels or romances. The Greco-Roman romances are stereotypical tales of young love frustrated by Tyche, the goddess of fortune. In these novels, an unusual sequence of events separates a young, well-born, and remarkably handsome couple. They vainly search for one another through a series of adventures in exotic locales, until they are finally reunited at the end of the story. As examples, Tolbert cites the two pre-Sophistic Greek novels: *An Ephesian Tale*, by Xenophon of Ephesus; and *Chaereas and Callirhoe*, by

---

[61] Ibid., 36.

[62] Ibid., 33.

[63] Ibid., 60.

Chariton.[64] These romantic novels are roughly contemporary with Mark, and, as Tolbert points out, they reflect a similar popular style. Tolbert notes that the essence of their generic unity is "a common myth, a common heritage, and a common conventionalized style." She further identifies the common myth as "the Hellenistic myth of the isolated individual in a dangerous world."[65]

Tolbert does not propose that Mark is a Greek novel.[66] She only suggests that the same general tendencies that influenced the Greek novels may also have influenced Mark and its audience.[67] The connection between Mark and the Greek novel is most apparent in the "rhetorical, stylistic, and linguistic similarities" that they share.[68] Mark's popular and unsophisticated Greek and lively narrative style more closely resemble romance than biography.[69] The evidence is sufficient to establish Mark as an example of popular Hellenistic literature. This in itself is an important observation since it significantly narrows the range of literary types to which we can favorably compare the Gospel of Mark.[70] Nevertheless, popular narrative is too broad a category to constitute a literary genre.

---

[64] For a convenient collection of Greek novels in English translation, see B. P. Reardon, ed., *Collected Ancient Greek Novels* (Berkeley: University of California Press, 1989).

[65] Tolbert, *Sowing the Gospel*, 64. As Tolbert notes, these claims are more fully developed by B. P. Reardon, "The Greek Novel," *Phoenix* 23 (1969): 291–309; and Tomas Hägg, *The Novel in Antiquity* (Berkeley: University of California Press, 1983), 89–90. See also B. P. Reardon, "Aspects of the Greek Novel," *GR* 23 (1976): 118–31; and Niklas Holzberg, *The Ancient Novel: An Introduction*, trans. Christine Jackson-Holzberg (London: Routledge, 1995), 29–31.

[66] Tolbert, *Sowing the Gospel*, 65.

[67] Ibid., 66.

[68] Ibid., 78.

[69] For an examination of Mark's stylistic similarity to popular Greek literature, see Marius Reiser, *Syntax und Stil des Markusevangeliums im Licht der hellenistischen Volksliteratur*, WUNT 2.11 (Tübingen: J. C. B. Mohr [Paul Siebeck], 1984); idem, "Der Alexanderroman und das Markusevangelium," in *Markus-Philologie: Historische, literargeschichtliche und stilistische Untersuchungen zum zweiten Evangelium*, hrsg. Hubert Cancik, WUNT 33 (Tübingen: J. C. B. Mohr [Paul Siebeck], 1984), 131–63; and idem, "Stellung der Evangelien," 1–27.

[70] Apart from considerations of space, it is not clear why Tolbert limited her comparison of Mark with popular literature to romance. In his review of Tolbert's book, Vernon Robbins notes that the striking difference in content between Mark and the Greek romance limits somewhat the usefulness of Tolbert's approach

Although the Gospel of Mark shares a common social environment with the Greco-Roman romance, this does not mean that it responds to that environment in the same way. While the myth of the "isolated individual in a dangerous world" also influenced first century Jewish and Christian literature, these works treat this theme in a completely different way. In Jewish and Christian literature, interest in the alienated individual does not overwhelm a concern for the larger community as it does in the Greek novel. A traditional concern for the larger community remains at the center of Jewish and Christian literature, even when the action of the narrative revolves around a representative individual.[71]

Moreover, Jewish and Christian literature treats the twin themes of isolation and alienation differently. In the Greek romances, romantic love and devotion to the gods provide solace for these anxieties. The author of a Greek novel uses prayers and introspective monologues to reveal the inner turmoil of the characters. In these moments, when not consumed by despair and thoughts of suicide, the main characters take refuge in their unfailing love for one another. In addition, they frequently offer prayers to their patron goddess, Eros. The message of the Greek novel is that romantic love provides comfort and security in the midst of an alien and hostile world. In the romance, characters persist in piety and passively wait for the fortunes to change.

Christian and Jewish literature typically involves a more active response to hostile circumstances. As in the Greek romance, there is an emphasis on piety, yet in Christian and Jewish literature there is an ever-present expectation of divine intervention and vindication. God's people cry out for divine deliverance, and live in expectation of it.

("Text and Context in Recent Studies of the Gospel of Mark," *RelSRev* 17 [1991]: 18). Similarly, Lawrence Wills suggests that a comparison of the Gospel of Mark with novelistic works from an even lower social stratum would have strengthened Tolbert's argument. As examples of this type of literature, Wills names *Life of Aesop*, *Alexander Romance*, and the Jewish novels. See Lawrence Wills, *The Jewish Novel in the Ancient World*, Myth and Poetics, ed. Gregory Nagy (Ithaca: Cornell University Press, 1995), 29, n. 53.

[71] In addition to the gospels and Acts, I have in mind here the Greek versions of Daniel and Esther, III Maccabees, Judith, and Tobit. An exception would be *Joseph and Aseneth*, which exhibits a more sustained focus on an individual character. In part, this is to be explained by the importance of romantic love in *Joseph and Aseneth*, which suggests that it has been influenced to a greater degree by the Greek novel.

Thus, Tolbert comes closer to capturing the essence of Mark's Gospel when she describes it as an "apocalyptic message in a popular narrative framework."[72] It is the apocalyptic perspective that makes Mark's story qualitatively different from the Greek novel. In Mark, salvation comes for the "isolated and alienated individual," not as romantic love, but as divinely inaugurated deliverance.

Tolbert's use of the Greek novel to illuminate the shadowy reader of Mark's Gospel is therefore not entirely successful. Although it expands our understanding of the narrative techniques of popular literature, we should be wary of inferring the ideological interests of a text solely from its narrative technique.[73] The Gospel of Mark may well reflect the narrative style that was popular among a broad segment of first century Greco-Roman society. This helps us place Mark in a broad class of generally accessible literature. Nevertheless, that general similarity helps us neither identify the particular form, nor specify the function of Mark's narrative. The cultural distance between these two groups of readers is more pronounced than Tolbert seems to allow. As with Burridge's use of Greco-Roman biography, at a high level of generality, there is some value to the comparison but it does not resolve questions about the gospel's generic influences.

Adela Yarbro Collins has also expressed dissatisfaction with the comparison of the Gospel of Mark with Greco-Roman biography. Collins is especially critical of Burridge's failure to investigate possible connections with Jewish literature.[74] Collins insists that the formal similarities which exist between Mark and Greco-Roman biography are insufficient to account for Mark's depiction of Jesus as the agent of God who comes to institute the fulfillment of God's salvation. According to Collins, the Gospel of Mark is only secondarily interested in presenting Jesus as an ethical and paraenetical model. As Collins sees it, Mark is primarily "an apocalyptic historical monograph."[75] Collins finds antecedents for this apocalyptic perspective in the "Apocalypse of

---

[72] Tolbert, *Sowing the Gospel*, 302.

[73] Ibid., 65–70, 74–78.

[74] Adela Yarbro Collins, "Genre and the Gospels," *JR* 75 (1995): 241.

[75] Adela Yarbro Collins, *Is Mark's Gospel a Life of Jesus?: The Question of Genre*, Père Marquette Lecture in Theology (Milwaukee, Wis.: Marquette University Press, 1990); reprinted in idem, *The Beginning of the Gospel: Probings of Mark in Context* (Minneapolis: Fortress, 1992), 26–27 (page numbers refer to the reprint).

Weeks" in *1 Enoch*, Daniel, the *pesharim* of the Qumran community, and the histories of Josephus. All these works share an "apocalyptic view of history," the belief that "earthly events are controlled by heavenly powers."[76]

Although Collins' emphasis on the apocalyptic-historical perspective of the Gospel of Mark is persuasive, it leaves the narrative form of the gospel largely unexplained. Apart from Mark 13, the visionary material in *1 Enoch* and Daniel 7–9 is unlike the bulk of Mark's narrative, and *pesharim* and historiography are also poor generic matches. Among the apocalyptic literature cited by Collins, the closest parallels would seem to be the narrative sequences in Daniel 1–6, which Collins describes as "historical romance or historical fiction." However, Collins passes over this material and gives greater attention to Daniel 7–9.

Conclusion

From this brief survey of recent approaches to the problem of Markan genre, I draw the following conclusions. First, if Mark is related to Greco-Roman biography, it is only loosely so. The biographical qualities of the Gospel of Mark consist mainly in its focus on the life and activities of a single individual in a rough chronological framework. Second, the syntax and style of Mark strongly suggest that it is some type of popular literature. Third, an explanation of Mark's genre must account for its apocalyptic understanding of history. An apocalyptic sense of time and an awareness of divine purpose are at the very center of Mark's Gospel. This apocalyptic perspective makes it much more likely that we will find a generic match for the gospel within Jewish, rather than Greco-Roman, literature.

Difficulties in the Investigation of Gospel Genre

The history of research into the genre of the gospels has shown steady progress in recognizing the literary qualities of the gospels. Over the course of time, New Testament scholars have shifted away from historical methods and embraced literary methods of investigation. This is as it should be. Genre is primarily a matter of human expression, and its investigation demands tools appropriate for its basic nature. Of

---

[76] Ibid., 34.

course human expression also has a history, and it is in this sense that genre is ultimately engaged in historical investigation. Genre is then not primarily a matter of taxonomy, a search for appropriate labels and categories, but an attempt to trace lines of influence. These lines of influence may, it seems, be both conscious and unconscious. In some cases, we can detect a direct connection between works, while elsewhere the influence is more general, related to broad cultural conditions and common human interests. We can conclude from this, that there is more at stake in the investigation of gospel genre than finding an appropriate label. Describing the genre of the gospels is in the final analysis about relating them to a tradition of human expression, and this is a task best pursued using the tools of literary research.[77]

Thus, the task of describing Mark's genre has less to do with schematic classification than it does with investigating Mark's literary heritage. The investigation of genre should help us orient the individual work within the larger framework of literary history. As Northrop Fry describes it,

> The purpose of criticism by genres is not so much to classify as to clarify such traditions and affinities, thereby bringing out a large number of literary relationships that would not be noticed as long as there were no context established for them.[78]

This would be easier if we knew more about the literary conventions of the first century. Unfortunately, by that time rhetoric had almost completely overwhelmed scholarly interest in literary criticism. Even when classical scholars addressed literary problems, they seldom commented on popular literary forms. Therefore, if we wish to understand the literary practices of the first century, we must proceed inductively by examining its extant literature. Because there is a dearth of literature from the first century, it is often necessary to cast the net even wider. Nevertheless, the fundamental question remains the same. When the author of Mark composed his gospel, albeit from the various oral and written traditions preserved by the early church, what literary model, or models, informed his arrangement of those materials?

---

[77] Jean-Marie Schaeffer, "Literary Genres and Textual Genericity," in *The Future of Literary Theory*, ed. Ralph Cohen (New York: Routledge, 1989), 174.

[78] Northrop Frye, *Anatomy of Criticism: Four Essays* (Princeton: Princeton University Press, 1957), 247.

In surveying past research on the genre of the gospels, we have noted a number of persistent problems. I believe there are three main issues. First, should we treat the gospels as a discrete class or sub-class of literature? Second, what is the best way to trace the literary influences of an individual work? Third, what is an appropriate scope for such an investigation?

Are the Gospels a Unified Group?

Investigations of gospel genre frequently begin by assuming the gospels are a unified class of literature. Burridge, Aune, and Talbert, for example, all assume that the gospels are biographical and then attempt to relate them to the Greco-Roman tradition of biography. This assumption is understandable, since before the composition of the canonical gospels, the ancient world knew nothing of a gospel genre. The gospels must therefore be a subset of some more widely known genre. But is it in fact necessary, or even desirable, to assume that the gospels form a unified class of literature before tracing their literary influences separately?

The assumption that the Synoptic Gospels form a unified literary class no doubt derives in part from their close source critical relationship. The presence of a large amount of common material conclusively demonstrates their mutual interdependence. This common material in turn guarantees that the Synoptic Gospels will contain much of the same content and many of the same literary forms. The use of common material, however, does not necessarily mean that the evangelists arranged their material under the influence of the same genre. Indeed, the redactional differences between the Synoptic Gospels suggest that at some level, each author was dissatisfied with the other's presentation.[79] By adding birth narratives and resurrection appearances to their narratives, both Matthew and Luke make their accounts conform more closely to ancient standards of biography.[80] This suggests either that

---

[79] Willi Marxsen, *Mark the Evangelist: Studies in the Redaction History of the Gospel*, trans. James Boyce et al. (Nashville: Abingdon, 1969), 212–13. Others who have advocated treating the gospels separately rather than as members of the same class include: Samuel Sandmel, "Prolegomena to a Commentary on Mark," in *Two Living Traditions: Essays on Religion and the Bible* (Detroit: Wayne State University Press, 1972), 153; Wilder, *Early Christian Rhetoric*, 29; Güttgemanns, *Candid Questions*, 278; and Petersen, "Can One Speak of a Gospel Genre?" 139.

[80] David E. Aune, "The Gospels as Hellenistic Biography," 9. Aune else-

Mark was not a biography, or that it was at least a deficient one. Either way, the precise nature of the literary influences that shaped the Gospel of Mark remains unresolved.

It would obviously be fallacious to assume that Mark is a biography because Matthew and Luke are. Any attempt to describe the Gospel of Mark as a Greco-Roman biography must stand or fall based upon evidence derived from Mark itself. Yet, the assumption that the Synoptic Gospels form a unified literary class too often leads to the superficial conclusion that all three gospels form a subset of Greco-Roman biography. Such a conclusion tends to obscure significant differences in the presentations of the evangelists. As free and creative individuals, each of the evangelists may have written under the influence of different genres. It should be the goal of any investigation of gospel genre to explore these creative influences. As we have already noted, the investigation of gospel genre is not merely an exercise in taxonomy, but an exploration of literary history. As such, the investigation of gospel genre should probe the literary influences at work in the composition of the gospel narratives. Rather than assume the literary unity of the gospels, it would be better to investigate first the literary influences on each of the individual gospels. Having done this, we would be in a better position to evaluate their unity as a literary class.

The Nature of Genre

Intramural disputes among literary critics over the criteria by which to make genre classifications make the investigation of gospel genre even more difficult. Nevertheless, at the most rudimentary level, genre refers to a set of expectations that guide a reader's understanding of a literary work.[81] These expectations are typically divided into two complementary categories: outer form and inner form. The outer form

---

where refers to this process as "literaturization" ("The Problem of the Genre of the Gospels," 45).

[81] For a brief introduction to the study of genres, see Wellek & Warren, *Theory of Literature*, 226–37. For a more detailed survey, see Heather Dubrow, *Genre*, The Critical Idiom, ed. John D. Jump, 42 (London: Methuen, 1982), 34–37. On literary conventions in general, see *The New Princeton Encyclopedia of Poetry and Poetics*, s.v. "Conventions," by Martin Steinmann and Lawrence Manley. Oswald Ducrot and Tzvetan Todorov provide a survey of generic typologies based on both form and content in their *Encyclopedic Dictionary of the Sciences of Language*, trans. Catherine Porter (Baltimore: Johns Hopkins University Press, 1979), 152–56.

of a literary work concerns matters such as length, mode of address, and overall structure. Inner form includes the topic that a work addresses, as well as its attitude, tone, and purpose. According to this approach, we may claim that a work belongs to a certain genre when its similarity to other works extends to both inner and outer form.

An author uses conventional literary patterns of inner and outer form to evoke a horizon of expectations in the reader.[82] These expectations, in turn, govern the reader's understanding of the literary work. Inner form and outer form are inseparable. An author never depends completely on one aspect to the exclusion of the other. In describing a work's genre, the critic must carefully balance both inner and outer form. As René Wellek and Austin Warren explain:

> Genre should be conceived, we think, as a grouping of literary works based, theoretically, upon both outer form (specific metre or structure) and also upon inner form (attitude, tone, purpose—more crudely, subject and audience). The ostensible basis may be one or the other...but the critical problem will then be to find the other dimension, to complete the diagram.[83]

Although the interdependence of inner and outer form is widely recognized, the dynamic relationship that exists between them is more difficult to describe. Nevertheless, any attempt to describe the genre of a literary work must account for both.

New Testament scholars have floundered precisely on the critical problem of finding "the other dimension" of this delicate balance. In comparing the gospels with the literature of the Hellenistic period, their tendency is to place undue stress on either inner form or outer form. Those who see the gospels as in some sense unique tend to emphasize their kerygmatic content; those who detect a relationship between the gospels and the literature of antiquity emphasize their formal similarities. The former position tends to deny the fundamental nature of writing as a socially bounded activity. The latter fails to account adequately

---

[82] I will use the term 'reader' throughout the study in its most basic sense to refer to a real perceiving subject. In this context, it does not, and cannot, refer to any hypothetical reader such as Mark's intended reader or implied reader. By using the term 'reader,' I also do not mean to imply that the original audience of the gospel was literate. In all likelihood, first century Christians read the gospel aloud in the first century. Nevertheless, it will be convenient to refer to the perceiving subjects of the gospel as "readers."

[83] Wellek & Warren, *Theory of Literature*, 231.

for the essential unity of content and form in literary production. Of these two positions, the second is the one that poses more subtle dangers. Analogies between the gospels and Greco-Roman biography attract attention, in part, because there are indeed similarities between them. It is not clear, however, that the accumulation of similarities is sufficient to demonstrate a meaningful generic connection.

In order for a comparison to be probative and interesting, it must point to features that are not merely accidental, but essential to the works in question. Comparisons are like definitions, which, as Aristotle observed, are only useful when built on essential qualities.[84] If we compare literary works based on accidental characteristics, the comparison may appear persuasive, but it will ultimately prove to be inconsequential.[85] This means that any successful comparison must not only demonstrate that a work is similar to other works, but also show that those similarities are significant. In terms of our inquiry into gospel genre, it is not enough to show that the gospels share certain qualities with Greco-Roman biography. If those qualities are not essential to the nature or quiddity of both literary classes then the comparison is at best questionable, and at worst misleading. As Aristotle observed, "to show that [two things] are the same is not enough to establish a definition."[86]

As some literary critics have pointed out, we may not be able to state the essence of a genre definitively.[87] Genre is a flexible category of description whose boundaries are elusive. Rather than a fixed set of characteristics, genre, as Alastair Fowler observes, is more akin to "family relations."[88] Yet, even here the distinction between the acciden-

---

[84] *Top.* 101b35.

[85] For example, Louis Agassiz notes that the father of modern biological classification, Carolus Linnaeus (1707–1778), first described *mammalia* as *quadrupedia*, before he realized that having four legs was only accidental and not essential to the class he was describing. Louis Agassiz, *Essay on Classification*, ed. Edward Lurie, John Harvard Library, ed. Bernard Bailyn (Cambridge: Harvard University Press, Belknap Press, 1962), 211.

[86] *Top.* 102a14–16.

[87] Fowler, *Kinds of Literature*, 274; E. D. Hirsch, Jr., *The Aims of Interpretation* (Chicago: University of Chicago Press, 1976), 121.

[88] The metaphor of "family relations" originated with Wittgenstein's philosophical investigation into the nature of games (Ludwig Wittgenstein, *Philosophical Investigations*, 3rd ed., trans. G. E. M. Anscombe [New York: Macmillan, 1958], 31–33). On its use among literary critics to describe the nature of genre, see David Fishelov, *Metaphors of Genre: The Role of Analogies in Genre Theory* (University Park, Penn.: Pennsylvania State University Press, 1993), 53–83.

tal and the essential is important. Families possess identifiable traits, although individual members will often lack one or more of them. In fact, it is often the case that family members will share no single trait. Likewise, literary works share "family traits" with other works, but frequently lack a complete repertoire. The indeterminacy of this approach to literary genre leaves at least two questions unanswered: How many shared traits are sufficient to establish a family resemblance? And, are all traits equally important? To answer such questions we must have some notion of what is most characteristic of the genre in question, even if we cannot provide a definitive list of characteristic features.

Unless we have a clear understanding of the literary object as a product of creative human expression, we are liable to be misled by traits that are merely accidental to the work in question. This is why the investigation of genre depends, in the first place, on a consistent theory of literature. If we can arrive at even a rudimentary understanding of the principles that govern the production of literature, we can then begin to distinguish between those features that are essential, and those that are not.

The Scope of Comparison

Another consequence of the assumption that the gospels form a discrete class of literature is that it has often foreshortened the scope of related investigations. When, for example, Burridge and Aune begin with the assumption that the gospels are biographical in nature, they quite naturally look for other biographical literature with which to forge a comparison. Although the origins of ancient biography are oriental, in the first century C.E. the best-known examples of the genre are Greco-Roman.[89] Judaism produced few, if any, biographies, at least of the type represented by Greco-Roman members of the class. The investigations of Burridge and Aune are therefore decidedly skewed in favor of Greco-Roman influences, to the detriment of Jewish influences. As Tolbert notes, this comparison runs counter to the decidedly popular flavor of Mark's narrative style, and as Collins observes, it cannot account for the gospel's apocalyptic themes.

At least in the case of Mark, an undue emphasis on comparisons with Greco-Roman literature is especially surprising. As the numerous

---

[89] Momigliano, *The Development of Greek Biography*, 35–37; and Dihle, "The Gospels and Greek Biography," 366.

citations and allusions to the Old Testament attest, the gospel's only overt literary dependencies are to Jewish writings. Moreover, Mark nowhere betrays knowledge of common Greco-Roman literary motifs, nor does the gospel ever allude to, or explicitly cite, Greco-Roman literary sources. If, therefore, the gospel's most overt point of contact with other literature is with Jewish Scripture, why would it not also be influenced predominately by Jewish literary forms? The fact that Mark writes in Greek is certainly no indicator either way, since by this time a great deal of distinctively Jewish literature was being read and perhaps even composed in Greek. Thus, any investigation into the Gospel of Mark's literary heritage must take its relationship to Jewish literature into account.

When Burridge broadens the definition of Greco-Roman biography to encompass the gospels, his objective seems primarily taxonomic. Likewise, Aune, in distinguishing between Christian and Jewish content and Greco-Roman form, seems determined to find a suitable place for the gospels among the literary genres of antiquity. If, however, the question of genre has more to do with tracing creative influences, such comparisons are incomplete. Biography may in fact have had some influence on the creation of the gospels, but how far did this influence extend? If, however, the gospels are significantly dissimilar to Greco-Roman biography, what other influences, if any, can account for these differences? To account fully for the literary influences on the gospels the scope of the inquiry cannot be limited to a comparison with Greco-Roman biography.

The inherent circularity of the practice adopted by Burridge and Aune is as obvious as it is unavoidable. In order to compare a literary work with other literary works, one has to begin with some notion as to which types of literature are suitable for comparison.[90] I would suggest, however, that the assumption that the gospels are some type of biography is unnecessarily restrictive. The gospels are in the first instance narratives. Although this is inadequate as a description of their genre, it does present a broad range of generally comparable materials. If with Tolbert we also propose that the gospels are popular narratives, we can limit the range of comparable materials further without becoming overly restrictive.

---

[90] Dubrow, *Genre*, 46.

Conclusion

Having surveyed previous research and reflected critically upon
it, I will now propose a new investigation of the genre of the Gospel of
Mark. First, I do not intend to address the question of "gospel" genre.
Whether or not the gospels form a discrete class of ancient literature is
beyond the scope of this investigation. I am interested only in tracing,
as much as possible, the literary influences that guided the creation of
Mark's Gospel. These influences may be multiple. Therefore, I propose
to compare the Gospel of Mark to a broad cross-section of literature.
This set of literature will include both Greco-Roman and Hellenistic-
Jewish works. In order to make the comparison manageable, I will limit
my examination to popular narrative works roughly contemporaneous
with the Gospel of Mark.

Since I have maintained that the investigation of genre depends
upon an adequate theoretical understanding of literature as a form of
creative human expression, my investigation must therefore begin with
a theoretical inquiry into the nature of literary production. I do not propose to investigate literary theory *ob ovo*; rather I will summarize the
literary theory of Mikhail Bakhtin and apply his understanding of genre
to the Gospel of Mark. Although previous works in biblical studies
have used Bakhtin,[91] the fruitfulness of his theory of genre has re-
mained largely unexplored. Other disciplines, such as classical studies,
folklore studies, and literary criticism have made use of Bakhtin's theory of genre,[92] but no one has yet applied this aspect of Bakhtin's work
to the Gospel of Mark. I contend that Bakhtin's approach to literary

---

[91] For example, Kenneth M. Craig, Jr., *Reading Esther: A Case for the Lit-
erary Carnivalesque*, Literary Currents in Biblical Interpretation, ed. Danna Nolan
Fewell and David M. Gunn (Louisville: Westminster John Knox, 1995); and Walter
L. Reed, *Dialogues of the Word: The Bible as Literature According to Bakhtin*
(New York: Oxford University, 1993).

[92] For classical studies see the special issue of *Arethusa*: John Peradotto, et
al. eds., "Bakhtin and Ancient Studies: Dialogues and Dialogics," *Arethusa* 26
(1993); and Barbara K. Gold, "A Question of Genre: Plato's *Symposium* as Novel,"
MLN 95 (1980): 1353–59. For folklore studies see John D. Dorst, "Neck-riddle as a
Dialogue of Genres: Applying Bakhtin's Genre Theory," *Journal of American
Folklore* 96 (1983): 413–33. For Bakhtin's importance to genre theory see Evelyn
Cobley, "Mikhail Bakhtin's Place in Genre Theory," *Genre* 21 (1988): 321–38;
Gary Saul Morson, "Bakhtin, Genres, and Temporality," *New Literary History* 22
(1991): 1071–92; and Clive Thomson, "Bakhtin's 'Theory' of Genre," *Studies in
Twentieth Century Literature* 9 (1984): 29–40.

genre offers new prospects for addressing the problem of Markan genre.

Chapter Two

BAKHTIN'S THEORY OF GENRE

In his critique of Russian Formalism, Pavel Medvedev claims "poetics should really begin with genre, not end with it."[1] The failure to

---

[1] M. M. Bakhtin / P. N. Medvedev, *The Formal Method in Literary Scholarship: A Critical Introduction to Sociological Poetics* (*FM*), trans. Albert J. Wehrle (Baltimore: Johns Hopkins University Press, 1978), 129. Bakhtin scholars disagree over the proper attribution of several works published under the names of Pavel Medvedev and Valentin Vološinov. There is some evidence to support the claim that Bakhtin was the original author of at least three book length works that originally bore the name of his colleagues: Medvedev, *The Formal Method in Literary Scholarship*; Vološinov, *A Marxist Philosophy of Language*; and idem, *Freudianism: A Critical Sketch*. Nicholas Rzhevsky, "Kozhinov on Bakhtin," *New Literary History* 25 (1994): 429–44; and Sergey Bocharov, "Conversations with Bakhtin," *PMLA* 105 (1994): 1009–24, offer the best evidence to date in support of this claim. Rzhevsky provides the transcript of an interview with Vadim Kozhinov, one of the executors of Bakhtin's literary estate. Kozhinov, who frequently visited Bakhtin before his death, reports that Bakhtin himself claimed to have authored these works. The article by Bocharov corroborates Rzhevsky's claims with additional reminiscences of Bakhtin's comments supporting his authorship of these works.

Others, such as Gary Saul Morson and Caryl Emerson, *Mikhail Bakhtin: Creation of a Prosaics* (Stanford: Stanford University Press, 1990), 102–19, steadfastly maintain that the books in question belong to Medvedev and Vološinov. All three books contain material, mostly of a Marxist bent, inconsistent with views Bakhtin espoused throughout his life. No matter which position one adopts, few would dispute that Bakhtin, Medvedev, and Vološinov shared similar philosophical views, which they developed over the course of a long association. Even if Bakhtin originally authored these works, it seems likely that Medvedev and Vološinov

understand the unity of a work severs its individual components from the context that makes them intelligible. Note that Medvedev does not say reading must begin with genre, only poetics. To a certain extent, this circumvents a vicious circularity. At first, we read the text without knowing precisely what type of work it is. As we read, we either subconsciously or uncritically supply a genre, or we correctly infer the text's genre from the clues embedded in the text. The ease with which we are able to identify the genre of a text depends on the extent to which we are familiar with its literary conventions and cultural values. When poetics takes up the critical task of evaluating the significance or meaning of the aesthetic work, it presupposes familiarity with the work as a whole.[2] Critical evaluation therefore begins with the determination of genre.

Like Medvedev, Bakhtin argued for the primacy of genre in literary studies. For Bakhtin, genre is a descriptive category that embraces the axiological, or evaluative unity of the whole work. In describing the

---

would have had some editorial control over the texts before their publication. The true nature of the authorship of the works in question was further obscured by the tragedy of the Stalinist purges, which claimed the lives of Medvedev and Vološinov. In light of these difficulties, it is perhaps preferable to speak of the Bakhtin School, and leave the problematic question of authorship unresolved. I will henceforth refer to the above-mentioned works as if they were authored by the person under whose name they originally appeared, and assume a high degree of continuity between the theoretical positions which they present.

For further information on the question of authorship see the articles by Gary Saul Morson, I. R. Titunik, and Katerina Clark and Michael Holquist in the *Slavic and East European Journal* 30 (1986): 81–102; Nina Perlina, "Bakhtin-Medvedev-Voloshinov: An Apple of Discourse," *The University of Ottawa Quarterly* 53, no. 1 (1983): 35–47; I. R. Titunik, "Bakhtin &/or Vološinov &/or Medvedev: Dialogue &/or Doubletalk?" in *Language and Literary Theory: In Honor of Ladislav Matejka*, ed. Benjamin A. Stolz, I. R. Titunik, Lubomír Doležel, Papers in Slavic Philology, 5 (Ann Arbor: University of Michigan, Department of Slavic Languages and Literatures, 1984), 535–64; and Albert Wehrle, "Introduction: M. M. Bakhtin/P. N. Medvedev," in M. M. Bakhtin / P. N. Medvedev, *The Formal Method in Literary Scholarship: A Critical Introduction to Sociological Poetics*, trans. Albert J. Wehrle (Baltimore: Johns Hopkins University Press, 1978), ix–x.

[2] As the chapter progresses, it will be increasingly important to recall the etymological meaning of the term "aesthetic." The Greek term αἰσθητικός refers to sensory perception (LSJ, s.v. αἰσθητικός). This is frequently the sense of the term that Bakhtin intends rather than the more popular meaning that equates "aesthetic" with artistic appreciation.

axiological unity of a text, he distinguished between its compositional form (the techniques that give it mechanical unity) and its architectonic form (the ideational perspective that gives it axiological unity).[3] Although Bakhtin did not oppose the investigation of compositional form, he claimed that compositional form is unable to account for the unity of an aesthetic object. Only architectonic form, which Bakhtin defines more precisely as "the expression of the axiologically determinate creative activity of an aesthetically active *subiectum*," is able to account for this unity.[4] In other words, the author's "expressed valuation" gives the work its architectonic unity. This expressed valuation governs the choice of compositional forms and unifies the content, material, and form of the artistic work.

For Bakhtin, the investigation of literary works begins with the problem of our perception of the world and the articulation of those perceptions in language. By examining certain aspects of perception, Bakhtin was able to specify further the fundamental nature of the poetic object. This in turn allowed him to state more precisely the basic tasks of a socio-historical poetics and, as a direct consequence, the essential nature of literary genre. Bakhtin maintained that the problem of perception relates directly to the aesthetic description of time and space, and ultimately this will lead us to his notion of chronotope, but first we must examine the dialogic implications of human perception.

Our perception of the world is always filtered through our own unique set of assumptions and values. Since our perception is always mediated and indirect, interaction with others becomes an important means of supplementing our limited field of vision. Dialogue is therefore a crucial aspect of literary production since, as Bakhtin maintains, the literary text is primarily an instance of human communication. The dialogic dimensions of literature are twofold. The text is both externally dialogic in relation to its reader and may be, to one degree or another, internally dialogic in the context of its characters and story-world. These dialogic relations tend to coalesce around specific social and his-

---

[3] M. M. Bakhtin, "The Problem of Content, Material, and Form in Verbal Art," in *Art and Answerability: Early Philosophical Essays by M. M. Bakhtin* (*A&A*), ed. Michael Holquist and Vadim Liapunov, trans. with notes by Vadim Liapunov, supplement trans. Kenneth Brostrom, UTPSS, ed. Michael Holquist, no. 9 (Austin: University of Texas Press, 1990), 269–70.

[4] Ibid., 305.

torical circumstances into semi-stable conventional forms. These conventional forms are what we normally refer to as genres.

As semi-stable patterns of human communication, literary genres also express a specific axiological or value-laden orientation to content by means of literary form. To understand this aspect of the text better we first need to clarify the relationship between author and linguistic material. Language is a dynamic and flexible medium of expression. Although this dynamic quality provides the necessary condition for creative freedom, it also creates significant challenges for authors. These challenges are not unique to literary works; they also affect other modes of aesthetic expression. For example, Bakhtin predicates the importance of genre in poetics upon its role in common speech acts.[5] An examination of the importance of the axiological, or value-laden aspect of speech genres will, by analogy, substantiate the claim that genre is fundamentally characterized by its axiological orientation.

Finally, we will turn to the aspect of aesthetic expression that most clearly reveals the text's genre; namely, its representation of the hero in time and space. How an author configures a work's temporal and spatial boundaries and, more importantly, her evaluative stance toward that time and space are for Bakhtin the essential indicators of a work's genre. This will bring us full circle to a reconsideration of the temporal and spatial dimensions of human perception. In the case of the literary chronotope, however, we will be interested in its effect on the creation of artificial worlds and the possibilities such worlds present for the meaningful activity of their hero.

Fundamental Principles of Bakhtin's Poetics

Bakhtin claims that one of the first tasks of poetics is the description of the architectonic structure of the aesthetic work.[6] Linguistic analysis and what we today call reader-response criticism are secondary

---

[5] Bakhtin is not idiosyncratic in this respect. Independent of Bakhtin, some contemporary linguists have also stressed the relationship between speech events and literary creation. See Deborah Tannen, "Involvement as Dialogue: Linguistic Theory and the Relation between Conversational and Literary Discourse," in *Dialogue and Critical Discourse: Language, Culture, Critical Theory*, ed. Michael Macovski (New York: Oxford University Press, 1997), 137–42, as well as the literature cited there.

[6] Bakhtin, "Problem of Content," 267.

and tertiary considerations. Architectonic structure is crucial because it refracts the authorial values that shape the work as a whole. Its importance notwithstanding, the glue that binds a text into a single cohesive unit is difficult to describe. The literary text is a complex combination of content or subject matter, set in a specific literary form, conveyed in the material of language. It was Bakhtin's contention that an atomistic or reductionistic analysis of the literary text could not do justice to the literary work as a whole, not to mention other forms of creative human activity. Such analytical procedures are indeed possible, and even beneficial, as long as one carefully observes their limitations. A proper assessment of the literary text, however, must take account of the text's overall unity.

If, as Bakhtin claims, all perception is socially conditioned, the only thing that we can say with certainty about reality is that our knowledge of it is limited. Indeed, Bakhtin refers to this aspect of reality as its "unfinalizability." Although our knowledge of reality is essentially unfinalizable, we are obliged nevertheless to make sense of our experience. We do this by creating finalized images of reality. The process of finalization has definite implications for a socio-historical poetics. By examining the process of finalization, we will be able to specify further the nature of human creativity and aesthetic perception.

Not only is the aesthetic work a crystallization of socially shared patterns of perception; it is also a fundamentally social act. Authors write not merely as an act of self-expression; they write to communicate a message. This message might be political or academic, informational or entertaining. No matter what its purpose, when we consider an aesthetic work as a social act, which is to say as *parole* rather than *langue*, it has specific social dimensions. Bakhtin calls these socially and historically embedded acts of communication "utterances." As an utterance, the aesthetic work internalizes various aspects of the social relations that attended its creation. Because the aesthetic work is an act of communication, these social relations are fundamentally dialogic. The aesthetic work is an implicit dialogue between two or more distinct perspectives. One of the functions of a socio-historical poetics is to investigate these internal dialogic relations. In the next section, we will anticipate the importance of dialogic relations for a socio-historical poetics by exploring their precise nature.

Unfinalizability and Dialogue

Bakhtin maintains that the dialogical nature of existence extends to consciousness itself.[7] Our very existence is steeped in dialogue. Even our self-awareness is the product of social and ideological interaction with others.[8] We acquire our language through our interactions with others and, as Bakhtin points out, language is more than lexicon and grammar; it is also inherently social and evaluative. Words provide us with both a perceptual framework and an evaluative orientation. We use language not only to describe reality, but also to establish our axiological relationship to it. Words, in both their descriptive and evaluative aspect, shape the way we perceive reality, or conversely, we only perceive reality through the words and values given to us by our culture.

Apart from our socially conditioned perception, reality is essentially unknowable. That is, we cannot know the essential nature of reality in any objective and absolute sense. Of course, by means of reductionism, the physical sciences are able to state, with a high degree of objectivity, certain facts about the real world. Nevertheless, even these scientific statements are socially conditioned and, more importantly, they achieve their precision only by bracketing the more complex variables of existence. In the words of Gary Saul Morson, "The complexities of existence cannot be approached, without ludicrous reduction, by assuming that somehow, underneath it all, there are simple processes

---

[7] M. M. Bakhtin, "Toward a Reworking of the Dostoevsky Book," in *Problems of Dostoevsky's Poetics* (*PDP*), ed. and trans. Caryl Emerson, with an introduction by Wayne C. Booth, THL, ed. Wlad Godzich and Jochen Schulte-Sasse, vol. 8 (Minneapolis: University of Minnesota Press, 1984), 287; also V. N. Vološinov, "Discourse in Life and Discourse in Art: Concerning Sociological Poetics," in *Freudianism: A Critical Sketch*, ed. I. R. Titunik in collaboration with Neal H. Bruss, trans. I. R. Titunik (Bloomington: Indiana University Press, 1987), 114–15.

[8] Of course, Bakhtin is not the only one who has described knowledge as socially conditioned. See, for example, Max Scheler, *Problems of a Sociology of Knowledge*, ed. with an introduction by Kenneth W. Stikkers, trans. Manfred S. Frings, International Library of Sociology (London, Routledge & Kegan Paul, 1980); Karl Mannheim, *Essays on the Sociology of Knowledge*, ed. Paul Kecskemeti (New York: Oxford University Press, 1952); David Bloor, *Knowledge and Social Imagery* (London: Routledge & Kegan Paul, 1976); Peter L. Berger, and Thomas Luckman, *The Social Construction of Reality: A Treatise in the Sociology of Knowledge* (Garden City, N.Y.: Doubleday, 1966); and Michael Polanyi, *Personal Knowledge: Towards a Post-Critical Philosophy* (Chicago: University of Chicago press, 1974).

captureable by a theory just revealed by some master."[9] The conditional nature of our perception of reality is one of Bakhtin's central ideas, a concept that he refers to as "unfinalizability." By unfinalizability, Bakhtin means that the phenomenal world is too complex to be reduced to any abstract theoretical system of rules. For Bakhtin, reality is a rich and variegated realm of human creativity and freedom. No abstract theoretical system of thought can adequately convey the true nature of reality while preserving the possibility of human creativity and freedom. Every attempt to circumscribe the unfinalizability of life necessarily imposes some order, some system, upon it. At best, these systems only fail to account for freedom and creativity; at worst, they render them meaningless categories.

Bakhtin notes that while the unfinalizability of life is *given*, we *create* the interpretative constructs we use to make sense out of life. We have a natural tendency to gravitate toward the given since "it is much easier to study the *given* in what is created . . . than to study what is *created*."[10] It is the created, however, that constitutes the true realm of human activity and is therefore the proper field of study for the human

---

[9] Gary Saul Morson, "Prosaics Evolving," *Slavic and East European Journal* 41 (1997): 64. Along similar lines, see Stephen Toulmin, "The Marginal Relevance of Theory to the Humanities," *Common Knowledge* 2 (1993): 75–84.

[10] M. M. Bakhtin, "The Problem of the Text in Linguistics, Philology, and the Human Sciences: An Experiment in Philosophical Analysis," in *Speech Genres and Other Late Essays* (*SpG*), ed. Caryl Emerson and Michael Holquist, trans. Vern W. McGee, UTPSS, ed. Michael Holquist, no. 9 (Austin: University of Texas Press, 1986), 120. It is characteristic of Bakhtin to note carefully the distinction between the given and the created. He believed the failure to observe this distinction was the source of many errors in literary criticism. See M. M. Bakhtin, "Forms of Time and of the Chronotope in the Novel: Notes toward a Historical Poetics," in *The Dialogic Imagination: Four Essays by M. M. Bakhtin* (*DI*), ed. Michael Holquist, trans. Caryl Emerson and Michael Holquist, UTPSS, ed. Michael Holquist, no. 1 (Austin: University of Texas Press, 1981), 253. In New Testament studies, a more careful distinction between these two ontological planes would go far in resolving confusion surrounding the question of the historical Jesus. As Bakhtin remarks, "from within the aesthetic architectonic there *is* no way out into the world of the performer of deeds, for he is located outside the field of objectified aesthetic seeing" (M. M. Bakhtin, *Toward a Philosophy of the Act* (*TPA*), ed. Vadim Liapunov and Michael Holquist, trans. with notes by Vadim Liapunov, UTPSS, ed. Michael Holquist, no. 10 [Austin: University of Texas Press, 1993], 73). As a character in the gospels, Jesus can never be equated without qualification to the real, deed-performing Jesus of history.

sciences. There is an inherent tension between the created and the given, which Bakhtin describes as the tension between two opposing forces. The complexity of life—its unfinalizability—is a centrifugal force tending toward disorder and is full of potential. The interpretive constructs that we create are centripetal forces that attempt to rein in centrifugal disorder and limit its potential.[11] Abstract theoretical approaches, which Bakhtin labels "theoretism," resolve this tension by suppressing life's unfinalizability. A proper approach to the human sciences and, in particular, a valid approach to poetics must preserve this tension.[12] Even when we finalize life through our aesthetic acts of perception and evaluation, we must remember that those acts are temporal and conditional.

Bakhtin identifies two extreme forms of theoretical finalization: dogmatism and relativism. Neither is capable of accounting for life's unfinalizability. Dogmatism, or absolutism, insists that its finalization of life is the only correct view. It attempts to overcome unfinalizability by overpowering it. Relativism claims that finalization is meaningless.[13] It capitulates in the face of life's unfinalizability by rejecting the task of finalization. Both dogmatism and relativism possess a ready-made answer to any specific circumstance. Dogmatism either accounts for a free and creative act within the confines of its rigid system, or it rejects the act as an aberration. Relativism denies outright the moral validity of the act since it rejects all normative systems. As Gary Saul Morson observes,

> Relativism . . . presumes morality must be a matter of abstract norms, but it denies that such norms can exist. The possibility that ethics might be

---

[11] M. M. Bakhtin, "Discourse in the Novel," in *DI*, 272–73.

[12] Compare Alastair Fowler's comparable warning against the dangers of "theoretism" genre studies in "The Future of Genre Theory: Functions and Constructional Types," in *The Future of Literary Theory*, ed. Ralph Cohen (New York: Routledge, 1989), 301–2.

[13] Clearly, I am using the term relativism in a somewhat imprecise and pejorative sense. When Bakhtin refers to relativism, he seems to have in mind something more akin to alethic nihilism, i.e., the rejection of the possibility of truth. Bakhtin's own views are more akin to alethic relativism since he claims that truth claims are true only in relation to specific social groups. For clarification on the meaning(s) of the term 'relativism' see William Max Knorpp, "What Relativism Isn't," *Philosophy* 73 (1998): 277–300.

real without being a system of norms at all is not even seriously considered.[14]

The particular events of existence have no effect on the way dogmatism and relativism finalize life. This lack of contact with the specific circumstances of life is only symptomatic of their abstract theoretical nature.

According to Bakhtin, the ready-made answers of such abstract theoretical systems can never explain human creativity and freedom. We can only explain creativity and freedom in the context of specific socio-historical circumstances. Free and creative acts depend upon the possibility of meaningful and responsible action in the specific circumstances of life. Only the particularity of our actions renders them ethical and responsible. According to Bakhtin, a judgment is morally necessary, not because of its putative "veridicality-in-itself," but only within the context of a specific moment of being.

> The ought arises only in the correlating of truth (valid in itself) with our actual act of cognition, and this moment of being correlated is historically a unique moment: it is always an individual act or deed. . . . the ought gains its validity within the unity of my once-occurrent answerable life.[15]

Because dogmatism and relativism both abstract meaning from the circumstances of existence, they are unable to account for free and creative responsible activity. Thus, dogmatism and relativism are simply two complementary aspects of theoretism. In contrast to the finalizing strategies of dogmatism and relativism, Bakhtin attempts neither to overpower the centrifugal force of unfinalizability, nor to capitulate to it. Instead, he accents the potential that exists within life's centrifugal forces. For Bakhtin, this potential for responsible activity constitutes the *sine qua non* of human creativity and freedom.

Although it is necessary to think about life in a disciplined and rational way, in light of life's unfinalizability, our interpretive constructs are of necessity always contingent and incomplete. Bakhtin claims "this world is fundamentally and essentially indeterminable either in theoretical categories or in categories of historical cognition or

---

[14] Gary Saul Morson, "Prosaics, Criticism, and Ethics," *Formations* 5, no. 2 (1989): 89.

[15] Bakhtin, *TPA*, 5.

through aesthetic intuition."[16] Theoretical categories are incapable of grasping the significance of an act in its existential unity. An act possesses three simultaneous aspects: it has cognitive content, historical particularity, and is capable of aesthetic evaluation. Any attempt to explain an act in terms of one of these aspects, while excluding the others, will necessarily fail to provide a full explanation of its unity. Nevertheless, aesthetic finalization, when properly understood, provides the best avenue for fully describing an act.[17]

Aesthetic perception is a more promising mode of finalization than theoretical analysis since it maintains a balance between the cognitive content and the historical particularity of the event. It preserves this balance by sympathetically entering the event and reanimating it by means of dialogical participation. There is, however, always the danger that aesthetic finalization may merge with the axiological values of the event and lose the distinctiveness of its own perspective. Before we can fully understand the process of aesthetic finalization, we need to explore further the social nature of finalization. On the surface, the act of finalization appears to be an individual act, but since cognition is itself socially conditioned, finalization is also a social act. Bakhtin discusses the social nature of finalization as another aspect of dialogue, to which I now turn.[18]

The liminal nature of human consciousness—its social and intersubjective dimension—is the initial condition for our dialogic relation with others. The primary medium of our dialogic interaction is, of course, language. Language conveys the substance of our dialogic interaction, which consists of both cognitive content and evaluative ori-

---

[16] Ibid., 16.

[17] Ibid., 18.

[18] Morson and Emerson note that Bakhtin uses the term dialogue in at least three distinct ways. First, all utterances are by definition dialogic in the sense that they require two participants: a speaker, and a responder. Second, some utterances preserve within themselves an orientation toward the responder. These utterances are dialogic, in contrast to utterances that have only a single dominant orientation. Such utterances are monological. Third, Bakhtin also uses dialogue to refer to his concept that truth, as we perceive it, is multifaceted. We can only apprehend "truth" by listening to many different voices and perspectives, and therefore truth is also dialogic (Gary Saul Morson and Caryl Emerson, "Extracts from a *Heteroglossary*," in *Dialogue and Critical Discourse: Language, Culture, Critical Theory*, ed. Michael Macovski [New York: Oxford University Press, 1997], 264–66).

entation. Bakhtin believed that the evaluative aspect of language had received too little critical attention due to the influence of structuralism. Ferdinand de Saussure had initiated the scientific study of language as *langue*, but only at the expense of *parole*.[19] Bakhtin insisted that only *parole* or utterance has a necessary relationship to life and can therefore be evaluative.[20] *Langue* exists only as a theoretical abstraction divorced from actual linguistic performance. In life, language does not function as a static and fixed code into which we encrypt ready-made cognitive content.[21] Instead, in our everyday usage, language is a malleable medium of creative human expression.

Every dialogue constitutes a unique and unrepeatable moment. Each occurs at a specific time and place and is resonant with its own values. Although the dialogic moment is unique to a particular time and place, it is not isolated from the flow of history. Dialogues relate to one another by the words they use. Dialogues participate in the ongoing life of words by exploiting their history, and the use of words in dialogue in turn shapes their future. In a sense then, when we speak we are participants in a variety of on-going conversations. Each of these conversations has a rich history that is measurable only against the backdrop of what Bakhtin calls "great time." Over great time, language changes as it encounters other languages, each with its own peculiar perspective. Dialogue then, becomes the necessary condition for the change and growth, not only of language's reservoir of lexicon and grammar, but also of its perceptual possibilities. Our aesthetic perception of the world grows as we interact with, and learn from, the language of others.

Since Saussure and his followers left the precise nature of the utterance as dialogic event unexamined, Bakhtin assumed for himself the task of its scientific description. He began by establishing its boundaries. An utterance is a linguistic event that occurs in the dialogic space

---

[19] Ferdinand de Saussure, *Course in General Linguistics*, ed. Charles Bally and Albert Sechehaye, in collaboration with Albert Riedlinger, trans. with introduction and notes by Wade Baskin (New York: McGraw Hill, 1966), 7–15.

[20] Evelyn Cobley, "Mikhail Bakhtin's Place in Genre Theory," *Genre* 21 (1988): 321–38.

[21] A well-known example of this approach to language is Roman Jakobson's communication model, which explicitly refers to the linguistic conventions shared by addresser and addressee as code. See Roman Jakobson, "Linguistics and Poetics," in *Language and Literature*, ed. Krystyna Pomorska and Stephen Rudy (Cambridge: Belknap, 1987), 66.

between an "I-for-myself" and an "other." Thus, a creating subject that anticipates a response delimits the utterance on the one side, and a perceiving subject that responds delimits it on the other. The axiological significance of an utterance exists only in the context of the dynamic relationship between these two subjects.

The "I-for-myself" and the "other" represent two distinct perspectives on life. They are not separate ontological categories. Instead, every person exists simultaneously as "I-for-myself" and "myself-for-others."[22] The "I-for-myself" refers to the individual's own internal self-perception. From within, the individual is totally free and open to the future. This future orientation constitutes the "I-for-myself's" essential unfinalizability and is a prerequisite of creativity. Since the "I-for-myself" is always in the process of becoming, no particular finalization of it can ever be valid. The most important aspect of the "I-for-myself's" self-perception is an awareness that it occupies a unique place in existence, one that can never be occupied by another.

Bakhtin refers to the external aspect of the individual, that aspect which others perceive, as "myself-for-others." In contrast to the "I-for-myself," the "myself-for-others" occupies a definite existential position with specific temporal and spatial boundaries. From the standpoint of its unique place in existence, the "I-for-myself" organizes the life of the "other" according to an "emotionally and axiologically ponderable time."[23] Bakhtin refers to this qualitative difference between the perspective of the "I-for-myself" and the "other" as "outsidedness." Because of its external orientation to the "other," or its "outsidedness," the "I-for-myself" possesses a unique perspective on life that is inaccessible to the "other."[24] It is based on this external perspective that the "I-for-myself" is able to finalize or provisionally consummate the life of the "other." This act of finalization is, nevertheless, always incomplete. Every attempt to finalize the "other" fixes the "other" temporally and spatially and therefore implicitly denies the "other's" openness to the future as its own "I-for-myself." The act of finalization is merely the "I-for-myself's" transitory attempt to establish an axiological position with respect to the "other."

---

[22] Bakhtin, "Reworking of the Dostoevsky Book," 293.
[23] M. M. Bakhtin, "Author and Hero in Aesthetic Activity," in *A&A*, 110.
[24] Ibid., 22–27.

To Bakhtin, the outsidedness that makes the finalization of the "other" possible stems from what we might call perceptual surplus. The "I-for-myself" occupies a temporal, spatial, and axiological position different from and, in certain respects, superior to that of the "other." To illustrate his point, Bakhtin uses the metaphor of vision. When someone looks at me, he sees me against a background against which I cannot see myself. This background is temporally and spatially static (that is it is synchronic rather than diachronic). At that particular moment, he experiences my personality against this fixed background in a way that differs from my own self-understanding. From the standpoint of this perceptual surplus, the "I-for-myself" finalizes the "other" by making evaluative judgments about him. Nevertheless, this act of finalization never fully corresponds to the internal freedom of the "other" as an "I-for-myself." As an "I-for-myself", a person is always free either to conform to, or rebel against, the "other's" finalizing act.

Only the dialogic interaction of statement and response within a specific context can realize the potential meaning of an utterance. The freedom of the "I-for-myself" in the face of finalization by the "other" constitutes the basis for the "I-for-myself's" dialogic response. What is essential is precisely this evaluative response. A response may serve to confirm, deny, or qualify the "other's" finalization of the "I-for-myself." It is only in the dialogic exchange of statement and response that anything close to an accurate finalization of the "I-for-myself" is possible. Although no amount of dialogic exchange can ever circumvent the essential freedom of the "I-for-myself," such a dialogic exchange can offer a corrective to an incomplete and inaccurate finalization. Ultimately, however, even the "I-for-myself" is unable to offer an authoritative self-evaluation.

> Only the other is capable of being formed and consummated *essentially*, for all the constituents of an axiological consummation (spatial, temporal, and those of meaning) are axiologically transgredient to an active self-consciousness. . . . As long as I remain *myself* for myself, I cannot be active in the aesthetically valid and consolidated space and time.[25]

Since the "I-for-myself" cannot adopt a perspective external (or "transgredient") to itself, it cannot evaluate its own actions in the world. Be-

---

[25] Ibid., 188.

cause of its unique perspective on life and its outsidedness in relation to the "other," the "I-for-myself" can evaluate the actions of others, but internally, "only prayer and penitence are possible." For axiological consummation, the "I-for-myself" is always dependent upon "the mercy of *the other*."[26]

Thus, there is an ethical dimension to the dialogic relation between the "I-for-myself" and the "other." To evaluate the acts of others properly, we must situate those acts in the particular circumstances in which they were performed. To do this we must enter into dialogue with the "other" through a process Bakhtin describes as "live entering," or "living into" their experiences. He describes this as a good faith attempt to see the world from another's perspective.

> I must empathize or project myself into this other human being, see his world axiologically from within him as *he* sees the world; I must put myself in his place and then, after returning to my own place, "fill in" his horizon through that excess of seeing which opens out from this, my own, place outside him.[27]

The act of finalization, therefore, resembles a typical conversation. Just as we should make a good faith effort to understand what someone is trying to say before we offer our reply, we must also try to evaluate the "other" from the standpoint of his or her own values. It is just as perverse and tendentious to evaluate the "other" by dogmatically imposing our values upon them, as it is intentionally to misconstrue someone's meaning for rhetorical purposes. Nevertheless, every statement deserves a response, and once we have tried to understand the "other," we must reply honestly from our own axiological perspective.

The abdication of one's unique perspective on life, which is the essence of relativism, is no less perverse than the dogmatic imposition of our values on others. In order for dialogue to enrich our mutual understanding, it must sustain the distinct perspectives of both dialogic partners. As Bakhtin remarks:

> *Creative understanding* does not renounce itself, its own place in time, its own culture; and it forgets nothing. . . . it is immensely important for the

---

[26] Ibid., 128.
[27] Ibid., 25.

person who understands to be *located outside* the object of his or her creative understanding—in time, in space, in culture."[28]

The goal of dialogue is therefore neither a dialectic synthesis of oppo-
sites nor the assimilation of one perspective by another; it is rather the
mutual enrichment of both parties achieved through the free exchange
of perspectives. Elsewhere, Bakhtin refers to creative understanding as
"interested attention," a concerned, engaged investigation of life.[29] His
emphasis on personal involvement is exactly opposite the feigned objectivity that is often popularly associated with the task of scientific inquiry. Bakhtin demands that we approach the scientific task fully aware
of our values, not so that we can set them aside to achieve a semblance
of neutrality, but precisely so that we can bring them into dialogue with
the values of the "other."

For Bakhtin, unfinalizability and dialogue are the two principal
conditions for human creativity and freedom. Unfinalizability ensures
that we will never arrive at a point where we know the truth in full.
Such a discovery would mean the end of human creativity, since there
would be nothing left to explore. Nevertheless, unfinalizability does not
eliminate the possibility of knowledge; dialogue helps us achieve at
least a measured certainty. We confirm or correct our perception of reality, in part, by comparing notes with others. Dialogue and unfinalizability are therefore essential aspects of perception. This is, in summary
form, the basis of Bakhtin's criticism of all forms of theoretism and the
starting point for his own approach to poetics.

What relevance do these philosophical ruminations have for a
general theory of poetics and a theory of genre in particular? One expression of our social and ideological perception of reality, and perhaps
its most sensitive indicator, is creative aesthetic expression. As something created (in contrast to the givenness of reality), a literary work is
an author's attempt to "finalize" life. An author creates a finalized image of reality that is both individual and social. It is a unique image
created out of socially conditioned semi-stable patterns of words and
values. Its uniqueness lies in its temporal, spatial, and axiological connection with a specific individual. A text represents one person's at-

---

[28] M. M. Bakhtin, "Response to a Question from the *Novy Mir* Editorial
Staff," in *SpG*, 7.
[29] Bakhtin, *TPA*, 62.

tempt to present a unified and evaluative vision of the world, whether that world is real or imaginary. For Bakhtin, the finalizing aspect of the aesthetic work constitutes the proper object of poetics.

The finalizing aspect of the aesthetic work confronts us with two levels of dialogue; the text is both internally and externally dialogic. Internally, Bakhtin describes the finalization of reality in the aesthetic work as analogous to the way the "other" finalizes the "I-for-myself." The author possesses a perceptual surplus over the hero and his world. This perceptual surplus provides the author with the objectifying distance necessary for the characterization of the hero. It is this evaluative perspective that shapes and animates the entire aesthetic work, including the life of the hero. Thus, for Bakhtin, a literary text is a type of utterance both internally and externally.

Externally, texts are the material remains of the "other's" voice. This voice confronts the reader with a unique perspective on the world. To preserve the integrity of the "other's" voice, the reader must assume the task of engaging it in dialogue. For this dialogue to succeed, the reader must sympathetically enter the world of the text. The reader must recognize the organic connection between the text's finalized representation of life and the space and time of the author. Thus, as Bakhtin remarks:

> The text as such never appears as a dead thing; beginning with any text— and sometimes passing through a lengthy series of mediating links—we always arrive, in the final analysis, at the human voice, which is to say we come up against the human being.[30]

Because the voice in the text possesses its own perceptual surplus, it confronts the reader with an otherwise inaccessible perspective on life. To understand this perspective, the reader must try to enter the perceptual world of the text. Nevertheless, as an "I-for-myself," the reader also enjoys a perceptual surplus over the "other" in the text. This perceptual surplus enables the reader to formulate a reply, without which dialogue would cease to exist.

It is against the general framework of unfinalizability and dialogue that Bakhtin develops his understanding of genre. His approach is distinctive because it privileges neither form nor content, but treats

---

[30] Bakhtin, "Forms of Time and of the Chronotope," 252–53.

the text as a unified utterance. By treating the text as an utterance, Bakhtin is able to describe its axiological potential, its unique, value-laden perspective on life. Considered as an utterance, we must evaluate the meaning of the text within the context of its temporal and spatial location. The importance of time and space in the evaluation of texts, and the need to place the text qua utterance in a larger context of meaning, will eventually lead us to the related notions of chronotope and genre. First, however, we must consider the social nature of language.

Language and Heteroglossia

Within any text, there are two main aspects: the repeatable and the unrepeatable.[31] The repeatable aspect of the text is its language system. The unrepeatable aspect is its plan or created purpose. An author employs the relatively stable conventions of language as material for the expression of a unique and unrepeatable, goal-directed end. Language, as the material of aesthetic expression, presents the author with rich possibilities for creativity. As with any form of aesthetic expression, the potential within the material is an obstacle that the artist must overcome. For example, a block of marble presents almost limitless possibilities for plastic representation. The sculptor can shape it into a myriad of images. The final product depends completely upon the intention and the ability of the sculptor. Likewise, language is an artistic medium with rich potential for self-expression. But unlike marble, which has no meaning apart from its use in art, words have a rich history of meanings and accents. Consequently, language is not a neutral medium of aesthetic expression; rather it bears the distinctive marks of previous artists. Thus, language is an especially challenging and problematic artistic medium.[32]

Bakhtin refers to the rich and complex nature of language as "heteroglossia." Heteroglossia refers to more than the diversity of the vocabulary of a language or the richness of its semantic constructions. It refers instead, to the variegated ways we use language to express our

---

[31] Bakhtin, "Problem of the Text," 105.

[32] V. N. Vološinov [M. M. Bakhtin], "Literary Stylistics," in Ann Shukman, ed., *Bakhtin School Papers*, trans. Noel Owen and Joe Andrew, Russian Poetics in Translation, ed. Anne Shukman, no. 10 (Oxford: RPT Publications, 1983), 94.

axiological relationship to the world. As Bakhtin writes, all the languages of heteroglossia

> are specific points of view on the world, forms for conceptualizing the world in words, specific world views, each characterized by its own objects, meanings and values. . . . As such, these languages live a real life, they struggle and evolve in an environment of social heteroglossia.[33]

Elsewhere, Bakhtin states the matter more succinctly: language is "shot through with intentions and accents."[34] Every word has its own values and intonations because of its social life. Words never have a simple, unaccented, axiologically neutral correspondence to their object.[35] Each word carries overtones of its previous use. Consequently, language is an ideologically saturated medium of expression. Whenever an author chooses a word, there is always the risk that it will say less, or more, than she wished to say. The chosen word may leave an impression, reflect an attitude, or convey an evaluation, different from that which the author wished to express.

The heteroglossic, or heteroglot, nature of language poses special problems for aesthetic expression. An author must force the heteroglot nature of language "to submit" to his "own intentions and accents."[36] Elsewhere Bakhtin describes the artist's task as "the surmounting of material."[37]

> One could say that the artist fashions the world by means of words, and to this end words must be immanently surmounted as words and must become an expression of the world of others and of the author's relationship to that world.[38]

Words do not belong to an author; they are the common property of society. It is impossible to sanitize the meaning of words, to cleanse them of their prior meanings and contexts and thereby make them exclusively one's own. In language, words are always "half someone

---

[33] Bakhtin, "Discourse in the Novel," 291–92.

[34] Ibid., 293.

[35] Ibid., 276; and M. M. Bakhtin, "Toward a Methodology for the Human Sciences," in *SpG*, 161.

[36] Bakhtin, "Discourse in the Novel," 294.

[37] Bakhtin, "Author and Hero," 193.

[38] Ibid., 195. Also, "Problem of Content," 297.

else's."[39] They only become the author's words when she successfully uses them to express her own socially conditioned intention with her own distinctive accent and intonation.

An author draws on the rich heteroglot possibilities of language by carefully choosing words and constraining their meaning by juxtaposing them with other words. In this way, an author can even relate words with different accents and intonations to one another dialogically. Authorial expression is the product of this dialogical interaction. It is therefore not the individual words, considered in isolation from one another, that express the author's intention but the complex dialogic interaction between words pregnant with heteroglot potential. Thus, we must discern the meaning of a text by considering the work as a whole. Any attempt to transcribe the content of a work by restating its meaning propositionally invariably loses the specific accents and intonations produced by the text. A text is a unified utterance, and we can only comprehended it properly by considering it as an architectonic whole.[40]

When Bakhtin speaks of authorial intention, he uses the term author in a carefully qualified sense.[41] The author reflected in the form and content of the material text is not identical to the author who created the text. These two authors exist on separate ontological planes. Borrowing the language of Duns Scotus, Bakhtin writes that the real author who creates a text is *natura non creata quae creat* (nature not created that creates), while the image of the author in the text is *natura creata quae non creat* (created nature that does not create).[42] Thus, Bakhtin claims:

---

[39] Bakhtin, "Discourse in the Novel," 293.

[40] Bakhtin, "Methodology for the Human Sciences," 160.

[41] Since the publication of "The Intentional Fallacy," by W. K. Wimsatt and Monroe C. Beardslee in 1946 (reprinted in W. K. Wimsatt, *The Verbal Icon: Studies in the Meaning of Poetry* [Lexington: University of Kentucky Press, 1954], 3–18), the significance of authorial intention in literary criticism has been much debated. Those who have defended its importance include, among others, E. D. Hirsch, *Validity in Interpretation*. For a recent work that defends the notion of authorial intention along dialogic lines similar to those advanced by Bakhtin, see Patrick Swinden, *Literature and the Philosophy of Intention* (New York: St. Martin's, 1999).

[42] Bakhtin, "From Notes made in 1970–71," in *SpG*, 148; also, "Methodology for the Human Sciences," 160–61; and, "Problem of the Text," 110.

> Every utterance in this sense has its author, whom we hear in the very utterance as its creator. Of the real author, as he exists outside the utterance, we can know absolutely nothing at all. . . . A given work can be the product of a collective effort, it can be created by the successive efforts of generations, and so forth—but in all cases we hear in it a unified creative will, a definite position, to which it is possible to react dialogically. A dialogic reaction personifies every utterance to which it responds.[43]

The author in the text is an image, or impression, created by the real author, either intentionally or unintentionally, whether the author is individual or corporate. As an image contained within the text, the created author is finalized against a specific spatial, temporal, and axiological background. The real author, by contrast, always remains free and unfinalized. It is the real author's free and unfinalized position outside the text that provides the perceptual surplus necessary for the creation of the world of the story, of which the finalized image of the author is only one component. When we speak of the authorial intention that shapes a text, we are referring to the intention of the author fixed within the text and not the intention of the real author. Here Bakhtin adduces, independently of modern literary theory, the figure we have come to refer to as the implied author. The psychological intention of the real author remains unknown and unknowable. Even when the real author is available to explain her intention, all that we have is the author's own finalized representation of the original intention and not the intention itself. In the process of reading, the reader dialogues not with the real author, but with the image of the author sympathetically recreated from the text.

When Bakhtin claims that the formal and linguistic elements of the utterance are the "sclerotic deposits of an intentional process," he gives the impression that the meaning of the text is rigid and unchanging.[44] Bakhtin maintains, however, that this is not the case. If it were, the text would be meaningful only for those who shared the socio-ideological values of the author. We cannot confine the meaning of a work to its author's original intent in a narrow sense, nor, on the other hand, can the text mean anything someone wants it to mean. The meaning of the text exists in a dialogic space between these two extreme positions. Bakhtin suggests that a text is able to mean more than its author

---

[43] Bakhtin, *PDP*, 184.
[44] Bakhtin, "Discourse in the Novel," 292.

consciously intended because it may contain intuited meaning. Many texts live a long and productive socio-ideological life. One need only think of the works of Shakespeare. Because great literary works draw on the rich heteroglot potential of language, they possess semantic potential of which the author may be only partially aware. This potential only surfaces in later generations when the text encounters new socio-ideological perspectives. Dialogic exposure to positions of genuine alterity often reveals previously unrecognized meaning in great literary works.[45]

The semantic potential of great literary works results from both their heteroglot potential and their use of relatively stable forms of linguistic expression. Linguistic expression assumes distinct patterns when the heteroglot potential of language coalesces into semi-stable forms of perception and evaluation. These semi-stable forms, or genres, are also rich in accumulated meanings and axiological intonations. Like words, genres also have a socio-ideological life and reflect the heteroglot nature of language. Nevertheless, while the grammatical rules that govern the use of words are relatively rigid and obligatory, there are no such rules for the use of generic forms. Generic forms are "much more flexible, plastic, and free."[46] Even so, as part of the repeatable, ready-made material of language, an author must also surmount the rich potential of genre to express an intention.[47] An author uses a specific genre because of its axiological intonation and then adapts it to suit his intention. Just as it is impossible to sanitize words of their evaluative overtones, it is likewise impossible to cleanse genres of their peculiar intonation. Nor would this necessarily be desirable. Genres are a rich and interesting medium of expression precisely because of their evaluative overtones. When an author uses these evaluative overtones skillfully and creatively, they contribute to the semantic potential of great literary works over the course of 'great time.'[48]

If, as Bakhtin claims, genres are semi-stable patterns of heteroglossia, then genre is a matter of metalinguistic, rather than material, form. Regular formal patterns in the linguistic material of the text may be only accidental to any particular genre. The essence of a genre is its

---

[45] Morson & Emerson, "*Heteroglossary*," 262–63.
[46] Bakhtin, "The Problem of Speech Genres," in *SpG*, 79.
[47] Bakhtin, "Author and Hero," 197.
[48] Morson & Emerson, "*Heteroglossary*," 264.

metalinguistic form or pattern; what Bakhtin calls its "form-shaping ideology." It is, therefore, the overarching, axiologically guided form or architectonic structure of the aesthetic work that constitutes the author's primary activity. Architectonic form is not merely the manipulation of linguistic devices (as the Formalists proposed), but the orchestration of the heteroglot potential of language to achieve a specific metalinguistic expression.[49] An author achieves this metalinguistic expression through the careful juxtaposition and dialogic arrangement of words and genres in light of their previous intonations and accents. What guides the over-all process is the form-shaping ideology of the author. It is this author-ial activity that produces the overall form of the aesthetic work and gives it not only its mechanical and compositional unity, but also more importantly its metalinguistic and architectonic unity.

Speech Genres, Literary Genres, and Chronotope

Bakhtin claimed that the main fault of genre study in the past was that it had overlooked "the basic social tone" of literary works.[50] Everything that we have said up to this point underscores the critical nature of this oversight. The sociological aspect of genre and the cru-cial role it plays in the understanding of literature became the guiding presupposition of Bakhtin's work. Within the literary work, "living so-cial forces intersect; each element of its form is permeated with living social evaluations."[51] A valid approach to poetics must be able to ac-count for and analyze the specific ways the literary work refracts these social forces.

The function of living social forces within generic forms is per-haps easiest to observe in the realm of everyday speech. Every sphere of social life has specific patterns of speech associated with it. We use these patterns of speech, or speech genres, to express meaning appro-priate to a given social situation. The choice of speech genre is dictated in part by the genres available within a language appropriate to the cir-cumstances of the utterance and in part by the intention of the speaker. Speech genres range from the purely phatic convention of greeting

---

[49] Bakhtin, "Problem of Content," 300–1, 304.

[50] Bakhtin, "Discourse in the Novel," 259.

[51] Bakhtin, "Three Fragments from the 1929 Edition, *Problems of Dosto-evsky's Art*," in *PDP*, 276.

someone in passing, to more elaborate conventionalized linguistic rituals, such as the job interview.[52] The use of a speech genre in the wrong social context often results in a serious social blunder. As Bakhtin notes, mastery of a language entails more than familiarity with its phonics, grammar, and lexicon. To be fluent, you must also master the speech genres of the language.[53] In other words, you must know what tones, grammatical structures, and words are appropriate in specific social circumstances.

Bakhtin labels the patterns of speech found in everyday language "primary speech genres." These are the myriad forms of conventionalized speech used in our daily contact with others: greetings, requests, casual conversation, and so forth. "Secondary speech genres" are more complex and specialized forms of discourse related to specific areas of communication, such as the scholarly treatise, the academic lecture, or the business letter.[54] Secondary genres are derivative of primary genres. They are formed through the incorporation and modification of various types of primary speech genres for specific purposes.[55] In the process of this transformation, the primary genre becomes stylized. It loses its immediate connection to the circumstances that governed its original function in life. Formal and axiological aspects of its original function become part of the created world of the secondary genre, and there they serve the overarching (architectonic) purpose of the secondary utterance. Within the secondary genre, the primary genre serves a more complex ideological function than the one it once had in everyday speech.[56] Within the secondary genre, it functions as an indirect indicator of condensed social evaluations.

---

[52] On the various functions of words see J. L. Austin, *How to Do Things with Words*, ed. J. O. Urmson and Marina Sbisa, 2d ed. (Cambridge: Harvard University Press, 1975).

[53] Bakhtin, "Speech Genres," 80.

[54] Ibid., 62. Bakhtin observes that, in contrast to primary speech genres, which are oral, secondary speech genres are often written.

[55] For example, the conventional greeting in a business letter ("Dear Sir") is a highly stylized adaptation of a formal greeting in everyday speech. Such forms of address serve the function of establishing contact and initiating an exchange of information. The written form would sound overly formal, however, if uttered in the context of everyday speech.

[56] Bakhtin, "Speech Genres," 62.

Speech genres are the point of contact between the history of society and the history of language. No linguistic phenomenon "can enter the system of language without having traversed the long and complicated path of generic-stylistic testing and modification."[57] A consequence of this process is that the ideological values of the epoch are reflected in the style of its speech genres, especially in those genres that are characteristic of the age.[58] When these characteristic speech genres begin to lose their currency, authors create new ones by borrowing and reaccenting speech genres from other social spheres. For example, the ironic or parodistic use of a speech genre typically reserved for formal occasions creates a new type of expression by reaccenting an existing genre. Authors also form new speech genres by intentionally mixing genres from disparate social spheres.[59] As the expressive potential of a speech genre dissipates over time, either it falls into disuse, or it becomes incorporated into new speech genres. This process never exhausts the linguistic resources of language since the social forces that animate language are constantly changing.

The notion that speech genres are rigid patterns of communication is derived from the mistaken idea that genres are linguistic forms of greater magnitude than the sentence. As Bakhtin demonstrates, this is not the case. The sentence is the most complex level of linguistic composition. Its construction is governed by the rules of grammar and its success as a meaningful unit of language depends upon adherence to those rules.[60] When properly composed, we can conceive of the potential meaning(s) of a sentence, but we cannot generate a response to it. We can only evaluate the isolated sentence by comparing its structure to grammatical rules. As an isolated unit of speech, the sentence is only capable of abstract meaning. We cannot characterize these abstract

---

[57] Ibid., 65.

[58] Ibid., 65. Tzvetan Todorov also notes this aspect of genre when he writes, "Each epoch has its own system of genres, which stands in some relation to the dominant ideology." See Tzvetan Todorov, *Genres in Discourse*, trans. Catherine Porter (Cambridge: Cambridge University Press, 1990), 19.

[59] Bakhtin, "Speech Genres," 79–80.

[60] As *langue*, either it conforms to grammatical rules or it does not. No other level of evaluation is possible. See Gary Saul Morson and Caryl Emerson, "Introduction: Rethinking Bakhtin," in *Rethinking Bakhtin: Extensions and Challenges*, ed. Gary Saul Morson and Caryl Emerson, Series in Russian Literature and Theory, ed. Gary Saul Morson (Evanston, Ill.: Northwestern University Press, 1989), 14.

meanings as good or bad, inspiring or depressing, serious or humorous, until we relate them to a definite situation. To generate an active response, someone must speak the sentence within a specific context, which is to say it must become part of an utterance.[61] Only then is it possible to adopt an evaluative position with respect to the meaning of the sentence.

Unlike the sentence, the utterance assumes a definite position with respect to content; it evaluates its subject, deems it adequate or condemns it as inadequate, declares it beautiful or base, pure or defiled. The utterance orients the potential meaning of the sentence to a specific time and place and sets it within the scope of a discrete set of social values. The performed sentence or utterance can only generate a response within this metalinguistic context. Only here can the reader or hearer judge the appropriateness of the utterance, deeming it right or wrong, fair or unfair, good or bad. Bakhtin emphasizes that the utterance's ability to generate a response is a necessary condition for human communication. Without a response, there can be no dialogue and therefore no human discourse. Consequently, every utterance is always oriented toward other utterances. It is simultaneously a response to previous utterances and the basis for subsequent utterances. These metalinguistic aspects of the utterance constitute its active social life. Bakhtin claimed that since the social dimension of the utterance was beyond the scope of the sentence as a linguistic unit, its meaning was completely beyond the range of the science of linguistics.

As we have noted, Bakhtin defined speech genres as "relatively stable thematic, compositional, and stylistic types of utterances."[62] Therefore, speech genres share the complex social and ideological qualities of the utterance. In fact, speech genres condense these metalinguistic factors into semi-stable patterns. What is typical about a speech genre is not simply its linguistic form but its socio-ideological orientation. As a metalinguistic rather than linguistic category, a speech genre is a semi-stable axiological pattern associated with a particular material form and semantic content. It shares this pattern with similar utterances, to which it relates dialogically. In everyday use, the individ-

---

[61] Bakhtin, "Speech Genres," 82–83. Compare Todorov's observations in *Genres in Discourse*, 16–17.

[62] Ibid., 64.

ual utterance may either draw on the metalinguistic resources typical of the speech genre, or nuance the generic pattern by intoning the utterance with a slightly different accent. In this way, a speaker is able to use the resources of a genre to express either agreement or disagreement with its tradition. The creative use of a speech genre also affects its future trajectory. Over time, as the innovative use of the generic pattern becomes conventional, the metalinguistic orientation of the speech genre shifts. These alterations refract historical changes in social values, as well as the use of the speech genre in new spatial and temporal locations.

Because literary works are a type of utterance, they have both an external and an internal orientation. Externally, on the level of performance, the literary genre is a complex, aesthetically created secondary genre. When it is read, the literary work is oriented toward real readers (or listeners) in a particular time and place under specific social conditions. Internally, the literary genre is a self-contained dialogically organized utterance. Like speech genres, literary works internalize aspects characteristic of both speaker and responder. The literary work not only makes claims, evaluations, and judgments concerning previous utterances; it also makes assumptions, and anticipates and parries possible counter responses. These two dialogic dimensions of the text produce what narratology refers to as the implied author and the implied reader. Every literary work is in some sense a dialogue between these two positions.

In everyday speech, the speaker and the responder are aware of their social relationship, the time and place of their encounter, and the thematic content of their exchange. The speaker's awareness of, and attitude toward, these circumstances dictates the most appropriate forms of speech. The metalinguistic information provided by the situation supplies the necessary context for meaningful discourse. If a literary work is to live beyond the immediate circumstances surrounding its composition, it cannot assume the metalinguistic context of its external performance. Instead, the author must weave metalinguistic information into the fabric of the literary text. The author draws on the resources of genre to convey this metalinguistic information. By either following the conventions of a single genre or juxtaposing several genres, an author creates "a zone and a field of valorized perception" that communicates the metalinguistic context necessary for a proper understanding of the literary work. [63] In the case of the "writer-craftsman," genre may merely serve as "an external template," but "the great artist" knows how to use "the semantic possibilities" of genre to create a specific socio-ideological context for the literary work.[64] Although the author's finalizing vision ultimately determines the precise socio-ideological dimensions of the literary work, genre is a critical resource in its production.

It is important not to confuse the internal and external aspects of the literary work's metalinguistic context. The external conditions of the literary work's performance are given. These external conditions are unique and unrepeatable, and therefore completely beyond the control of the author. Every performance of a literary work—whether public or private—has significance in its immediate context that can never be duplicated. Each performance enters history as a unique event. A literary work is only able to live beyond the circumstances of its performance because of its internal context.[65] This internal context creates an axiologically charged, spatially and temporally finalized world that provides a specific metalinguistic context for the literary work. In great literary works, the richness and complexity of this internal context allows them to live beyond the immediate circumstances of their production and initial performance. As Bakhtin remarks,

> Trying to understand and explain a work solely in terms of the conditions of its epoch alone, solely in terms of the conditions of the most immediate time, will never enable us to penetrate into its semantic depths. . . . Works break through the boundaries of their own time, they live in centuries, that is, in great time and frequently (with great works, always) their lives there are more intense and fuller than are their lives within their own time.[66]

Thus, the significance of a literary work lies in its ability to transcend its own epoch. The literary work is reanimated when the socio-ideological context of its present day performance awakens the semantic potential it possesses as a whole utterance. The locus of this dialogic vitality is neither in the material form of the literary work, nor in its

---

[63] Bakhtin, "Epic and Novel," in *DI*, 28.

[64] Bakhtin, "Response to a Question," 5.

[65] Bakhtin, "Notes made in 1970–71," 134. Also Bakhtin, "Forms of Time and of the Chronotope," 256; and Bakhtin / Medvedev, *FM*, 131.

[66] Bakhtin, "Response to a Question," 4.

cognitive content. What brings the text to life and makes it meaningful is the dialogic interaction between distinct axiological positions. On the one hand, there is the axiological position of the implied author fixed within the material of the text, and on the other, there is the ever-changing axiological position of the reader who responds to the text.

The dialogue between author and reader takes place within an axiologically charged world of the author's creation. This created world reflects the values of the author's aesthetic perception of the world, and the aesthetic and axiological dimensions of this created world constitute a work's architectonic form. Because architectonic form is what gives the literary work its unity, it constitutes the essence of a work's genre. Over the course of his career, Bakhtin explored three main ways in which the axiological perspective of the author was refracted in the literary work: the relationship between author and hero, the relationship between the author and addressee, and the axiological qualities of the work's time and space, an aspect of the text that he preferred to call its "chronotope."[67] The last of these was the most significant for Bakhtin.[68] Albert Einstein originally coined the term chronotope—from the Greek terms for time (χρόνος) and place (τόπος). For Bakhtin, however, its connection with the Theory of Relativity was unimportant.[69] Bakhtin

---

[67] On the relationship between author and hero, see Bakhtin, "Author and Hero," 89–90. On the influence of the author's conception of the addressee on genre, see Bakhtin, "Speech Genres," 95, 98.

[68] Bakhtin, "Forms of Time and of the Chronotope," 84–85. For helpful discussions of Bakhtin's notion of chronotope and its relation to his theory of genre, see Tzvetan Todorov, *Mikhail Bakhtin: The Dialogical Principle*, trans. Wlad Godzich, Theory and History of Literature 13 (Minneapolis: University of Minnesota Press, 1984), 80–5; and Gary Saul Morson and Caryl Emerson, *Mikhail Bakhtin: Creation of a Prosaics* (Stanford: Stanford University Press, 1990), 271–305, and 366–432.

[69] The concepts of time and space were also of particular importance to Immanuel Kant. He calls them the "two pure forms of sensuous intuition" (*Critique of Pure Reason*, A 22, B 37). In a note, Bakhtin remarks that although he "employs the Kantian evaluation of the importance of these forms in the cognitive process," he differs from Kant by "taking them not as 'transcendental' but as forms of the most immediate reality." Bakhtin's intention is "to show the role these forms play in the process of concrete artistic cognition" ("Forms of Time and of the Chronotope," p. 85, n. 2). Later in the same article, Bakhtin refers his readers to Ernst Cassirer, *The Philosophy of Symbolic Forms*, for a more detailed explanation of the role of time in language ("Forms of Time and of the Chronotope," 251). On the connection between Bakhtin's notion of chronotope and Kantian epistemology,

used chronotope somewhat metaphorically to stress "the inseparability of space and time" in literature.[70]

Since, for Bakhtin, all meaning is contextual—organically related to a specific time and place—the values inherent in the chronotope of the literary work are an especially useful index of the author's values.[71] Thus, for Bakhtin chronotope became the primary basis for the description of genres: "The chronotope in literature has an intrinsic *generic* significance. . . . it is precisely the chronotope that defines genre and generic distinctions."[72] The chronotope possesses this significance because it reflects, in an especially clear way, the text's form-shaping ideology. Thus, Bakhtin claims, "every entry into the sphere of meaning is accomplished only through the gates of the chronotope."[73]

The chronotope of the literary work has little to do with its time and place of performance.[74] The time and place of performance is open and unfinalized, and therefore unrepresentable. Nor is chronotope another word for *mise-en-scène*. Chronotope includes axiological overtones that are absent in the notion of *mise-en-scène*. The chronotope is the literary work's finalized vision of the world; the world the way the author envisions it. A world filled with the author's values and judgments; an ideal world created by the author for the meaningful activity of the hero.[75] Within this artistically created world,

> spatial and temporal indicators are fused into one carefully thought-out, concrete whole. Time, as it were, thickens, takes on flesh, becomes artistically visible; likewise, space becomes charged and responsive to the

---

see Bernard F. Scholz, "Bakhtin's Concept of 'Chronotope': The Kantian Connection," in *The Contexts of Bakhtin: Philosophy, Authorship, Aesthetics*, ed. David Shepherd, Studies in Russian and European Literature, ed. Peter I. Barta and David Shepherd, 2 (Amsterdam: Harwood, 1998), 141–59.

[70] Bakhtin, "Forms of Time and of the Chronotope," 84. Bakhtin's best discussion of the axiological unity of time and space is "The *Bildungsroman* and Its Significance in the History of Realism," in *SpG*, 10–59.

[71] Bakhtin, "Forms of Time and of the Chronotope," 150.

[72] Ibid., 84–85.

[73] Ibid., 258.

[74] Ibid., 256.

[75] Bakhtin, "Author and Hero," 99, 100.

movements of time, plot and history. This intersection of axes and fusion of indicators characterizes the artistic chronotope.[76]

Chronotopic time and space always possess an "evaluating aspect . . . colored by emotions and values."[77] Within the chronotope, time, space, and evaluation merge into an inseparable, organic unity. This axiologically charged vision of the world supplies the necessary metalinguistic context for the discourse within the text.

An example may help to indicate the importance of chronotope in generic distinctions. Form critics often use the German literary terms *Märchen*, *Sage*, and *Legende* to identify Old Testament literary genres. At times, the application of this terminology among biblical scholars has lacked precision due to infelicitous translations and confusion with Scandinavian terminology. John J. Scullion has tried to clarify the meaning of these three terms. His proposed definitions are remarkable because he describes these literary genres in chronotopic terms, quite apart from any familiarity with Bakhtin and the notion of chronotope. Nevertheless, Scullion describes the differences between these three genres according to variations in their temporal and spatial qualities. For example, he describes the characteristics of *Märchen* as follows:

> The world of the *Märchen* is the world of "the beyond" where the preternatural and the supernatural, in modern terms the "unreal", predominate; it is a world that does not know the limitations of space, time and causality; it transcends the limits of our experience of reality. The places are nameless, the characters are nameless, and there is little sense of time.[78]

Now compare his definition of the German *Sage*.

> *Sage* is a story...concerned with particular persons, places and times, in which extraordinary events occur in ordinary places. The element of the numinous, the awesome, is often there. The story is believed to have taken place and so is in some way determinative of the present belief of the people among whom it is now handed down and recited.[79]

---

[76] Bakhtin, "Forms of Time and of the Chronotope," 84. For further remarks on the importance of chronotope and the way that it reflects the values of the author, see: Ibid., 250; Bakhtin, *"Bildungsroman,"* 42.

[77] Bakhtin, "Forms of Time and of the Chronotope," 243.

[78] John J. Scullion, *"Märchen, Sage, Legende*: Towards a Clarification of Some Literary Terms Used by Old Testament Scholars," *VT* 34 (1984): 322.

[79] Ibid., 331.

What is remarkable about these definitions is that they stress precisely those chronotopic aspects that Bakhtin suggests are determinative of genre. The space of the *Märchen* is the realm of the fantastic, beyond the limits of normal causation. It is temporally indeterminate, with historically unidentifiable characters. One of the characteristics of the *Märchen* identified by Scullion is that *Märchen* treats this "unreal world" as if it were completely normal. Thus, there is an axiological dimension to his description of the genre as well. Scullion also describes *Sage* according to its chronotopic aspect. *Sage* is set in a realistic space and time, peopled with familiar "persons, places and times." Nevertheless, this realistic world is the scene of fantastic events, and it is precisely the evaluation of the fantastic as paranormal that gives the *Sage* its peculiar accent. The axiological aspect of the *Sage* is also apparent in the implicit belief that the story actually happened and, because it happened, it is now determinative of present beliefs.

The most interesting aspect of the distinction between *Märchen* and *Sage* is the difference in aesthetic potential that each genre possesses. *Märchen* allows an author to address universal problems apart from the constraints of historical verisimilitude. Stereotypical characters are placed in extraordinarily demanding circumstances where there is rarely any middle ground between abject poverty and spectacular wealth, oppressive bad luck and miraculous good fortune. With its simplified set of values and nearly limitless narrative possibilities, the *Märchen* excels at morality tales wherein evil always comes to naught and goodness and purity are ultimately rewarded. In contrast, the genre of *Sage* has its own characteristic potential. The *Sage* recounts tales of heroic figures in the past surmounting obstacles of supernatural proportions through heroic perseverance and determination. Neither type of literature could fully replace the other. Each genre has a special way of constructing the world of the story and consequently each brings specific types of values to bear on the world of the hero. According to Bakhtin, these features define a literary work's genre.

Bakhtin claimed that literary works are generically similar when they finalize the world in similar ways. Therefore, genre is, strictly speaking, not about formal similarities, but about ideological trajectories, and the best indicator of these trajectories is the chronotope. Ideological trajectories represent a continuous chain of utterances that share a similar perspective on the world. As a chain of utterances, works that share this relationship are engaged in an ongoing dialogue about life. No single work stands alone in this chain of discourse; every work is both a reply to previous works and a new statement to which subsequent works reply. To understand a given literary work means that the critic must situate the work within the ongoing discussion of which it is a part. According to Bakhtin, it is impossible to evaluate an aesthetic work properly apart from an appreciation of its intrageneric dialogic context.

Conclusion

The problem of genre is the problem of creative human expression. We cannot dissect and analyze the meaning of such creative expressions according to their basic components. Human expression is social-historical discourse. As such its material, form, and content can be analyzed atomistically, but its meaning—its significance and relevance—can only be apprehended with reference to its specific context. Just as the linguistic event of a speech act depends upon a concrete context, even if assumed or imagined, aesthetic expression is rooted in a particular context.

Genre is thus not a matter of taxonomy: the final step that follows scientific analysis. It is rather an attempt to relate a work with other works that are engaged in the same ongoing dialogue. The comparison of literature according to formal similarities misses this aspect altogether. It compares similarities and patterns in the material, form, and content but ignores the unified expression of a definite axiological position. According to Bakhtin, this socio-historical axiological position is the essence of genre and the problem of genre is thus less a matter of scientific taxonomy than it is a matter of temporally extensive ("great time") conversations about values. If we take seriously Aristotle's dictum that a definition should state the essence of a thing,[80] Bakhtin's understanding of genre helps us state more precisely the essence of a literary work. The superficial, formal similarity of two or more literary works based upon similar themes or linguistic forms is an inadequate basis for a generic comparison since formal similarities may merely be accidental to the essential nature of a work. To be meaning-

---

[80] *Top.* 1.5, 101b36.

ful, we must base our determination of genre on essential qualities. Bakhtin's socio-historical poetics lays bare these qualities for us.

For Bakhtin, the function of the literary work as a communicative act primarily defines its essence. As such, its essence is not merely a matter of content or form. Communication is fundamentally about two people engaged in a dialogue. Each of these persons represents a distinct and unique perspective on life, with specific temporal, spatial, and axiological aspects. To understand the communicative act means that we must address the intentionality that motivates the dialogic exchange. Authorial intention is, therefore, properly located "at the center of organization where all levels intersect."[81] Because a literary work is a linguistically fixed expression of a communicative act, it represents an author's intention to communicate information, as well as evaluation and emotion. To understand the essence of a literary work, we must attend to its communicative intention. This communicative intention, as Bakhtin demonstrates, is what is essential to a work of literature because it is intention that gives the work its architectonic unity.

It is, of course, somewhat unfashionable to speak, in an unqualified way, of authorial intention. The authorial intention embedded in the text is elusive. We know it more from its effects than its material remains. Nevertheless, the material of a text—words, phrases, and sentences arranged in a particular way—implies the intentional work an author. Linguistic material alone, however, is a mute indicator of the author's intention. Linguistic material requires a context in order to communicate meaning. Form and redaction critics also recognized the connection between text and context.[82] They tried to elucidate the *Sitz im Leben* of a pericope, but too often, they abstracted the pericope from its generic context and indulged in overly speculative historical theories about its original cultic function. Oddly enough, Bakhtin confronted a similar situation with the literary critics of his own day who sometimes reduced the dialogue between competing ideological perspectives within a literary work to "actual real-life struggle[s] among schools and trends."[83] When we direct our attention to the author's personality, or

---

[81] Bakhtin, "Prehistory of Novelistic Discourse," 49.

[82] In certain respects, Form Criticism's use of the concept *Sitz im Leben* prefigured the recent interest in the social context of genre. See Joe Foley, "Form Criticism and Genre Theory," *Language and Literature* 4 (1995): 173–91.

[83] Bakhtin, "Epic and Novel," 7.

the hypothetical battles he may have been waging, we lose sight of "the specific demands [genre] makes upon language and the specific possibilities it opens up for it."[84] To prevent such farsightedness, Bakhtin redirects our attention to the importance of the text's ideological context. He claims that the most appropriate context for the interpretation of a text is the authorially determined ideological perspective that dictated its creation.

In literary communication, as in everyday speech, there are semistable patterns of communication, or genres. These patterns provide contextual clues that are necessary for communication to occur. The ability to sense the appropriate genre of an utterance, or text, is therefore essential for successful communication. Each genre, whether of speech or literature, conveys something of the axiological perspective of the speaker or writer. This is, of course, not to say that we can easily or necessarily equate the axiological position in the text with the ongoing axiological orientation of the speaker or author. The historical, physical, and psychological activity of the speaker or author is, for the duration of their life, in a constant state of flux. Nevertheless, each speech act—whether oral or written—is uttered from the axiological standpoint of an identifiable rhetorical persona, namely that of the implied author.

The dialogic exchange engendered by the text is therefore much more than the exchange of information through a neutral linguistic code. It is an exchange of ideas, perceptions, and attitudes conveyed as much by the linguistic material of words and genres as by the content of the exchange. What unifies this complex of material, form and content is the work's form-shaping ideology, and this is what gives a literary work its architectonic unity. Form-shaping ideology constitutes the true essence of a literary work and therefore comparing literary works that share similar form-shaping ideologies is superior to the isolation of potentially accidental patterns of form and content. Since ideology is inseparable from its expression in a specific space and time, the characteristic chronotope of a text is the best indicator of its form-shaping ideology and therefore the best indicator of its genre.

From the standpoint of what Bakhtin calls "great time," literary works that share a similar form-shaping ideology are engaged in an on-

---

[84] Bakhtin, "Prehistory of Novelistic Discourse," 43.

going conversation that may span centuries. This conversation may be direct or indirect; what establishes the generic connection is the way an author exploits the axiological potential of a particular form-shaping ideology. It stands to reason that no two aesthetic works will have identical axiological perspectives. Nevertheless, similarities between works whose axiological viewpoints overlap share a generic relationship, and often these similar axiological viewpoints coalesce into relatively stable formal patterns. Within these relatively stable patterns, we can expect to find both continuity and transformation. Both aspects are significant. Continuity preserves the particular pattern of perception while transformation adapts the pattern to new socio-historical contexts. Therefore, a Bakhtinian approach to the problem of Markan genre suggests that a comparison of Mark with formally similar works is less important than a comparison with ideologically similar works. In the following chapter, we will begin our search for such works.

Chapter Three

GRECO-ROMAN NOVELISTIC LITERATURE IN THE HELLENISTIC PERIOD

As an act of creative perception, the aesthetic work is forged from the socio-ideological material of language. This material consists of language itself, with its grammar and lexicon, and familiar patterns of usage, or genres. This linguistic material is thoroughly social in nature; it overflows with the potential of heteroglossia. An utterance refracts this heteroglot potential through the specific values governing its orchestration. One implication of the heteroglot nature of language is that no literary genre can ever be, strictly speaking, *sui generis*. Authors can create new genres, but only from the linguistic material at hand. Bakhtin writes:

> A newly born genre never supplants or replaces any already existing genres. Each new genre merely supplements the old ones, merely widens the circle of already existing genres. For every genre has its own predominant sphere of existence, in which it is irreplaceable. . . . But at the same time each fundamentally and significantly new genre, once it arrives, exerts influence on the entire circle of old genres: the new genre makes the old ones, so to speak, more conscious; it forces them to better perceive their own possibilities and boundaries, that is, to overcome their own *naiveté*.[1]

Thus, every literary work bears an essential relationship to its literary antecedents. This relationship is not one of mere imitation. Successful

---

[1] Bakhtin, *PDP*, 271.

works, works that live beyond the immediate circumstances of their composition, breathe new life into old forms. The new work, looking back on its predecessors from a new perspective, uses its perceptual surplus, its outsidedness or otherness, to exploit the unseen potential of those former works. In the process, it not only says something new; it also lends new significance to its source material.

The innovative use of the heteroglot potential of language to express new and relevant content constitutes the primary realm of authorial creativity, and the explication of this creative activity was, for Bakhtin, the legitimate task of poetics. Bakhtin devoted much of his writing to this task. His primary focus was the aesthetic development of the novel. The novel has always been a problematic genre.[2] It assumes so many different forms that invariably any definition of it must be broad and sweeping, collecting under some overarching generalization many different subtypes. Bakhtin never offered a precise definition of the novel as a genre. Instead, he investigated the processes that produced it. For investigating the Gospel of Mark, it might seem irrelevant to discuss the development of the novel, since the novel is a modern genre, the first true example being Cervantes' *Don Quixote* in the seventeenth century. Nevertheless, Bakhtin believed the origins of the novel were more ancient.[3]

> Long before the appearance of the novel we find a rich world of diverse forms that transmit, mimic and represent from various vantage points another's word, another's speech and language, including also the languages of the direct genres. These diverse forms prepared the ground for the novel long before its actual appearance. Novelistic discourse has a lengthy prehistory, going back centuries, even thousands of years.[4]

During its prehistory, novelistic discourse emerged from epic literary forms through a lengthy process of transformation. A brief explanation

---

[2] M. H. Abrams, *A Glossary of Literary Terms*, 5th ed. (Fort Worth: Holt, Rinehart & Winston, 1988), 117–22; and J. A. Cuddon, *A Dictionary of Literary Terms and Literary Theory*, 3rd ed. (Oxford: Blackwell Reference, 1991), 599–641.

[3] Bakhtin, "Discourse in the Novel," 324. Also Abrams, *Glossary*, 118; Cuddon, *Dictionary of Literary Terms*, 602.

[4] M. M. Bakhtin, "From the Prehistory of Novelistic Discourse," in *DI*, 50. In his discussion of the novel, J. A. Cuddon claims that the novel's roots extend as far back as the 12th Dynasty Middle Kingdom of Egypt (ca. 1200 B.C.) (*Dictionary of Literary Terms*, 601).

of this process will reveal the basic features of novelization. Since novelistic activity was quite pronounced in the Hellenistic period, this in turn might illuminate certain aspects of the literary evolution of Mark's Gospel.

Novelization in the Hellenistic Period

Bakhtin believed that the novel emerged as the result of profound social change during the Hellenistic period. He traced the origins of the novel to Greco-Roman biography, romance, and Menippean satire, all of which flourished in the early Roman Empire. Bakhtin viewed each of these literary types in their relation to older epic forms of literature stemming from the classical period. As culture began to shift, the values preserved in epic literature could no longer be sustained. New literary forms were created to meet this need, and thus the prototypes of the novel were born.

Epic and Novel

Bakhtin summarizes the main characteristics of the epic as consisting of three main features. First, the subject of the epic is the "national epic past." It is not simply that the epic tells a story of past events. Rather, epic is preoccupied with the pivotal moments in the history of a people. The epic is especially interested in "'beginnings' and 'peak times' in the national history."[5] These pivotal moments in the nation's past are the source of socio-ideological norms in the present. As the primal source of social norms and values, the epic past is finished and complete; within it, nothing can be indeterminate. All that is best in the world of the present flows from the epic past. Therefore, the epic past is not merely a temporal category but an evaluative orientation as well.

Second, the source of the epic is national tradition and not personal experience. Since the epic past is the source of national values, it follows as a corollary that the epic cannot be a work solely of the author's creative imagination. Artistic perception is subsumed under the demands of the epic.[6] Epic discourse is traditional discourse; discourse handed down from one generation to another. There is no room in epic

---

[5] Bakhtin, "Epic and Novel," 13.
[6] Ibid., 18.

for personal perspectives and judgments. The author can only look back on this past from a distance and tell the epic story with piety and reverence. The epic past is "sacrosanct." To allow individual opinions and criticisms to intrude upon the epic would erode the national tradition, the very tradition that gives stability to the prevailing social order. The axiological framework that governs the epic is therefore thoroughly social rather than personal.

Third, with the epic past as its subject and the national tradition as its source, an "absolute epic distance" separates the epic from the authorial present. It is not merely that the epic recounts completed events in the past. The epic allows only one evaluative point of view: a point of view anchored in the epic past. Epic is therefore complete and rounded off not only in the sense that the events it depicts were accomplished in the past, but also in the sense that its values are completely stable and rooted in the past. The epic knows nothing of the incomplete present with its moral ambiguity and future expectations.

> The epic world achieves a radical degree of completedness not only in its content but in its meaning and its values as well. The epic world is constructed in the zone of an absolute distanced image, beyond the sphere of possible contact with the developing, incomplete and therefore re-thinking and re-evaluating present.[7]

Within the completed world of the epic past, the stature of the hero is uncontested.[8] This does not mean that the epic hero passes through life unopposed. The epic hero frequently confronts obstacles, often of significant proportion. The epic hero is uncontested in the sense that his worth as a champion is never impugned. The moral character of the epic hero is unassailable, both within the story where he invariably prevails and outside the story in the authorial present where he receives only praise and reverence. Reverence for the values of the past ensures the inviolable quality of the epic hero's character.

From the standpoint of the epic, everything that is important and meaningful has been accomplished. The uncertainty of the present is never allowed to affect the understanding of the epic past. When epic shapes a culture's values, it lacks the language necessary to assess its epic traditions critically. In Bakhtin's terms, the epic present is so

---

[7] Ibid., 17.
[8] Bakhtin, "Discourse in the Novel," 334.

strongly influenced by the past that it lacks the outsidedness or perceptual surplus necessary to critique the past. The present only acquires the
requisite outsidedness when it encounters other languages and hence
other values.

In a culturally diverse world, languages and ideas collide with
one another and compete for the loyalty of their adherents. This is the
essence of what Bakhtin calls polyglossia. Polyglossia provides new
ideological perspectives that allow the present to reassess the epic past.
When the epic past is exposed to new words and values, the "religious,
political, and ideological authority" that drew strength from the epic
past also begins to decay.[9] Under the influence of polyglossia, the epic
as the source of socio-ideological values becomes a "semiconventional,
semimoribund genre."[10] Of course, this process is not instantaneous. It
takes centuries for polyglossia to weaken the hold of the epic past. The
decentering of the epic, however, eventually resulted in a new form of
literature: the novel.

Polyglossia and Novelization

Bakhtin refers to the long process that led to the creation of the
novel as novelization. This process has, as one of its main consequences, the dissolution of the absolute distance of the epic past. Novelization brings the epic, and other similar genres, into "a zone of contact with reality."[11] This is essentially a dialogic zone that brings contrasting ideas and alien perspectives into direct contact with one another. The polyglossia that brought about the deterioration of epic genres gave rise in the novel to a "Galilean perception of language."[12] In
other words, through its exposure to the perceptual possibilities and
alien values of other languages, novelization began to realize the heteroglot potential of language. The main problem of the novel, or the

---

[9] Ibid., 370.

[10] Bakhtin, "Epic and Novel," 17.

[11] Ibid., 39.

[12] Bakhtin, "Discourse in the Novel," 366–67. Bakhtin's metaphorical use
of the term "Galilean" contrasts the decentered view of language characteristic of
the novel with the "Ptolemaic" view of the epic. On the novel's relation to heteroglossia, see Bakhtin, "Discourse in the Novel," 417.

proto-novel, therefore became the orchestration of the heteroglot potential of language revealed to it by polyglossia.[13]

When, under the influence of polyglossia, the epic past encounters the values of the present, values collide. Such a world is ideologically unstable. Epic ideas and values must now defend themselves and
prove their worth in relation to alien ideas and values. These new centrifugal forces supplant the centripetal forces that created the epic
world's sense of ideological security. Conventional solutions to life's
problems, solutions once rooted in the epic past, must now yield to the
concerns of the present moment. In place of the stability of the epic
past, the present offers indeterminacy and openness to the future. Life
is, consequently, less certain, and there is a renewed quest for answers
to ultimate questions since the answers handed down in the epic tradition are now suspect. In this axiological vacuum, the artist begins to
explore new answers to the problems posed by present experience. The
literary artist novelizes older forms of literature to work out answers to
these questions by aesthetically representing a heteroglot perception of
the world. In such novelistic literature, diverse characters express this
new sense of ideological uncertainty. This novelistic approach to the
polyglossic present introduces a host of aesthetic and artistic problems,
problems that were unknown to the epic author.

The most significant problem facing the novelistic author is that
of orchestrating the dialogic encounter between ideas and perceptions.
For the literary artist this becomes a problem of *"artistically representing language."*[14] If, as Aristotle claimed, the main goal of narrative is
the mimesis of people in action, in the novel it is, for Bakhtin, the mimesis of languages in dialogue.[15] In the novel, "the speaking person
and his discourse" become the "object of *verbal* artistic representation
. . . *by means of* (authorial) *discourse.*"[16] The novel reveals its Galilean
perception of language by artistically shaping heteroglossia into dia-

---

[13] Thus, Bakhtin describes the novel as "a diversity of social speech types
(sometimes even diversity of languages) and a diversity of individual voices, artistically organized" (ibid., 262).

[14] Ibid., 336, 366.

[15] *Poet.* 1448a1. Don H. Bialostosky makes a similar observation in
"Booth's Rhetoric, Bakhtin's Dialogics and the Future of Novel Criticism," *Novel*
18 (1985): 216.

[16] Bakhtin, "Discourse in the Novel," 332.

logues between speaking persons. Each character in the novel becomes, to a certain extent, "an *ideologue*, and his words are always *ideologemes*."[17] In the novel, it is not so much the personal trials of the characters—their fortunes or misfortunes—that matter, it is the idea represented by each character and their dialogic contact with other characters. In the novel, every character is "ideologically demarcated." Each character represents a distinct perspective on life, distinct in both its perceptual and axiological aspects. The artistic challenge confronting the author is the successful orchestration of these distinct socio-ideological positions into a coherent architectonic whole.

In Bakhtin's opinion, the novelistic depiction of Galilean discourse reached its zenith in the work of Dostoevsky. Nevertheless, he believed "the germs of novelistic prose" were located in the literature of antiquity.[18] He claimed that in its development over many centuries novelization followed two main lines: the monologic and the polyphonic.[19] The polyphonic line eventually produced works such as Dostoevsky's novels. With minimal interference from the author, such polyphonic works achieve a high degree of dialogization through the internal interaction between ideological positions. Through aesthetic legerdemain, the ideological position of the author disappears into the background, and all that remains are characters engaged in intense dialogue with one another. As Bakhtin notes, the polyphonic line of novelization was only partially realized in the literature of antiquity. Since this literature is our primary interest, we will forego a more detailed discussion of polyphonic novelization and concentrate instead on the monologic line of development.

In the monologic novel, the ideological position of the author permeates every aspect of the work. As in the polyphonic novel, the characters of the monological work represent discrete ideological positions, but the author never permits them to speak authentically from their own ideological perspective. The author, who literally puts words

---

[17] Ibid., 333.

[18] Ibid., 371.

[19] Ibid., 375. In "Discourse in the Novel," published in the mid-1930's, Bakhtin refers to these two main lines as "the First Stylistic Line" and "the Second Stylistic Line." Here we are using the language of Bakhtin's later work, *Problems of Dostoevsky's Poetics*, published in Russia in 1963. In spite of the terminological variation, it seems likely that Bakhtin is talking about the same basic phenomenon.

in their mouths, finalizes them beforehand. As free individuals (each one as an "I-for-myself"), the characters would not necessarily acknowledge the words given to them by the author as their own. Of course, we are speaking metaphorically. Bakhtin's point, however, is that the monological author does not grant these created personas their own unique and authentic existential perspective on life. The author does not permit them to speak consistently out of their own "lived-life," even if that "lived-life" is also a fictional creation of the author. Instead, their words are created for them from the standpoint of the author's own axiological position. Therefore, the words of the monologic character are always the finalizing words of the "other"; words that presume to fix the ideological framework of the character temporally, spatially, and axiologically from an external vantage point. Whereas characters in the polyphonic novel speak for themselves out of unique and authentic, self-sufficient perspectives on life, characters in the monological novel are ideological proxies. They represent various aspects of the author's ideologically shaped perception of social heteroglossia.

The monologic novel still manifests a Galilean consciousness of language, but awareness of "heteroglossia remains *outside* the novel...as a dialogizing background in which the language and world of the novel is polemically and forensically implicated."[20]

> Even in those places where the author's voice seems at first glance to be unitary and consistent, direct and unmediatedly intentional, beneath that smooth single-languaged surface we can nevertheless uncover prose's three-dimensionality, its profound speech diversity, which enters the project of style and is its determining factor.[21]

In the monologic novel, heteroglossia is molded into distinct ideological positions from the vantage point of the author's own ideological perspective. These ideological positions are represented in the novel by means of the discourse of the characters. Within the created world of the story, characters come into contact and their dialogue with one another exposes their distinctive ideological positions. Bakhtin borrows two terms from Socratic dialogue to explain this fundamental technique of dialogic orchestration. First, there is syncrisis (σύγκρισις) wherein

---

[20] Bakhtin, "Discourse in the Novel," 375.
[21] Ibid., 315.

two or more positions are brought into close contact with one another. This is supplemented by anacrisis (ἀνάκρισις) whereby "the juxtaposition of various points of view on a specific topic" teases out the full expression of a particular point of view.[22] While in the polyphonic novel the use of syncrisis and anacrisis produces an authentic encounter between dialogic positions, in the monologic novel it is more likely to seem artificial and contrived. Nevertheless, whether polyphonic or monologic, what characterizes the novel is the careful and intentional orchestration of divergent ideological perspectives.

In the monologic novel, the hero invariably represents the axiological position of the implied author.[23] The hero represents a particular ideological point of view that the author wishes to test. The testing of the hero and his discourse is one of the defining features of the monologic novel.[24] The function of the plot is then to expose the hero's ideological perspective to other heteroglot perspectives in order to test that ideological position and set it in sharper relief. All the formal literary devices in the text along with their intonational accents possess meaning only through their axiological relation to the hero and his test.[25]

The author creates the entire world of the story, in all of its chronotopic distinctiveness, as the stage for this test. For the testing of the hero and the idea that he represents to be relevant and convincing, the novelistic presentation of the hero must possess a certain degree of verisimilitude, even if the story itself is "impossible or improbable."[26] Even an unrealistic story-world can serve as an interesting proving ground for an idea, as long as the idea itself is relevant to contemporary ideological values.

In this way, novelistic literature begins to pull epic literature into closer contact with the realities of the present. The world of the novelistic present is a place where rival ideologies flourish. The purpose of the novel is to test these ideas by bringing them into dialogue with one another. In the critical assessment of the novel and novelistic literature, the primary task is to determine "the heteroglot background outside the

---

[22] Bakhtin, *PDP*, 110–11.
[23] Bakhtin, "Author and Hero," 197.
[24] Bakhtin, "Discourse in the Novel," 388–89; and *PDP*, 111–12.
[25] Bakhtin, "Author and Hero," 198.
[26] Ibid., 199.

work that dialogizes it."[27] In other words, a metalinguistic poetics must identify the "form-shaping ideology" that has set the parameters of the dialogue. This form-shaping ideology is revealed primarily through the chronotopic qualities of the narrative and by the nature of the author's relationship to the hero.

Novelization in the Hellenistic Period

In the course of the historical evolution of the novel, specific patterns of form-shaping ideology shaped its development. Bakhtin surveyed these trends, and it is not necessary for us to survey all of his results here. Nevertheless, those innovations that emerged out of the polyglossia of the Hellenistic period are relevant to our investigation and may shed further light on the genre of the Gospel of Mark.

Classical Greek culture produced many highly developed artistic literary forms such as epic, drama, and lyric, all of which were composed in metre. The Greeks reserved prose for scientific and philosophical topics. In the classical period, historiography was the most sophisticated genre of prose composition. Like the more popular romances, historiography is essentially a narrative genre.[28] The historian tells a story, but unlike the romance, the purpose of the story is not merely to entertain. Historiography uses narrative to convey serious information about the events of the past. Nevertheless, the histories of Thucydides, Herodotus, and Xenophon preserved novelistic tales and short stories, or novelle, which found their way into these works under the guise of anecdotal history.[29] These novelistic tales suggest the existence of prose narrative as an oral genre, but in the classical period, such tales lacked the requisite seriousness to circulate independently as literature.

It would be difficult to think of an era more characterized by polyglossia than the Hellenistic period inaugurated by the conquests of

---

[27] Bakhtin, "Discourse in the Novel," 416.

[28] Note, for example, Theon's claim that "history is nothing other than a collection of narratives" (οὐδέ γὰρ ἄλλο τί ἐστιν ἱστορία ἡ σύστημα διηγήσεως), 1.29–30. See James R. Butts, "The 'Progymnasmata' of Theon: A New Text with Translation and Commentary" (Ph.D. diss., Claremont Graduate School, 1983), 98–99.

[29] Sophie Trenkner, *The Greek Novella in the Classical Period* (Cambridge: Cambridge University Press, 1958), 23–30.

Alexander the Great. Under Greek hegemony, the language and culture of classical Greece spread throughout the Mediterranean region and eastward into Asia. Unlike the repressive tactics of previous empires, the Greeks assimilated the best of those cultures with which they came in contact. This intentional syncretism, in turn, had a corresponding affect on the cultures of the Near East, each culture absorbing and modifying aspects of the other. The interplay of languages and cultures continued unabated under Roman rule. Because of its cultural polyglossia, the Hellenistic and early imperial periods saw numerous innovations in politics, religion, art, and literature. Among the more notable innovations in literature were Greco-Roman biography, Greek romance, and Menippean satire.

In the Hellenistic period, novelistic innovations are especially apparent in the romances and satires. In these genres, the forces of novelization are brought directly to bear on the traditions of the epic past. These genres rework epic themes by bringing them into direct contact with the values of the polyglossic present. In so doing, they attempt to assess the value of the epic past in the light of the competing values of a culturally diverse present. The traditional epic values are put to the test by evaluating them under the conditions of the present. This does not mean that the stories are necessarily set in the present; some are not. What is important is that the story-worlds represent present conditions. Chief among these conditions is the unavoidable contact with alien perspectives. In this ideological conflict between the epic values of the past and the cultural diversity of the present, the ultimate issue is whether epic values are worth preserving. Biography, romance and Menippean satire represent radically different answers to this question.

These new literary genres were the product of the social polyglossia of the Hellenistic period. The old epic literary forms no longer served the creative needs of authors in this turbulent ideological milieu. The traditional epic forms of literature were dependent upon a stable, homogeneous cultural environment: an environment that no longer existed. Without that stable background, such works seemed hollow and unsatisfying. Of course, there were those in Greece who were nostalgic for the epic past. In the second century C.E., their fondness for the literature of the past led to the intellectual movement known as the Second Sophistic. Nevertheless, for others the old epic forms had lost their currency. This is not to say that the old epic forms could simply be discarded. Instead, through a process of novelization, old epic literary forms were brought into closer contact with the polyglossic conditions of the present. Martin Braun has traced the cultural effects of Hellenistic rule on literary composition.[30] He found that oriental cultures responded to the threat of Hellenism by turning to their traditional heroes. In the Hellenistic period, the achievements of these heroes were subject to legendary expansion and romantic elaboration. This literary activity could take two forms: a conservative, socially sophisticated form, or a popular romantic form. Historiography and biography represent the former, novelistic romance the latter. Bakhtin traced a third form as well, Menippean satire, a form that introduced modifications to both biography and romance.

Greco-Roman Novelistic Literature

Bakhtin saw the earliest antecedents of the modern western novel in three types of Greco-Roman literature: biography, romance, and Menippean satire. Each in its own way contributed to the novelization of older epic forms by presenting a distinct answer to the problems posed by the polyglossia of the Hellenistic period. In this section, we will examine the characteristic chronotope of each of these Greco-Roman genres. Then, in the next chapter, we will compare them to the Gospel of Mark and extend the discussion with a chronotopic examination and comparison with popular Jewish novelistic genres. In comparing the Gospel of Mark with the novelizing genres of the Hellenistic period, the peculiar chronotopic qualities of the Gospel of Mark will begin to emerge.

Greco-Roman Biography and its Chronotope

Greek biography emerged as a distinct literary form in the fifth century B.C.E. The historians Herodotus and Thucydides sometimes incorporated biographical accounts in their histories, and as Arnaldo Momigliano notes, it is very likely that independent biographies were already being written at this early date.[31] Nevertheless, the earliest sur-

---

[30] Martin Braun, *History and Romance in Graeco-Oriental Literature*, with a preface by Arnold Toynbee, Ancient Greek Literature, ed. Leonardo Tarán (Oxford: Basil Blackwell, 1938; reprint, New York: Garland, 1987), 35.

[31] Momigliano, *The Development of Greek Biography*, 32, 109.

viving independent biographies are encomiastic compositions by Isocrates and Xenophon. These works, written to praise the lives of deceased kings, are products of what D. R. Stuart called the "commemorative spirit."[32] Yet, although they recount the lives of figures from the past, their interest is more than antiquarian. Instead, they praise their subject's virtues and urge the present generation to imitate them. It is this rhetorical intention that determines their overall composition. Isocrates and Xenophon write biographies not to preserve an accurate record of the great accomplishments of Evagoras or Agesilaus, but to recommend their lives as models for future generations.[33]

It is not necessary to infer this intention since it is explicitly stated. In the *Evagoras*, Isocrates tells Evagoras' son Nicocles that

> I have undertaken to write this discourse because I believed that for you, for your children, and for all the other descendants of Evagoras, it would be by far the best incentive, if someone should assemble his achievements, give them verbal adornment, and submit them to you for your contemplation and study.[34]

Nicocles should contemplate and study his father's life and accomplishments so that he might imitate his greatness and so live up to his ancestral heritage. Like Isocrates, Xenophon also clearly states the nature of his objectives. His is not the historian's interest to preserve an accurate record of Agesilaus' life; rather he undertakes "an appreciation of Agesilaus that shall be worthy of his virtue and glory."[35] The praise of Agesilaus' perfection is the overarching objective of Xenophon's biography.

Xenophon proved an adept innovator of the biographical form. His autobiographical account of the Greek mercenaries' retreat following the death of Cyrus the Younger, the *Anabasis*, contains semi-independent biographical memorials to the fallen Greek generals, as well as a biographical account of Cyrus. His account of Socrates' life

---

[32] Duane Reed Stuart, *Epochs of Greek and Roman Biography*, Sather Classical Lectures, vol. 4 (Berkeley: University of California Press, 1928; reprint, New York: Biblo and Tannen, 1967), 1–29 (page references are to the reprint edition).

[33] In this respect, it is better to describe the *Agesilaus* and the *Evagoras* as biographic rather than biography. On this distinction, see Edwards, "Biography and the Biographic," 229–31.

[34] *Evagoras*, 76.

[35] *Agesilaus*, 1.1.

and teaching, the *Memorabilia*, is also biographical, although Xenophon filters everything through his own interpretation of Socrates'
teaching. Therefore, while the *Anabasis* and the *Memorabilia* are
loosely biographical, interests other than pure biography govern both
works. Xenophon's most important innovation in the composition of
biographies was his *Cyropaedia*. Ostensibly, the *Cyropaedia* is a biographical account, among other things, of the life and education of
Cyrus the Great.[36] It is, however, such a blend of fact and fiction, history and romance that it is more properly the earliest example of a historical novel. Although the historical value of the *Cyropaedia* is, at
times, suspect, its literary style was nevertheless very influential in the
development of both biography and romance.

Biography continued to develop within the peripatetic school
during the early Hellenistic period. Aristotle's interest in moral virtue
prompted his disciples to produce biographies that focused on the life-
styles of famous men.[37] For example, Aristoxenus composed biographies of a number of philosophers including Pythagoras, Socrates and
Plato. These biographies now exist only in fragments, but from what
remains it seems that Aristoxenus assembled these lives to serve a definite polemical purpose.[38] In Alexandria, from the third century B.C.E.
onward, biography assumed a more scholastic form. For philological
and text critical reasons, the Alexandrian librarians found it useful to
attach reliable historical and chronological information to the works in
their collection. The data available to them was largely chronological
and anecdotal, and therefore their biographies were often imaginative
recreations based on inferences from the author's works. [39] Scholastic
interests dominated Alexandrian biography and, consequently, they
lacked the overriding ethical interests of peripatetic biography. There-

---

[36] On the range of Xenophon's interests in the *Cyropaedia* see Deborah Levine Gera, *Xenophon's "Cyropaedia": Style, Genre, and Literary Technique*, Oxford Classical Monographs (Oxford: Clarendon, 1993), 1–13.

[37] Edna Jenkinson, "Nepos—An Introduction to Latin Biography," in *Latin
Biography*, Studies in Latin Literature and Its Influence, ed. T. A. Dorey (London:
Routledge & Kegan Paul, 1967), 6–7.

[38] Momigliano, *The Development of Greek Biography*, 75.

[39] On the widespread use of biographical inferences drawn from an author's
works see Mary R. Lefkowitz, *The Lives of the Greek Poets* (Baltimore: Johns
Hopkins University Press, 1981); and Janet Fairweather, "Fiction in the Biographies of Ancient Writers," *Ancient Society* 5 (1974): 231–75.

fore, while their approach to biography aspired to greater historical accuracy, it lacked the literary creativity that characterized the work of Xenophon and the Peripatetics.

We know very little of biography during the second century B.C.E. since most of these works have been lost. It seems likely, however, that biographies continued to be written since Greek biography reached its zenith in the first century C.E. with Plutarch's *Parallel Lives*. Plutarch's *Lives* reflects the ethical concerns of the peripatetic biographical tradition. Indeed, Plutarch claimed that this ethical interest is what distinguishes his biographies from history. He writes in the preface to his biography of Alexander that his primary aim is the "expression of character" (ἔμφασιν ἤθους).[40] Thus, Plutarch excuses himself from the responsibility of recounting all of Alexander's famous exploits, since even historically insignificant things can reveal a person's character. Nor is Plutarch's interest in moral character benign. In the *Lives*, Plutarch stands over his characters as a moral judge.[41] Plutarch presents examples of both good and bad character, all with the goal of illustrating the importance of virtuous living. Of particular importance is his belief that men who are sensitive to the favorable moment for action become great. The man blinded by an undisciplined life of vice fails to seize opportunities and is thereby brought to ruin.[42] Ultimately then the purpose of Plutarch's *Lives* is to illustrate for his contemporaries the importance of the moral life. Plutarch underscored this purpose by presenting the *Lives* in parallel pairs. Each pair represents a similar trajectory through life, and by comparing the rise and fall of two great men, Plutarch demonstrates the importance of moral virtue.[43]

---

[40] *Vit. Alex.* 1.2.

[41] Patricia Cox, *Biography in Late Antiquity: A Quest for the Holy Man*, Transformation of the Classical Heritage, ed. Peter Brown, 5 (Berkeley: University of California Press, 1983), 13; and A. J. Gossage, "Plutarch," in *Latin Biography*, Studies in Latin Literature and Its Influence, ed. T. A. Dorey (London: Routledge & Kegan Paul, 1967), 48.

[42] D. R. Shipley, *A Commentary on Plutarch's "Life of Agesilaos": Response to Sources in the Presentation of Character* (Oxford: Clarendon, 1997), 2, 14. A similar idea is expressed by Frederick E. Brenk, *In Mist Apparelled: Religious Themes in Plutarch's Moralia and Lives*, Mnemosyne, Bibliotheca Classica Batava, Supplementum, ed. W. den Boer et al., 48 (Leiden: E. J. Brill, 1977), 175, who emphasizes that Plutarch sees this as an opposition between *arete* and *tyche*.

[43] D. A. Russell, "On Reading Plutarch's *Lives*," *GR* 13 (1966): 151; and

Among the Jewish writings of the first century, we have Philo's *Life of Moses*. Although it predates Plutarch's biographies, Philo's account of Moses' life is comparable to Plutarch. Throughout his birth-to-death account of Moses, Philo demonstrates his concern to present Moses as a model leader. For Philo, Moses is "the greatest and most perfect of men," and this is what makes him a worthy subject of a biography.[44] Because of Moses' exceptional wisdom and virtue, Philo presents him as antiquity's greatest prophet, priest, king, and lawgiver.[45]

The Romans also composed biographies. The chief examples are the writings of Cornelius Nepos, Tacitus, and above all Suetonius. Although Greek biographical writing influenced these works, they are different enough to represent a distinct tradition. Like Greek encomiastic biography, Roman biography developed out of funeral speeches.[46] These speeches, which lavished praise upon the recently deceased, were preserved among family records as a lasting memorial to their ancestors. Since the purpose of these speeches was to praise the deceased, the facts of the person's life were often selectively presented. Tacitus' laudatory biography of his father-in-law Agricola is a notable example of this style of Roman biography.

Alongside Plutarch, the other towering figure of ancient biography is Suetonius. Suetonius differed from Plutarch by arranging his bi-

---

Christopher Pelling, "Is Death the End? Closure in Plutarch's *Lives*," in *Classical Closure: Reading the End in Greek and Latin Literature*, ed. Deborah H. Roberts, Francis M. Dunn, and Don Fowler (Princeton: Princeton University Press, 1997), 228.

[44] *Mos.* 1.1.

[45] Peder Borgen, "Philo of Alexandria," in *Jewish Writings of the Second Temple Period: Apocrypha, Pseudepigrapha, Qumran Sectarian Writings, Philo, Josephus*, ed. Michael E. Stone, CRINT, sec. 2, vol. 2. (Philadelphia: Fortress, 1984), 235. Compare the comments of Mariette Canevet, "Remarques sur l'utilisation du genre littéraire historique par Philon d'Alexandrie dans la *Vita Moysis*, ou Moïse général en chef-prophète," *RevScRel* 60 (1986): 189–206, who argues that Philo follows the conventions of Greek historiography to present Moses as both general and prophet. The overall effect is to present Moses "comme un modèle pour l'homme universel" (204).

[46] Ronald Mellor, "Roman Historiography and Biography," in *Civilization of the Ancient Mediterranean: Greece and Rome*, ed. Michael Grant and Rachel Kitzinger (New York: Charles Scribner's Sons, 1988), 3.1555; and B. Baldwin, "Biography at Rome," in *Studies in Latin Literature and Roman History*, vol. 1, Collection Latomus, vol. 164, ed. Carl Deroux (Brussels: Latomus, 1979), 101.

ographies according to an analytic scheme. He apparently composed several works of this nature. One work, known only from fragments, was a survey of important grammarians and rhetors, but the best extant example of Suetonius' technique is *The Twelve Caesars*. Covering the lives of the Caesars from Julius to Domitian, Suetonius presents an "objective" account of each ruler's reign. Birth and death roughly circumscribe each biography, but within these bounds, Suetonius organizes his lives schematically rather than chronologically.[47] Suetonius' biographies lack the overt ethical perspective that pervades the work of Plutarch, but his schematic presentation nevertheless betrays a preconceived notion of moral character.[48] Although Suetonius may be subtler than Plutarch, his interest in the moral dimension of his subjects is no less clear.

Bakhtin claimed that Greco-Roman biography and autobiography exerted an important influence on later novelistic prose. What interested Bakhtin was not biography's development as a branch of historiography, but its fictional representation of a person's life and deeds in writing. In modern parlance, we refer to such works as biographical novels and distinguish them from works of serious biography. The writers of antiquity did not observe such a sharp distinction. Although the classical past produced few biographical works that were purposefully fictitious, fact and fiction were frequently mixed together in what seems, to modern sensibilities, a rather uncritical combination.[49] The aspect of this biographical enterprise that attracted Bakhtin's attention was the new sense of "biographical time" organized around an individual "who passes through the course of a whole life."[50] Bakhtin claimed that it was this sense of time, bracketed by birth and death, that exerted an important influence on the development of the novel.

---

[47] Arnaldo Momigliano, "History and Biography," in *The Legacy of Greece: A New Appraisal*, ed. M. I. Finley (Oxford: Oxford University Press, 1984), 170; and G. B. Townend, "Suetonius and His Influence," in *Latin Biography*, Studies in Latin Literature and Its Influence, ed. T. A. Dorey (London: Routledge & Kegan Paul, 1967), 82.

[48] Townend, "Suetonius and His Influence," 92; and Cox, *Biography in Late Antiquity*, 15.

[49] Even in the overtly fictional biographies, "fictionalization is not the recipe for the narrative, but simply one ingredient" (Holzberg, *Ancient Novel*, 15).

[50] Bakhtin, "Forms of Time and of the Chronotope," 130.

In Greco-Roman biography, time adheres to the Aristotelian principle of entelechy.[51] Individuals are unaffected by events in their life. Instead, events serve merely as opportunities for them to display their true character. Therefore, the human image in Greco-Roman biography never undergoes a process of "becoming" or "development." Encomiastic biographies, for example, begin with an "idealized image of a definite life type."[52] In the encomium, there is no sense that the hero developed into an exemplary figure over the course of his life, nor is there any interest in the hero's life apart from what bears directly on his professional conduct. The author of an encomium views the life of the hero abstractly, at the point of "greatest maturity and fullness of life."[53] The author then shows that at the apex of his life, the hero was an exemplary member of his class, the ideal embodiment of his profession.

Bakhtin posits two types of Greco-Roman biography: energetic and analytic.[54] In the energetic biographies, such as those of Plutarch, inner character is displayed through actions and statements. Unless the protagonist is acting or speaking, he ceases to exist within biographical time. The author only quotes words and actions to illustrate the case he is making for the protagonist's virtue. For the biographical description of a person's character, the chronological ordering of actions or statements is inconsequential, since biographical character does not develop over time. In this sense, biographical time in the Greco-Roman biography is reversible; there is no development from one action or statement to another. As Bakhtin remarks,

> Biographical time in Plutarch is specific. It is a time that discloses character, but is not at all the time of a man's 'becoming' or growth…. Historical reality itself, in which disclosure of character takes place, serves merely as a means for the disclosure…but historical reality is deprived of any determining influence on character as such, it does not shape or create it, it merely manifests it. Historical reality is an arena for the disclosing and unfolding of human characters—nothing more.[55]

Since character does not develop in the energetic biography, time exists only to be filled with examples. The biography achieves its goal when

---

[51] Ibid., 140.
[52] Ibid., 136.
[53] Ibid.
[54] Ibid., 140–42.
[55] Ibid., 141.

the reader's initially imperfect knowledge of the protagonist's character is, at the end of the work, full and well rounded.

Suetonius is the main example of the analytical biography. In the analytical biography, life is examined according to "well-defined rubrics," such as "social life, family life," and "conduct in war." Suetonius draws examples from the hero's life to illustrate the propriety of his behavior within these categories. The temporal sequence of these analytical accounts is even less important than it was in Plutarch. "From such a point of view time is of no importance at all, nor is the order in which various parts of this whole make their appearance."[56]

The Greco-Roman biography reveals the character of the protagonist only through his public life. Unlike modern biographies, there is no awareness of interior psychological growth and development. Everything is external to the individual. Bakhtin claimed that it was only with "the Hellenistic and Roman epochs" that literature began to translate "whole spheres of existence . . . onto a *mute register*, and into something that is in principle invisible."[57] The completely exterior nature of the hero in the Greco-Roman biography meant that the hero had no private life; he existed only for others. "A man was utterly exteriorized. . . . the *unity* of a man's externalized wholeness was of a *public* nature."[58]

Within the chronotope of Greco-Roman biography, with its abstract time and exterior public space, the presence of the monological perspective of the author is inescapable. The author overtly controls the presentation of the hero. This is preeminently evident in the narrative mode characteristic of Greco-Roman biography. Biography tells, rather than shows, its story; it is diegetic rather than mimetic. This distinction provides another important indicator of the abstract nature of the biographical chronotope. Telling gives the author complete control over the pace, order, and content of the presentation. Thus, in Greco-Roman biography, the protagonists are normally "quoted," which is to say the author abstracts their speech from life and places it within an artificially created context. Rather than "showing" the hero interacting naturally with others through dialogue,[59] the authors of Greco-Roman biography

---

[56] Ibid., 142.

[57] Ibid., 134.

[58] Ibid., 135.

[59] As Seymour Chatman has remarked, "Dialogue, of course, is the preemi-

simply cite examples and anecdotes to legitimize their evaluation of the protagonist.[60]

Our summary of Bakhtin's analysis of Greco-Roman biography underscores his interest in the relationship between the literary chronotope and its particular way of perceiving human existence. The Greco-Roman biography perceives existence as an outward, essentially social orientation. Its characters experience this reality, not with internal angst, but by simply being what they were born to be. Greco-Roman biography manifests these values, not by defending a set of propositions, but by citing concrete examples that illustrate a specific understanding of the world. Greco-Roman biographies form a cohesive genre, not simply because of their formal similarity to one another but more importantly because of their axiological similarity. In particular, the axiological orientation of Greco-Roman biography is conservative toward the values of the epic past. By recounting the virtuous lives of their contemporaries, the biographies try to defend the enduring value of tradition.

Ancient Romance and Its Chronotope

From a modern perspective, one of the most notable literary achievements of the late Hellenistic period was the development of the Greek novel or romance.[61] Oddly enough, romance entirely escaped the notice of ancient literary criticism. Ancient literary critics apparently deemed these popular narratives unworthy of critical attention. Of the few comments that acknowledge the existence of the genre, most are sharply critical of it. In the fourth century, the emperor Julian recommended against reading "erotic stories and all such works," branding

---

nent enactment." Seymour Chatman, *Story and Discourse: Narrative Structure in Fiction and Film* (Ithaca: Cornell University Press, 1978), 32.

[60] As I indicated in the first chapter, Auerbach was the first to call attention to this important difference between biblical narrative and Greco-Roman genres. See above, page 15.

[61] The Greeks never developed specific terminology to designate these works. See Daniel L. Seldon, "Genre of Genre," in *The Search for the Ancient Novel*, ed. James Tatum (Baltimore: Johns Hopkins University Press, 1994), 43. Both novel and romance have unfortunate overtones in modern parlance, nevertheless, the use of one or the other is unavoidable. I have preferred romance rather than novel to avoid confusion with Bakhtin's description of biography, romance, and Menippean satire as novelistic forms of literature.

them fiction (πλάσματα).[62] Julian objected to the presentation of fictitious stories in prose, since before the appearance of romance, prose literature was the exclusive domain of history, oratory, and philosophical
dialogue.[63] A narrative composed in prose gave the impression of serious literature, yet the contents of romance were far from serious. Its
romantic plots and manufactured adventures were obviously fictional,
and Greco-Roman literary culture relegated fiction to comedy and
mime. To their way of thinking, fiction masquerading as history was
tantamount to lying and thus unworthy of critical recognition.[64] Therefore, as B. P. Reardon remarks, "The Greek Académie appears to have
regarded prose fiction as a thoroughbred racehorse might regard a
camel, with puzzlement and disdain."[65] In spite of its poor reception
among literary critics, the Greek romance was nevertheless a vibrant
and productive, if not influential, genre in the late Hellenistic and early
Imperial periods.

Five works are normally considered the main examples of the
genre.[66] Chariton's *Chaereas and Callirhoe* is the earliest complete ro-

---

[62] The whole phrase reads ὅσα δέ ἐστιν ἐν ἱστορίας εἴδει παρὰ τοῖς
ἔμπροσθεν ἀπηγγελμένα πλάσματα παραιτητέον, ἐρωτικὰς ὑποθέσεις καὶ
πάντα ἁπλῶς τὰ τοιαῦτα (*Ep.* 301b, Wright). The only other reference to romance is equally dismissive. In a letter attributed to Philostratus, and addressed to a
certain "Chariton," the author suggests that writing romances is a poor way to build
one's literary reputation: Χαρίτωνι. Μεμνήσεσθαι τῶν σῶν λόγων οἴει τοὺς
Ἕλληνας, ἐπειδὰν τελευτήσῃς· οἱ δε μηδεν ὄντες, ὁπότε εἰσίν, τίνες ἂν εἶεν,
ὁπότε οὐκ εἰσίν; (Letter 66). See B. E. Perry, *The Ancient Romances: A Literary-
Historical Account of Their Origins*, Sather Classical Lectures, vol. 37 (Berkeley:
University of California Press, 1967), 98–99; and B. P. Reardon, *The Form of
Greek Romance* (Princeton: Princeton University Press, 1991), 46–48.

[63] George A. Kennedy, "The Evolution of a Theory of Artistic Prose," in
The Cambridge History of Literary Criticism, vol. 1, *Classical Criticism*, ed.
George A. Kennedy (Cambridge: Cambridge University Press, 1989), 184;
Reardon, *Form of Greek Romance*, 8, 52.

[64] J. R. Morgan, "Make-believe and Make Believe: The Fictionality of the
Greek Novels," in *Lies and Fiction in the Ancient World*, ed. Christopher Gill and
T. P. Wiseman (Austin: University of Texas Press, 1993), 175–93; also idem, "The
Greek Novel: Towards a Sociology of Production and Reception," in *The Greek
World*, ed. Anton Powell (London: Routledge, 1995), 132–33.

[65] Reardon, "Aspects of the Greek Novel," 120.

[66] For general introductions to the literature, see Tomas Hägg, *The Novel in
Antiquity*; Niklas Holzberg, *The Ancient Novel*; Perry, *The Ancient Romances*;
Reardon, *The Form of Greek Romance*; and *The Novel in the Ancient World*,

mance and dates from the first century C.E. Xenophon of Ephesus, who seems to have imitated Chariton, wrote *An Ephesian Story* sometime in the mid-second century C.E.[67] The Greek romance was further refined in the second and third centuries under the influence of the Greek cultural revival known as the Second Sophistic. *Leucippe and Clitophon* by Achilles Tatius, *Daphnis and Chloë* by Longus, and *An Ethiopian Story* by Heliodorus date from this period and reflect its characteristic interest in rhetorical stylization.[68] Although the details vary, as do their authors' literary abilities, these five romances share the same general pattern. Each is a stereotypical tale of young love frustrated by Tyche. Through an unusual sequence of events, a young, well-born, and remarkably handsome couple becomes separated. They vainly search for each other while enduring a series of spectacular adventures. In their adventures, they are transported—whether by kidnap, shipwreck, or forced flight— to exotic locales in the eastern Mediterranean. These adventures jeopardize their fidelity to one another and place them in mortal danger until they are finally reunited at the end of the story. The most notable exception to this general pattern is *Daphnis and Chloë*. Longus exchanges adventurous travel for the adventures of maturing love, and thus Daphnis and Chloë never leave the pastoral setting of Lesbos. Longus employs many of the themes and motifs associated with romance, but he also used them with greater sophistication and creativity.[69] This subtle exception to the general pattern only serves as a

---

Mnemosyne, ed. Gareth Schmeling, Bibliotheca Classica Batava, Supplementum, ed. J. M. Bremer et al., 159 (Leiden: E. J. Brill, 1996).

[67] Some, however, would date Xenophon before Chariton, as does James N. O'Sullivan, *Xenophon of Ephesus: His Compositional Technique and the Birth of the Novel*, Untersuchungen zur antiken Literatur und Geschichte, Bd. 44 (Berlin: Walter de Gruyter, 1995), 145–70.

[68] *An Ethiopian Story* is sometimes dated as late as the fourth century. I am dependent here on the dates provided in Reardon's introduction to *CAGN*, 5. Similar dates are given in Holzberg, *The Ancient Novel*; E. L. Bowie, "The Greek Novel," in *CHCL*, 1. 4, *The Hellenistic Period and the Empire*, ed. P. E. Easterling and B. M. W. Knox (Cambridge: Cambridge University Press, 1989), 124; and Perry, *The Ancient Romances*, 96–98, 343–44, and 345–46. Hägg supports the same relative order and approximate dates with the exception of Chariton, which he dates to the first century B.C.E. (*The Novel in Antiquity*, 6).

[69] Reardon, *Form of Greek Romance*, 32–34.

reminder that the romance paradigm was in no way prescriptive for individual authors.

The remarkable similarity of the surviving romances may be little more than a historical accident resulting from Byzantine Christian sensibilities that preferred stories about chaste and faithful characters.[70] Indeed, the fragmentary remains of romances like *Iolas* (first century C.E.) and *A Phoenician Story* (second century C.E.) suggest that the romance could often be crude and vulgar.[71] Other, even earlier, fragmentary romances reveal a particular interest in the legendary exploits of oriental heroes such as Ninus and Semiramis in Assyria, and Sesostris and Nectanebus in Egypt.[72] The legendary life of Alexander the Great,

---

[70] Censorship would be too strong a word. There is no evidence that certain forms of literature were destroyed because they did not meet Christian standards (Reardon, *Form of Greek Romance*, 178, esp. n. 15; and idem, "The Greek Novel," 294). Nevertheless, Christian romances such as the *Acts of Paul and Thecla*, the *Acts of Thomas*, the *Acts of Andrew*, and the *Acts of Xanthippe and Polyxena*, to name only a few examples, all exhibit a pronounced interest in sexual chastity and moral integrity (Perry, *Ancient Romances*, 30). Given their similarity to secular romance, these popular works were apparently written to provide Christians with an alternative to secular romance. The success of this Christian enterprise may be measured, in part, by the subsequent rarity of secular romance. See Johannes Quasten, *Patrology*, vol. 1, *The Beginnings of Patristic Literature* (Utrecht: Spectrum, 1950; reprint, Westminster, Md.: Christian Classics, 1986), 129.

[71] A selection of fragmentary romances in English translation is included in *CAGN*, 775–827. For a more complete collection with Greek texts, see Susan A. Stephens, and John J. Winkler, *Ancient Greek Novels: The Fragments: Introduction, Text, Translation, and Commentary* (Princeton: Princeton University Press, 1995).

[72] Braun, *History & Romance*, 1–43. Perry provides an informative discussion of the *Ninus* romance in *Ancient Romances*, 153–77, where he dates *Ninus* as early as the first century B.C.E. These oriental romances predate the Greek romance and, as some scholars have suggested, to a certain extent they may illuminate its genesis. This is the position of Elizabeth Hazelton Haight, "Oriental Stories in Classical Prose Literature," in *Essays on Ancient Fiction*, 1–45 (New York: Longmans, Green & Co., 1936); John Wintour Baldwin Barns, "Egypt and the Greek Romance," in *Akten 8. Internationalen Kongresses für Papyrologie: Wein 1955*, Mitteilungen aus der Papyrussammlung der Österreichischen Nationalbibliothek (Papyrus Erzherzog Rainer), n.Ser., hrsg. Hans Gerstinger, 5. F. (Vienna: Rudolf M. Rohrer, 1956), 35; Reardon, "Aspects of the Greek Novel," 126; and Hägg, *Novel in Antiquity*, 3. The most recent champion of oriental influence on the Greek romance is Graham Anderson, *Ancient Fiction: The Novel in the Graeco-Roman*

the *Alexander Romance*, probably originated at about the same time.[73] At times, ancient novelistic prose bordered on the fantastic, as in *A True Story* by Lucian and *The Wonders beyond Thule* by Antonius Diogenes. Both works recount remarkable adventures that beggar the imagination. There are also two Latin romances that stem from Greek literary traditions—Apuleius' *Metamorphoses* and the anonymous *Apollonius King of Tyre*—although in the case of Apuleius the trans-formation has been so complete as to obscure its Greek origins. Thus, when we place the five paradigmatic examples of romance alongside other contemporary works of prose fiction, we find more thematic di-versity than is often recognized.[74]

Most Greek romances, especially those that are pre-sophistic, can be accurately described as "historical novels."[75] The earliest romances show a pronounced interest in historical figures. Unlike biography, however, which typically recounts the most notable events of a per-son's life, romance specifically elects to narrate events that are more obscure. Romance is set in "the gaps in real history," and is very toler-ant of anachronisms and temporal loose ends.[76] B. E. Perry believed that the historical veneer of romance was a subterfuge by which its au-thors hoped to win respectability.[77] Recently, B. P. Reardon has offered the more plausible suggestion that romance used historical figures sim-ply because they provided "interesting people, with whom one could do interesting things."[78]

Whether or not romance couched its narratives in a historical form to conceal its fictions, it nevertheless mimicked the prose style of

---

World (London: Croom Helm; Totowa, N.J.: Barnes & Noble, 1984), especially pp. 1–24.

[73] Hägg, *Novel in Antiquity*, 125–27. Braun traces the origins of the *Alexan-der Romance* to pre-Christian times (*History & Romance*, 35).

[74] Perry, *Ancient Romances*, 28–29. See also Niklas Holzberg, "The Genre: Novels Proper and the Fringe," *The Novel in the Ancient World*, ed. Gareth Schmeling, Mnemosyne, Bibliotheca Classica Batava, Supplementum, ed. J. M. Bremer et al., 159 (Leiden: E. J. Brill, 1996), 11–28.

[75] Perry, *Ancient Romances*, 78. On the distinction between Sophistic and pre-Sophistic novels see ibid., 109.

[76] Morgan, "Make-believe," 199.

[77] Perry, *Ancient Romances*, 173. Holzberg also holds this position ("Genre: Novels Proper," 17; and *Ancient Novel*, 41), as does Morgan, "Make-believe," 187.

[78] Reardon, *Form of Greek Romance*, 126.

the Greek historiographers. Like historiography, romance uses a lengthy prose composition to tell a realistic story of past events mostly narrated in the third person.[79] Nor was the boundary between historiography and fictional storytelling impermeable. Greek historiography, from earliest times, had shown a predilection for reporting entertaining stories. Herodotus and Ctesias both decorated their historical narratives with inserted novelle.[80] They used these stories casually, without verifying their accuracy to such an extent that Aristotle dismissed Herodotus as a μῦθολόγος.[81] Directly or indirectly, these inserted novelle established a precedent for the prose narration of fictional events in later Greek literature.

In the fourth century, Xenophon expanded storytelling beyond the boundaries of novella and produced one of the first biographical novels, the *Cyropaedia*. The intermingling of fact and fiction in the *Cyropaedia* makes it a difficult work to classify precisely. It is historical in intention and form, yet its reconstruction of Cyrus' life is often fictional. The earliest forms of romance bore a strong resemblance to history, but, as Reardon observes, "that is because in Xenophon of Athens and some of his contemporaries, history, in at least some of its forms, was in practice romance."[82] Xenophon wrote about Cyrus because he was an example of a great leader, not simply to report the facts of his life. Thus, in its intention, the *Cyropaedia* preserved the seriousness of Greek narrative prose. It was the fictional aspect of Xenophon's tale, however, that paved the way for romance. Judging by the pseudonyms used by the authors of romance— Xenophon of Ephesus, Xenophon of Antioch, and Xenophon of Cyprus—the *Cyropaedia* exerted a special influence on the genre's development.[83]

Pre-sophistic romances, such as Chariton's, often used a historical kernel, perhaps preserved in a popular local legend, as the starting

---

[79] Holzberg, *Ancient Novel*, 35; Hägg, *Novel in Antiquity*, 112; and Morgan, "Make-believe," 208.

[80] Sophie Trenkner, *The Greek Novella in the Classical Period*, 23–30.

[81] *Gen. An.* 756b6.

[82] Reardon, *Form of Greek Romance*, 61. As Reardon notes, Momigliano also stressed that fourth century biography occupied "an ambiguous position between fact and imagination" (*Development of Biography*, 46).

[83] Perry, *Ancient Romances*, 146–47, 167; and Morgan, "Greek Novel," 137.

point for their compositions.[84] The use of received myths and legends to establish the main outlines of what would become a largely fictional account was a commonplace of classical Greek composition. What would have been highly irregular was the free composition of a story with no connection to myth or history.[85] Generally, the Greeks expected the plot (μῦθος) of a narrative to honor these familiar tales by following the main outlines of the traditional account. Romance, however, turned to the obscure rather than the familiar.

There is typically just enough historical information in romance to evoke a specific time and place, but rarely more. Having created a veneer of historical plausibility, the author of romance concentrates on the lesser-known events in the lives of his characters. These unknown episodes offered the maximum amount of freedom in the composition of the story.[86] Unconstrained by historical details, the author was at liberty to display greater imagination and skill as a storyteller. Unlike biography, romance does not simply report the lives of its heroes; instead, it creates a world in which they can act and speak for themselves. Nor does the author feel constrained to report historical information about them. Romance serves only to entertain. Thus, in spite of its similarity to the prose narration of historiography and biography, romance no longer intends to instruct but to entertain, and its form is mimetic rather than diegetic.

With respect to its mimetic and entertaining qualities, romance seems more likely to derive from New Comedy than from historiography. Like romance, New Comedy, which flourished during the late fourth century B.C.E., had also moved away from the heroic themes of classical epic and drama to emphasize the plight of common individuals. These sentimental, romantic dramas were preoccupied with love's intrigues and mistaken identities, and overall the genre shows much greater contact with contemporary values and concerns.[87] New Comedy

---

[84] Haight, "Oriental Stories," 9–10.

[85] Perry, *Ancient Romances*, 113–14, 152.

[86] Ibid., 69. On Chariton's romance and its relation to history, see ibid., 137–40.

[87] Reardon, *Form of Greek Romance*, 50, 74. Holzberg, *Ancient Novel*, 31–32, suggests that New Comedy developed under social conditions that paralleled those of Greek romance. On the social setting of New Comedy, see Wilfred E. Major, "Menander in a Macedonian World," *GRBS* 38 (1997): 41–73.

also prefigured romance in its interest in the psychological turmoil created by life's misfortunes. In New Comedy, the depiction of misfortune was used with comic rather than tragic intent by showing that fortunes are just as likely to take a turn for the better. Fate is fickle in both New Comedy and romance. Because New Comedy was devoted to entertainment, its free invention (πλάσμα) was more readily tolerated, especially since its composition in metre distinguished it from serious prose genres like history and biography. Nevertheless, the liberty with which New Comedy employed πλάσμα was also a symptom of the weakening hold of μῦθος on creative literature, and in this respect too, New Comedy paved the way for romance.[88]

It seems then that the origins of romance are complex. Scholars such as Perry and Reardon see romance as a combination of historiography's narrative prose form with New Comedy's plasmatic freedom and romantic content.[89] From historiography, romance derives its biographical interest in specific individuals and its narrative style. At the same time, it is also clear that we can describe romance as neither history nor biography. Romance is not guided by an intention to present reliable accounts of past events based on careful research.[90] Like New Comedy, romance is a self-consciously fictive and entertaining genre. Romance, however, was not intended for the stage, and its complex and expansive stories far exceed the scope of New Comedy. Nor did romance fabricate its stories out of whole cloth. Instead, beginning with

---

[88] On "plasmatic license" and its transference from drama to romance, see Perry, *Ancient Romances*, 72–79.

[89] Perry, *Ancient Romances*, 78, 140; Reardon, *Form of Greek Romance*, 126; idem, "Greek Novel," 292; and Holzberg, *Ancient Novel*, 10. Nor are the influences on romance limited to historiography and New Comedy. Epic, travel narratives, erotic poetry, and rhetoric (Hägg, *Novel in Antiquity*, 109), as well as oriental fiction (see above, page 91, note 72) all seem to have influenced romance.

[90] This is not just a modern view of history. See Plutarch's essay, "The Malice of Herodotus" (*Mor.* 855F), and Lucian's essay *How to Write History* (*Hist. Conscr.* 7, 9, 39, 41, 47). For pertinent excerpts from these two essays see D. A. Russell and M. Winterbottom, eds., *Ancient Literary Criticism: The Principal Texts in New Translations* (Oxford: Oxford University Press, 1972), 534–47.

the most attenuated connection with history, romance learned, like Hesiod's Muses, to "tell many lies that resemble the truth."[91]

Scholars who study the genesis of Greek romance no longer describe the relationship between romance and its generic predecessors as one of dependence or gradual evolution.[92] Without denying the importance of the formal similarities between romance and earlier genres, the tendency now is to focus on the social circumstances that produced romance. In his influential investigation of the origins of romance, Perry argued that genres do not evolve mechanically from other genres, but are created by individual artists in response to specific social and historical circumstances. As Perry observed, a genre cannot evolve into a new type of literature without "passing through zero, that is through the negation of its own *raison d'être*."[93] Romance cannot be a degenerate form of historiography precisely because it is guided by a very different purpose.[94]

Literature itself "has no procreative power."[95] Instead, new genres are born out of an author's creative response to the changing cultural conditions. As Perry noted, this creative transformation stems from a desire "to satisfy the new spiritual or intellectual needs and tastes that have arisen in a large part of society in a given period of cultural history."[96] Earlier literary traditions are never prescriptive, but only provide "loose structural patterns" and assorted "building materials" for creative artists. Artists rework these patterns and materials to achieve new forms of expression. In this sense and to the extent that an author is no mere epigone, every literary work is, strictly speaking, unique. Thus, for Perry, the notion of genre is useful only as a descriptive tool "*universalia post rem*" to describe certain patterns of similarity that exist among works shaped by a common purpose.[97]

---

[91] *Theog.* 27. Quoted from Russell & Winterbottom, *ALC*, 3. Lucian lays claim to this same art when he expresses his confidence that the readers of his *True Story* will find his miscellaneous lies convincing and believable (1.2).

[92] A position championed by Erwin Rohde, *Der griechische Roman und seine Vorläufer*, 3. Aufl. (Leipzig: Teubner, 1914).

[93] Perry, *Ancient Romances*, 10.

[94] Ibid., 39.

[95] Ibid., 25.

[96] Ibid., 9–10.

[97] Ibid., 18–20, 176.

According to Perry, the most important criterion for generic classification is authorial intention. Previous literary genres, traditional themes and motifs, mythical plots, and historical characters are little more than raw material for a creative author. To understand a work of literature we must understand the *idea* that controlled its composition.[98] It is this idea that binds the form and content of the work together and creates its unity as an aesthetic expression. The procreative power that shapes the available materials and fashions them into something new is the author's idea. Therefore, if we want to understand the final product, we must grapple with the idea that created it.

Of course, authors do not exist in isolation from the world around them. The creative idea that governs the shape of a work is informed by, and is in part a response to, external social conditions. Therefore, the creative idea must be related to contemporary social circumstances. In explaining the development of romance, Perry contrasted the social circumstances surrounding its appearance with that of epic poetry. Epic poetry flourished in the closed society of classical Greece. Until the waning years of the fifth century, Greece was relatively isolated from other cultures, and its social life revolved around the shared values of the city-state. In such a closed society, ideas were "centripetal," and society was guided by "custom and fixed beliefs about human values and mankind's relation to the beyond."[99] Epic literary genres flourished under these conditions. These works depicted the legendary exploits of figures like Jason, Heracles, and Odysseus, who undertake heroic labors and match wits with gods and mythical creatures. Although these adventures are set in a remote and mythical past, they nevertheless reflect an idealization of contemporary values. The epic hero represents all that is good and virtuous in the world— courage, honor, ingenuity. The epic never challenges these idealized values. It acknowledges no other axiological point of view and intro-

---

[98] Ibid., 30–32. Holzberg (*Ancient Novel*, 26) also asserts the importance of this criterion. Interestingly enough, Perry also remarks in passing that "antecedent literature" such as Greek aretalogy, historiography, and biography are of little use in "explaining the origin of the canonical Gospels and the message of Jesus." The generation of these literary forms can only be explained by examining the "ideas and purposes" that guided their creation (*Ancient Romances*, 31).

[99] Ibid., 335, n. 15.

duces no perspective that might compete with these heroic values.[100]
Thus, as we noted earlier, epic primarily serves a legitimizing function—to explain, validate, and celebrate the *status quo*.

Epic composition enjoyed brief revivals in the third century
B.C.E. with Apollonius Rhodius and in the first century B.C.E. with
Virgil, but slowly it gave way to literary forms in closer contact with
the realities of everyday life.[101] During the Hellenistic period, writers in
Mesopotamia, Syria, and Egypt revived stories of epic heroes to compensate for an increasing sense of powerlessness and inferiority.[102]
They cast the heroes of the past in new adventures in hopes of revitaliz-
ing the national tradition. The earliest examples of Greek romance also
resuscitate past heroes. The popularity of the *Alexander Romance*,
forged during the early Hellenistic period, is only one example. These
efforts to revive the epic with its legendary heroes and use it to address
contemporary concerns were nevertheless moribund. By the close of
the Hellenistic period, the heroes of the past seem to have lost their currency entirely.

In Hellenistic and early imperial times, the Greeks lived in an
open society. As the cultures of the eastern Mediterranean were drawn
into increasingly closer contact with one another, the resulting polyglossia produced feelings of alienation. Exposure to a wide array of
languages, beliefs, and customs began to weaken the values of the epic
past rooted in tradition, clan, and *polis*. The Greeks were simply one
more ethnic group living under the hegemony of a foreign empire—
first Macedonian, then Roman. In this strange and alien world, individuals often found themselves in unknown territory, both physically
and ideologically. In this open society, ideas were "centrifugal and
chaotic" and the political, moral, and religious ideas once nurtured in
the close confines of the Greek city-states now had to compete in a
world full of alternative ideas.[103] Although many still valued Greek
rhetoric and education, as a people, the Greeks lacked the political

---

[100] Hägg, *Novel in Antiquity*, 88–89.

[101] On Apollonius and Virgil, see J. W. H. Atkins, *Literary Criticism in Antiquity: A Sketch of Its Development*, vol. 1, *Greek* (Cambridge: Cambridge University Press, 1934; reprint, Gloucester, Mass.: Peter Smith, 1961), 177–79.

[102] Bakhtin, "Prehistory of Novelistic Discourse," 64. On the emergence of
novelistic prose in the Orient see the literature cited above (page 91, note 72).

[103] Perry, *Ancient Romances*, 335, n. 15.

freedom that was once the natural expression of their intellectual so-phistication. Nostalgia for the classical past was a natural response to this sense of political impotence.[104] Thus it is not surprising that most romances are set in the classical period when Greek culture was at its zenith.[105]

Unlike the epic, however, romance no longer celebrates the accomplishments of legendary heroes who oppose gods and undertake fantastic labors. Although its stories are often set in the past, it is no longer a legendary, but a realistic—even if romanticized—past.[106] At the center of Greek romance are everyday characters suffering typical misfortunes, isolated from the people and things that might offer them a sense of security.[107] Romance was not interested in kings and princes, political intrigues and wars, but in young lovers and the tribulations visited upon them by fate. Like epic characters, the characters of ro-mance are idealized, but they are no longer invincible and heroic. They are idealized only in the sense that they remain somewhat larger than life. The heroes of romance come from good families and normally possess all the requisite skills befitting their station in life. In addition, their appearance is always radiant enough to provoke the jealousy of the gods.[108] Alone and powerless, these resplendent characters must face the unknown and unfamiliar. The problem of romance is therefore not the validation or even celebration of the *status quo*, but the diffi-

---

[104] Hägg, *Novel in Antiquity*, 106; Morgan, "Greek Novel," 145; and E. L. Bowie, "Greeks and Their Past in the Second Sophistic," *Past and Present* 46 (1970): 30, 39.

[105] Holzberg, "Genre: Novels Proper," 23. Nostalgia for the classical past became even more pronounced in the second century during the 'Second Sophis-tic.' On the importance of this cultural movement and its effect on the development of Greek romance, see Bowie, "Greeks and Their Past," 3–41; B. P. Reardon, "The Second Sophistic and the Novel," in *Approaches to the Second Sophistic: Papers Presented at the 105th Annual Meeting of The American Philological Association*, ed. G. W. Bowersock, 23–29 (University Park, Penn.: American Philological Asso-ciation, 1974); and Graham Anderson, *The Second Sophistic: A Cultural Phenome-non in the Roman Empire* (London: Routledge, 1993), 156–70.

[106] Morgan, "Make-Believe," 198–99, 229; and Holzberg, *Ancient Novel*, 27.

[107] Perry, *Ancient Romances*, 7. See also, Hägg, *Novel in Antiquity*, 89–90; Holzberg, *Ancient Novel*, 98; and Reardon, *Form of Greek Romance*, 28–29, 172.

[108] The idealistic qualities of romance suggest a certain lack of contact with the present and to that extent, romance is only weakly heteroglossic.

culty of life in a strange and complex world. Where the epic offered certain *answers* to life's problems, romance sets the *problems* of the present at center stage.[109]

According to Perry, the Greek romance is a direct product of the open society of late Hellenism. Thus, Perry, in an oft-quoted passage, concludes that:

> The first romance was deliberately planned and written by an individual author, its inventor. He conceived it on a Tuesday afternoon in July, or some other day or month of the year. It did not come into being by a process of development on the literary plane. What had really developed was the complex cultural outlook, the *Weltanschauung*, of society as a whole in the Alexandrian age, in contrast to what it had been in the age of Pericles.[110]

Tomas Hägg states the matter more succinctly: the novel is "the open form for the open society."[111] In its innermost structure, the Greek romance reflects the social uprootedness of its age. It embodies new values not because it developed naturally from antecedent literary forms, but because individual authors brought the literary resources at their disposal to bear on the problems facing their own generation. In light of the possible influence of oriental narrative traditions, recently defended by Graham Anderson, we should recognize the hyperbole of Perry's statement.[112] Romance has a lengthy pedigree. Nevertheless, even the oriental practice of storytelling is little more than raw material for Greek romance. The many antecedent influences from which romance was created are, alone, insufficient to explain the development of the genre. To understand the development of romance we must come to terms with the creative activity of authors who saw fit to preserve and re-fashion antecedent materials into a distinct literary form.

---

[109] Perry, *Ancient Romances*, 335, n. 15. Other scholars who have addressed the importance of social conditions in the formation of romance are Reardon, "Aspects of the Greek Novel," 118–31; Holzberg, *Ancient Novel*, 28–42; Morgan, "Greek Novel," 137–38; and Hägg, *Novel in Antiquity*, 81–90. Even Graham Anderson, who stresses the importance of oriental influences in the development of the genre, notes that the task of romance was to "accommodate narrative material to a new cultural context" (*Ancient Fiction*, 27).

[110] Perry, *Ancient Romances*, 175–76.

[111] Hägg, *Novel in Antiquity*, 89.

[112] Anderson, *Ancient Fiction*, 25.

Bakhtin and Perry offer very similar explanations of the origins of Greek romance.[113] Both scholars stress the importance of authorial intention and the role of social factors in the production and development of new literary genres. Bakhtin's investigation, however, underscores the importance of polyglossia in the development of the novel. Polyglossia and its attendant awareness of heteroglossia provide an important linguistic and ideological background for the production of literature. This ideological background, in turn, is set in sharper relief by examining the chronotopic aspects of the text's story-world.

By creating a realistic story-world, romance provided a creative way to explore the varied social and cultural terrain of the Hellenistic world. It exhibited a heightened awareness of heteroglossia in part through its eclectic use of genres.[114] Romance incorporates many different primary and secondary genres, such as dialogues, descriptions (ἔκφρασις), letters, prayers, speeches, and short stories. Each incorporated genre possesses its own ideological overtones, and the juxtaposition of these varied genres therefore manifests an awareness of heteroglossia. By ignoring traditional generic boundaries, romance offers a subtle critique of social conventions and incorporates a new sensitivity to the possibilities of language.

Greek romance also reflects its sensitivity to heteroglossia in its use of multi-leveled discourse. In epic, monological discourse dominated the whole composition. The epic hero spoke the same ideological language as that of the author and reader. Romance, on the other hand,

---

[113] Bakhtin's most detailed discussion of Greek romance is in "Form of Time and of the Chronotope," 86–110. Although contemporaries, Bakhtin was still an obscure figure in the west when Perry wrote *The Ancient Romances*. An interesting point of possible contact between them is Henri Bergson. In elaborating the notion of an "open" versus a "closed" society, Perry cites Bergson, *Les deux sources de la morale et de la religion* (Paris, 1932). Along with Kant, Bergson was a special preoccupation of the Bakhtin Circle and an important early influence on Bakhtin (Morson & Emerson, *Mikhail Bakhtin*, 177–79; Katerina Clark and Michael Holquist, *Mikhail Bakhtin* [Cambridge, Mass.: Harvard University Press, 1984], 102–3; and Michael Holquist, *Dialogism: Bakhtin and His World*, New Accents, ed. Terence Hawkes [London: Routledge, 1990], 152–53). This common interest in Bergson may account for the similar way in which Perry and Bakhtin treat the development of literary genres.

[114] Bakhtin, "Forms of Time and of the Chronotope," 89. The eclecticism of Greek romance is also noted by Seldon, "Genre of Genre," 41–42; and Morgan, "Make-believe," 222.

uses many different ideological languages.[115] The characters of romance see the world in different ways. The author uses the speech of
the characters to introduce new perspectives into the story. Bakhtin,
however, observed that Greek romance "only weakly embodied this
new discourse that resulted from polyglot consciousness."[116] Greek romance never achieved the kind of ideological independence so characteristic of the modern novel. In romance, speech remains conventional
and stylized and is, therefore, a mere caricature of authentic speech.
Such speech never escapes the controlling influence of a monologic author. Therefore, while Greek romance exhibits an awareness of heteroglossia, it nevertheless remains a monologic genre.

As Reardon observes, "the imagined world is the heart of romance."[117] Therefore, if we hope to understand the essence of romance,
we must understand its fictive world. An examination of the chronotope
of romance yields further insights into its nature. Temporally, the
Greek romance is composed of events that lie outside "historical, quotidian, biographical . . . biological and maturational" time.[118] Biographical time is important only for establishing the boundaries of the
narrative events. At the beginning, two young people meet and fall in
love; at the end they are reunited, unscathed and unaffected by their in-
tervening adventures. Consequently, time produces no discernible effect on the characters or their world. The time of Greek romance is
simply a temporal void to be filled with adventures. The heroes of
Greek romance do not grow older, nor do they develop mentally or

---

[115] As R. Bracht Branham observes in comparing Menippean satire and
epic: "Achilles and Hector speak the same language in a way in which Eumolpus
and Trimalchio do not." They may all speak Greek but their social and ideological
location is quite different. See Branham, "Inventing the Novel," in *Bakhtin in Contexts: Across the Disciplines*, ed. Amy Mandelker and Caryl Emerson, Rethinking
Theory (Evanston, Ill.: Northwestern University Press, 1995), 82.

[116] Bakhtin, "Prehistory of Novelistic Discourse," 65.

[117] Reardon, *Form of Greek Romance*, 46.

[118] Bakhtin, "Forms of Time and of the Chronotope," 91. As Bakhtin notes,
Longus would, in certain respects, be an exception (ibid., 103). Daphnis and Chloë
mature over the course of the romance, growing in their understanding of love and
its delights. In this, and in other respects, *Daphnis and Chloë* is the most highly developed of the ancient romances, and therefore resists facile comparison with the
other romances. Nevertheless, in other respects, it still fits the overall pattern of the
romance genre.

emotionally. The extent and duration of the narrative events can rarely be measured accurately; all that matters is that time is extensive enough to contain the events of the narrative.[119] Bakhtin refers to the temporal quality of Greek romance as "adventure-time," time that merely provides space for adventure.

In the romance, biographical-time serves only to establish the boundaries of adventure-time. In the space between separation and reconciliation are travels and adventures. Since the lovers are unaffected by their separation, these travels and adventures could, if the author wished to do so, extend indefinitely; they only serve to keep the two lovers apart. Chance is the only factor governing the number and duration of adventures. The result is an "extratemporal and in effect infinite series" of adventures.[120] The sequence of events in romance is arbitrarily arranged according to a logic of "random contingency."[121] The contingent relationship between events in Greek romance is more important than their objective chronological relationship. What is of decisive importance is that events should happen "suddenly" and "at just that moment."[122] The artificiality of this arrangement opens up rich narrative possibilities for romance—possibilities that were unthinkable for epic forms like Greek tragedy, which were constrained by the need to tell a traditional story.[123]

In adventure-time, the potentially infinite series of events is artificially organized by means of "the road."[124] This simple device allows the author to create a plausible arrangement of narrative events, while avoiding the complex problem of necessary causation. As the characters move along the road, they naturally meet other characters. Bakhtin mentions two temporal moments, which are especially significant on

---

[119] For a detailed study of day/night sequences in three of the Greek romances, see Tomas Hägg, *Narrative Technique in Ancient Greek Romances: Studies in Chariton, Xenophon Ephesius, and Achilles Tatius*, Skrifter utgivna av Svenska Institutet i Athen 8°, 8 (Stockholm: Svenska Institutet i Athen, 1971).

[120] Bakhtin, "Forms of Time and of the Chronotope," 94.

[121] Ibid., 92.

[122] Ibid., 92. Vague temporal adverbs are especially prominent in Chariton (Hägg, *Narrative Technique*, 47). This artificial arrangement of events lacks precisely the kind of necessary or probable causation that Aristotle claimed was essential for a well-formed plot (*Poet.* 1452a19–21).

[123] Aristotle, *Poet.* 1453b25.

[124] Bakhtin, "Forms of Time and of the Chronotope," 98, 243–45.

the road. First, there is the moment of encounter, or non-encounter. The adventure-time of romance is filled with a series of chance encounters and near misses. The peculiar chronotopic qualities of the road, qualities it shares with the marketplace, facilitate the transgression of "social distances" and allow the author to bring people from widely divergent backgrounds into close contact. These encounters would be unthinkable in other contexts. Along the road, all types of people may meet: the rich and the poor, the wise and the foolish, the hero and the villain, and so forth. When these meetings occur on the road, they are completely natural and ideologically neutral. Along with encounters, there may also be near misses. These non-encounters serve to keep the main characters apart and create a sense of suspense and drama. This is especially the case when the main characters are in close proximity to one another, but their encounter is temporally and spatially unsynchronized.

The second moment that occurs along the road is that of recognition or non-recognition. Even when the main characters share the same narrative time and space, they are often prevented from recognizing one another. This may be due to a dramatic change in social circumstances, a change in costume, or physical limitations of one sort or another. As might be expected in a tale of separation, the dramatic high point of romance is the moment of encounter and recognition.[125] Normally this leads to reconciliation and the conclusion of the story, unless there is a subsequent separation. The use of recognition/non-recognition may also extend beyond the separation of lovers. The hero's identity may be obscured, as in Lucius' metamorphosis in *The Golden Ass,* or their aristocratic origins concealed, as in *Daphnis and Chloë.* These temporary non-recognitions create a necessary tension that keeps the plot of the story alive until the truth finally wins out at the end of the narrative. Non-recognitions also present another opportunity to transgress normal social boundaries. Since their captors know nothing of their aristocratic background, for the first time in their lives the heroes of romance are treated like slaves. Likewise, in the presence of the heroes, the captors behave in ways they would normally conceal even from their social

---

[125] Aristotle's ἀναγνώρισις, which also frequently involves a reversal or περιπέτεια (*Poet.* 1452a22–b9). See O. J. Schrier, "A Simple View of *Peripeteia,*" *Mnemosyne* 33 (1980): 96–118.

equals. In this way, romance creates a temporally random and socially ambiguous space for its adventures.

To compensate for the random arrangement of narrative events, romance often resorts to prophecy, dreams and omens. In addition to heightening the psychological tension of the hero and heroine, these devices prepare the reader for subsequent events and render narrative transitions less abrupt and more natural.[126] Like the road, these devices are quite artificial. Nevertheless, by foreshadowing ensuing events, they lend an air of ineluctability to the adventures. Within the story-world, the characters desperately want to know how their fates will un-fold. Divine revelation presents this knowledge in small portions, allay-ing the anxiety of the heroes but preserving the central tension of the story. This aspect of the romance chronotope suggests that uncertainty of the future was a significant concern for its Hellenistic audience. The epic past was complete and fully resolved, but the romantic present was preoccupied with an unknown and unpredictable future. While epic was backward looking and closed off from the present, romance opened a "zone of contact with reality" and cultivated a lively interest in the pre-sent and the immediate future.[127] The message of romance is that life must take its course, and the hero can only endure and wait for her luck to change.

The adventures of the Greek novel are normally set in foreign lands. The alien quality of these locations makes the random contin-gency of events in the novel seem more plausible. Quite apart from its entertainment value, travel to exotic foreign locations produces an overwhelming sense of isolation within the characters of the novel. Foreign laws and customs suspend the heroes' normal expectations and render them powerless in their new circumstances. In this foreign world, the characters are completely passive and unprotected from Tyche.[128] Typically, external forces, such as sea-storms or kidnappers, move them from one adventure to the next. These disasters render the heroes impotent. Because they are so overwhelmed with grief and self-pity, when action is necessary to advance the plot, a trusted companion must often act on their behalf. Thus, the spatial dimension of the ro-

---

[126] Bakhtin, "Forms of Time and of the Chronotope," 92.

[127] Branham, "Inventing the Novel," 82–83.

[128] Bakhtin, "Forms of Time and of the Chronotope," 105.

mance chronotope functions to neutralize the heroes and accentuate their helplessness. The counterbalance to this sense of helplessness is an emphasis on divine control. The gods control the fate of the characters, and only piety can placate their wrath and turn the tide of events.

Romance rarely limits its action to a single foreign land. Adventure-time requires a vast expanse of space.[129] In their adventures, the characters of romance travel throughout the lands of the eastern Mediterranean. The precise geographical location is of little importance; virtually any foreign land will suffice. All that matters is that it be unfamiliar and preferably exotic. Of course, these are relative terms. What is unfamiliar and exotic is so precisely in relation to the author's world.[130] For romance, the value of foreign space lies squarely in its difference from what the characters expect to be normal and conventional. When romance does describe its setting, it seldom provides political or geographical details. Virtually any ocean will serve as a setting for a shipwreck, and the details of political disturbances are irrelevant, except as a backdrop for the action of romance. What is important is that between one country and another there lies a vast sea or a long and perilous journey. With a few minor adjustments, any sea or highway will suffice. The external world merely provides the setting and is of little interest in its own right.

Quite apart from its value as entertainment, travel to exotic locations also serves another important function in the Greek romance. Foreign locations create a profound sense of isolation for the main characters. This alien world separates the heroes from the very things that normally keep fate in check—family, wealth, and social status.[131] In the absence of their social safety net, they are unprotected from Tyche's devices. Whereas epic space was public, impersonal, and spatiotemporally remote, romance is private, personal, and in close contact with the present.[132] The author of romance is less interested in explaining what is universally true and more interested in describing what is "isolated, single and unique."[133] This is true not only of foreign curiosities, but

---

[129] Ibid., 99.

[130] Ibid., 101.

[131] Ibid., 108. Perry makes a similar observation in *Ancient Romances*, 120.

[132] Branham, "Inventing the Novel," 83.

[133] Bakhtin, "Forms of Time and of the Chronotope," 101–2.

also of the fortunes and misfortunes of the main characters. Individual fate and private thoughts dominate the space of romance.[134]

The characters of romance express feelings and emotions that would have been familiar to Hellenistic readers. The general sense of insecurity, stemming from the hero's isolation from family, and especially from their beloved, expresses itself as sentimental anguish rather than heroic resolve. To the isolated individual, the world looms large, both as a threat and as a treasure house of new experiences and wonders. Consequently, the space of romance is intensely private. It explores the private longings and inner wonder of individuals caught up in an expansive world.

Although romance is set in a zone of close contact with the present, its main characters are in no way average Hellenistic citizens. Invariably, they are people of wealth and privilege from the upper strata of society. Nevertheless, in contrast to epic, Greek romance has a pronounced focus on individuals facing typical misfortunes. There are no battles with mythical creatures, only common, everyday pirates and brigands. According to Bakhtin, the idea that unifies the Greek romance as a genre is the "test of the hero's integrity."[135] The main characters are placed in Tyche's crucible to test the quality of their character or ἀρετή. There is nothing in the space and time of romance to limit the vicissitudes of chance.[136] Consequently, the world of romance is unpredictable and often hostile. The only fixed point in romance is love. In this test, extraordinary deeds of courage and bravery are of little value; only constancy in the face of unrelenting threats and pious submission to fate are sufficient to demonstrate the hero's virtue. Only by resisting unrelenting attacks on their virtue do the heroes demonstrate both their commitment to one another and thereby also their ἀρετή. These pivotal conflicts are staged in the psyches of the main characters, and the reader has access to this private world only by means of lengthy introspective soliloquies whereby the main characters reveal their private thoughts. This psychological space is the main interest of the Greek novel. The random adventures and alien space of the

---

[134] Perry, *Ancient Romances*, 7, 120; Hägg, *Novel in Antiquity*, 81–86; and Morgan, "Greek Novel," 144.

[135] Bakhtin, "Forms of Time and of the Chronotope," 106.

[136] Ibid., 100.

story-world of the novel only serve to accent the psychological struggles of the main characters.

Nor is the romance interested in the notable civic accomplishments of its characters, as is Greco-Roman biography. The characters of romance are politically disenfranchised. They are not civic leaders bearing the weighty responsibility of political affairs. Like their Hellenistic readers, the characters of romance are citizens of a large empire that is quite beyond their control. Instead of civic duty, what interests the author of romance is private, and often melodramatic, anguish. Romance highlights the psychological sufferings and trials of its heroes. Its characters are not on display as suitable models of epic heroism and civic virtue as they would be in epic and biography. In romance, the heroes suffer to recommend piety and perseverance to the reader, as well as to provide an entertaining diversion from the problems of imperial life. Romance offers its readers a momentary respite from their anxieties, along with the saccharine hope that things will ultimately lead to a happy ending.

The chronotope of Greek romance is therefore temporally abstract and spatially alien. The author of romance places idealized characters within this world to test their piety and romantic devotion. We might say then that romance presents a bourgeois approach to the social turmoil of the Hellenistic period. Its main concern is to explore how well-born Greeks should conduct themselves in the midst of a strange and often dangerous world.[137] The answer proposed by romance is that perseverance and piety will prevail, and while there may be no hope of recovering the glory days of classical Athens, romantic love is a tolerable substitute.

Menippean Satire and Its Chronotope

Polyglossia affected Hellenistic culture in a slightly different way in the Menippean satire.[138] Hellenistic examples of Menippean sat-

---

[137] In this context, the term "bourgeois" is of course anachronistic. I use it here to emphasize a general interest in conformity to standards of respectability, common among a class of people that is materially secure. I do not mean to imply that there was an economic "middle class" in antique society.

[138] Bakhtin comments on Menippean Satire in: *PDP*, 112–22; "Epic and Novel," 22, 27; "Forms of Time and the Chronotope," 221–24; and "Discourse in the Novel," 371, 390–91. There are also several book length studies on Menippean

ire span several centuries.[139] As a distinct genre, the Menippean satire dates from around the time of its eponymous ancestor, Menippus of Gadara (fl. ca. 250 B.C.E.), and it survived well beyond the collapse of the Roman Empire. Today the works of Menippus, Bion Borysthenes (ca. 325–ca. 255 B.C.E.) and Marcus Terentius Varro (116–27 B.C.E.) either exist in fragments or are known only indirectly through testimonia.[140] The fragmentary remains of Varro's works, however, are substantial and provide additional insight into the nature of the genre. One of the earliest fully preserved examples of the genre is Seneca's *Apocolocyntosis*, written shortly after Claudius' death during the reign of Nero. The most substantial extant collection of Menippean satires are those of Lucian of Samosata, who was active during the second century C.E. Menippean satire is also found in combination with other genres such as romance in Petronius' *Satyricon*, Pseudo-Lucian's *Asinus*, and Apuleius' *Metamorphoses*; and biography in *The Life of Aesop*, *The Life of Secundus*, and the letters of Hippocrates.

Unlike the amorous adventures of Greek romance, Menippean satire, or menippea, as Bakhtin preferred to call it, is organized around fantastic or picaresque adventures. On the surface, these adventures are merely entertaining, but on closer examination, they serve a more seri-

---

satire: Joel C. Relihan, *Ancient Menippean Satire* (Baltimore: Johns Hopkins University Press, 1993); H. K. Riikonen, *Menippean Satire as a Literary Genre: With Special Reference to Seneca's Apocolocyntosis*, Commentationes Humanarum Litterarum 83 (Helsinki: Finnish Society of Sciences and Letters [Societas Scientiarum Fennica], 1987). Shorter treatments may be found in: Frye, *Anatomy of Criticism*, 308–12; and Phillip Hoyt Holland, "Robert Burton's *Anatomy of Melancholy* and Menippean Satire, Humanist and English" (Ph.D. diss., University College London, 1979), 30–91. For general bibliography on the genre, see Eugene P. Kirk, *Menippean Satire: An Annotated Catalogue of Texts and Criticism*, Garland Reference Library of the Humanities, 191 (New York: Garland, 1980).

[139] The term Menippean satire was unknown in classical times. It is now commonly used, however, to refer to both Greek and Roman satirical writing, as well as the later satirical tradition that includes Cervantes, Rabelais, Swift, and Voltaire. See Joel C. Relihan, "On the Origin of 'Menippean Satire' as the Name of a Literary Genre," *Classical Philology* 79 (1984): 226–29.

[140] For an English translation of Varro's satires, see Charles Marston Lee, "Varro's Menippean Satires" (Ph.D. diss., University of Pittsburgh, 1937). The fragmentary remains of Bion's satires are published, with accompanying English translation, in Jan Fredrik Kindstrand, *Bion of Borysthenes: A Collection of the Fragments with Introduction and Commentary*, Acta Universitatis Upsaliensis, Studia Graeca Upsaliensia, 11 (Stockholm: Almqvist & Wiksell, 1976).

ous purpose. Whereas Greek romance tests the moral *character* of its heroes, menippea tests an *idea* through the adventures of the hero.[141] Bakhtin called menippea the *"universal genre* of *ultimate questions."*[142] Menippea exposes unexplored aspects of an idea by subjecting its representative to the extreme circumstances of everyday life. Thus, each character is an ideologue, not simply a character, but the bearer of an idea. In the course of the hero's adventures, this idea is exposed to the withering scrutiny of parody. Menippea does not treat its heroes with the reverence and dignity of epic literature. The Menippean protagonist is typically an anti-hero, presented as either a Cynic philosopher as in Lucian's satires, or a picaro as in Petronius and Apuleius. The motivation of these characters is far from heroic; they seek only to satisfy their own intellectual, and often carnal, curiosity. Nor are their adventures noble or tragic; they are either comic or simply vulgar.

Plato also knew how to expose the undetected weakness of an idea by bringing it into contact with competing ideas, as his Socratic dialogues demonstrate. Indeed, in this respect, menippea is organically related to Socratic dialogue, but, as Bakhtin notes, in menippea "the familiarizing role of laughter" is more pronounced.[143] The author uses laughter to mock the pretensions of monological ideas. Whenever centripetal forces offer abstract and monological solutions to life's problems, they become vulnerable to Menippean laughter. Therefore, menippea is essentially a comic genre, but it is a comic genre with a serious purpose. Menippea lampoons traditional answers to the serious problems of everyday life. It tests conventional wisdom against the prosaic demands of the present. The failure of traditional answers to measure up to this standard produces the comical element in Menippean satire. Thus, menippea is a characteristically σπουδογέλοιον, or seriocomic genre.[144] Under the guise of burlesque, menippea tests the seri-

---

[141] Bakhtin, *PDP*, 114. Following Bakhtin's practice, I will use the term "menippea" interchangeably with the more formal "Menippean satire."

[142] Ibid., 146. Compare Frye's comment: "The Menippean satire deals less with people as such than with mental attitudes." Thus, characters "are handled in terms of their occupational approach to life as distinct from their social behavior" (*Anatomy of Criticism*, 309).

[143] Bakhtin, "Discourse in the Novel," 26. Branham follows Bakhtin in noting the importance of laughter and its relation to "outsidedness" in menippea ("Inventing the Novel," 84–86).

[144] Bakhtin, *PDP*, 106. For further discussion, see Lawrence Giangrande,

ous issues of morality, religion, and philosophy by bringing them into contact with the prosaic realities of everyday life.

Bakhtin claimed that contact with the immediate present was the most characteristic feature of the novelistic tradition.[145] Nevertheless, each novelistic genre—whether biography, romance, or menippea—has its own particular way of creating such contact. In contrast to the conservative traditionalism of biography and the bourgeois piety of romance, menippea has a pronounced iconoclastic quality. This distinctive quality is apparent in both menippea's subject matter and its chronotope.

The menippea is temporally set in the closest possible contact with the immediate present. Through a technique Bakhtin calls familiarization, Menippean authors use laughter and parody to destroy "epic and tragic distance" and thereby transfer "all represented material to a zone of familiar contact."[146] Menippea bridges the distance that once separated the epic author from his subject matter. In menippea, the hero exists on the same ideological plane as the author. This does not mean that the menippea is always set in the present. Instead, even when the hero is a figure from the past, he represents the values of the present, and not those of his own time. Nevertheless, the menippea never gilds the present. It exposes the underside of everyday life. Menippea is especially interested in those aspects of life normally hidden from public view. Thus, menippea brings the idea represented by the main character into the closest possible contact with the prosaic present, and this contact often results in a vulgar realism, or "slum naturalism."[147] In menippea, vulgar realism sometimes manifests itself as a preoccupation with bodily functions and physical desires. While this sophomoric fascination with vulgar topics no doubt contributed to menippea's popularity as a form of entertainment, it also illustrates the novelistic impulse toward immediate contact with the present.

The Use of "Spoudaiogeloion" in Greek and Roman Literature, Studies in Classical Literature, 6 (Hague: Mouton, 1972); Kindstrand, *Bion of Borysthenes*, 46–49; Holland, "Burton's *Anatomy*," 36–37; and R. Bracht Branham, *Unruly Eloquence: Lucian and the Comedy of Traditions*, Revealing Antiquity, ed. G. W. Bowersock, 2 (Cambridge: Harvard University Press, 1989), 26–28.

[145] Bakhtin, "Epic and Novel," 7, 11.

[146] Bakhtin, *PDP*, 124.

[147] Bakhtin, "Discourse in the Novel," 26; and, *PDP*, 108, 115.

Like Greek romance, menippea has an attenuated sense of biological and quotidian time. Menippean characters never age or mature; they exist only in the present moment. While romance depicts events in a temporal hiatus within biological time, and biography naturally organizes its action around the chronology of the hero, menippea concentrates on exceptional moments in the hero's development.[148] Menippea is not interested in the hero's notable civic accomplishments, or his chaste passions. Instead, it is interested in individual transformations. These transformations are typically the result of a magical metamorphosis or a fantastic journey. Thus, in Apuleius' *Metamorphoses*, Lucius is transformed into an ass. Consequently, he experiences a very different side of life and in the end devotes himself to Isis and Osiris. In Lucian's *Icaromenippus*, Menippus fashions wings for himself so that he can fly to the heavens. There, he converses with the gods and, because of his journey, forswears the idle musings of the philosophers and becomes a Cynic. In neither case is the development psychological. Lucius and Menippus do not become better people through a natural process of maturation. They are better and wiser because of their unusual experiences.

In some examples of menippea, the novelistic impulse to establish a zone of contact between the epic past and the present leads to a complete abridgment of temporal distinctions. In these instances, we can only describe the Menippean sense of time as supratemporal. These works use a fantastic sense of time to contemporize epic figures and bring them into dialogic contact with the hero. Whole works, such as Lucian's *Dialogues of the Dead*, are composed on this premise. In such works, epic heroes, ancient poets, and classical philosophers must answer for their life's work. Their interrogator is the Menippean hero, who represents the ideological standpoint of the present. Frequently, these dialogues expose the deceitfulness and unreliability of the ancient traditions. This ideological shift, wherein menippea measures the past against the values of the present, dissolves the epic distance that once guaranteed reverence for epic heroes. Menippea exposes the imperfections of the epic heroes by weighing their great accomplishments and erudition against their lesser-known misdeeds and falsehoods. Invaria-

---

[148] Bakhtin, "Forms of Time and of the Chronotope," 111, 116.

bly, menippea finds the heroes of the past unworthy of unconditional admiration and praise.

Menippea also dissolves temporal distinctions in its critique of the contemporary defenders of traditional epic values. Anyone with a personal stake in conventional values, especially the rich and powerful, can become the target of Menippean satire. To expose the superficiality of these values, menippea frequently adopts a supratemporal perspective. From this perspective, menippea can view the entire span of a person's life and thereby show that death robs everyone of power, privilege, and wealth. Thus, menippea's constant refrain is that it is best not to become too attached to life's fleeting pleasures. Only someone like Menippus who has already renounced life's vain pursuits can laugh in the face of death.[149] In menippea, the ultimate source of laughter is vain attachment to wealth and power. Anyone who succumbs to the allure of earthly pleasures is vulnerable to ridicule and mockery, since, when death comes, the rich find that they are poor, the wise show themselves to be foolish, and the powerful become powerless.[150] Thus, the characteristic irony of menippea is that those who have nothing, those who know they are fools and embrace their powerlessness, are the ones better prepared for death. This irony, which is explicit in the satires of Lucian and Varro, is also apparent in the Menippean romances. The comic element in Petronius, Seneca, and Apuleius turns on the attachment of their main characters to wealth, power, and sensual pleasure. These are comical stories precisely because of the lengths to which their characters will go to satisfy their vain desires.

The menippea's spatial aspect also reinforces its serio-comic chronotope. Superficially, Menippean stories are organized by journeys, much like Greek romance, but unlike the idealized journeys of romance, Menippean journeys are either crudely realistic, or fantastic. For example, Lucian's Menippean dialogues are set in a fantastic space. His heroes freely cross spatial boundaries. Unconstrained by physical laws and forces, they travel upward to heaven or descend to Hades, and

---

[149] In one of Lucian's finest comic scenes, Menippus even refuses to pay Charon the toll to cross the river Styx (*Dial. Mort.* 2). Similarly, in *Dial. Mort.* 20, Menippus assists Charon and Hermes in unburdening the recently deceased of their earthly trappings.

[150] There is probably no better example of this post-death reversal in Menippean literature than that of the Emperor Claudius in Seneca's *Apocolocyntosis*.

from there, they make their observations about life. From the heights of heaven, they see people in their private moments and witness their secret hypocrisies. From the depths of Hades, they see people for what they truly are, stripped of earthly trappings of wealth and power.

Similarly, in Menippean romance the journeys are picaresque. In their travels, Lucius and Encolpius visit the unseemly places of antiquity. Their narrative worlds are filled with brothels, cheap apartments, robbers' caves, and graveyards. This is a striking contrast to the dignified public space of the Greco-Roman biography and the idealized private space of Greek romance. The space of Menippean romance lacks refinement and dignity, and its characters must therefore negotiate the rough habits and coarse language of the seamier side of the Hellenistic world.

In Pseudo-Lucian's *Asinus* and Apuleius' *Metamorphoses*, space is viewed from the unusual perspective of an ass. Since those around him see only a humble ass, Lucius observes them when their guard is down and therefore sees them as they really are. He witnesses their deceitfulness, hypocrisy, pettiness, and cruelty—traits they normally conceal from their friends and neighbors. Other Menippean works offer subtle variations on the theme of metamorphoses. For example, in Plutarch's *Bruta animalia ratione uti* Odysseus defends the advantages of being human against the arguments of a pig named Gryllus.[151] The pig, however, wins decisively since he had once been human and therefore knew better.

Elsewhere, menippea achieves the same effect by viewing life from the standpoint of a servant or thief. No matter what the technique, in each case Menippean space serves as a window on private human behavior. Menippea creates an unusual spatial position from which it surveys the truth about people. From its perspective above or beyond human space it finalizes human achievement and strips away privilege and pretension to reveal the truth about life.

Because of its peculiar chronotopic qualities, Bakhtin claimed that menippea was especially adept at absorbing and transforming any genre with which it came into contact.[152] Quintilian was the first to note the eclecticism of Menippean satire, as exemplified by Varro's min-

---

[151] *Mor.* 985–92.
[152] Bakhtin, *PDP*, 118, 119–21.

gling of verse and prose.[153] In the past, many have used Quintilian's observation to identify Menippean satire as a strictly prosimetric genre. Modern scholarship on menippea has abandoned this formalistic definition.[154] Even so, a characteristic feature of menippea is its ability to combine diverse genres. As H. K. Riikonen notes,

> in Greek and Roman Menippean satires it is not only a question of mingling prose with verse but of building up a new whole from parts of texts relying on conventions and/or subject matter peculiar to different genres.[155]

Menippea's combination of various genres is not haphazard but intentional. Menippea weaves disparate genres together to bring their ideological fields into contact. Since each genre views the world in its own particular way, the use of a genre also evokes its ideological perspective. Thus, such combination is no mere stylistic flourish, but a powerful way of achieving dialogic syncrisis between opposing positions.

The way Lucian incorporates poetry into some of his Menippean satires is a good illustration of the creative use of a genre's ideological overtones. In the opening scene of Lucian's *Menippus sive necromantia*, Menippus appears clothed in the epic garb of Heracles, Odysseus, and Orpheus spouting poetry in response to every question. When his friends finally persuade him to drop his poetic façade, Menippus tells them of his recent journey to Hades. He tells his friends that as a young man he became disillusioned with the epic poets and their scandalous tales of divine misbehavior.[156] When, however, he asked the philosophers what manner of life was best they gave him incompatible and inconsistent answers. Unable to find direction from either the poets or the philosophers, Menippus determined to travel to Hades so that he might

---

[153] *Inst*. 10.1.95.

[154] See Juanita Sullivan Williams, "Towards a Definition of Menippean Satire" (Ph.D. diss., Vanderbilt University, 1966), 274; Relihan, *Ancient Menippean Satire*, 12–36; and Frederick Joseph Benda, "The Tradition of Menippean Satire in Varro, Lucian, Seneca and Erasmus" (Ph.D. diss., University of Texas at Austin, 1979), 1–25.

[155] Riikonen, *Menippean Satire as a Literary Genre*, 12.

[156] Criticism of the epic tales for their depiction of divine immorality did not originate with Lucian. As Xenophanes (c. 565–470 B.C.E.) observed, "Homer and Hesiod attributed to the gods all the reproaches and disgraces of men—theft, adultery, deceit" (Russell & Winterbottom, *ALC*, 4).

press his question to the sage Teiresias. After journeying to Babylon to consult with the oriental magician Mithrobarzanes about the safest way to enter Hades, Menippus finally arrives in the land of the dead. There, he observes the sad fate that awaits rich and poor alike, and when at length he meets Teiresias, he learns that the simple life is best.[157] Lest we miss the irony, a line of Homeric verse follows Teiresias' comments. To get the point, we need only recall that Lucian is writing in the second century, during the heyday of Atticism. The pretentious speech of the poets, like the vain musings of the philosophers, is mere affectation. What really matters is "life of the common sort." Petronius achieves a similar effect in the *Satyricon* when Eumolpus launches into epic verse at the most inappropriate moments. For his indiscretion, Eumolpus regularly earns the abuse of those around him.[158] Commenting on Eumolpus' performance, R. Bracht Branham remarks, "epic can enter the novel, but when it does so, it ceases to be itself, and becomes a comic image of epic."[159] By juxtaposing the practiced dignity of epic poetry with the bawdy adventures of his picaresque heroes, Petronius clearly intends to lampoon epic literary style.

Menippea absorbed prose genres as well. These could be both speech genres and literary genres. In particular, Bakhtin argued that menippea absorbed the kindred genres of diatribe, soliloquy, and symposium.[160] In addition, encomiastic speeches, folk tales, symposia, fables, letters, and prayers also grace the pages of menippea. In each case, these genres are invoked to measure their form-shaping ideology against the standard of contemporary, prosaic values.

Not only was menippea capable of absorbing all sorts of speech genres, it also effected the wholesale transformation of entire literary genres.[161] For example, the Menippean adaptations of Petronius and Apuleius challenge the romanticism of Greek romance. Less frequently noted are biographical works that have fallen under the influence of menippea. The *Life of Aesop* and the epistolary *Life of Hippocrates* are both examples of Menippean biography, as is most likely the *Life of*

---

[157] *Men.* 21.
[158] *Sat.* 89–91.
[159] Branham, "Inventing the Novel," 83.
[160] Bakhtin, *PDP*, 119–20.
[161] Ibid., 120–21.

Secundus the Silent Philosopher.[162] In contrast to the conservative nature of the typical Greco-Roman biography, these works are openly iconoclastic. For example, in the *Life of Aesop*, Aesop's misshapen looks and low station place him in a unique position to ridicule the pretensions of all those who think themselves more intelligent and fortunate.[163] It is no accident that Aesop's master, Xanthos, is an arrogant philosopher. As a slave, Aesop is often in a position to observe Xanthos in his most private moments, and Aesop seldom fails to use these situations to his own advantage. Aesop pits his earthy wisdom and common sense against Xanthos' sophistication and learning, but in this battle of wits, Xanthos is no match for Aesop. Like other Menippean genres, the *Life of Aesop* again shows that everyday values are superior to the traditional Greek values of cultural sophistication and philosophical erudition.[164]

The Pseudo-Hippocratic letters also exhibit pronounced Menippean qualities.[165] When the philosopher Democritus is overcome with laughter, the people of Abdera believe he has gone mad and ask Hippocrates to examine him. When he does so, Hippocrates learns that De-

---

[162] Bakhtin only mentions the Menippean qualities of the Hippocratic letters in passing (ibid., 113). The Hippocratic letters are treated in detail by Holland, "Burton's *Anatomy*," 70–77. Bakhtin never refers to the *Life of Aesop* as a Menippean work, but its similarities to menippea are obvious. Niklas Holzberg, for example, relates the *Life of Aesop* to the *Satyricon* and *Metamorphoses*, two works with well-established Menippean qualities. See Holzberg, "Novel-Like Works of Extended Prose Fiction II," *The Novel in the Ancient World*, ed. Gareth Schmeling, Mnemosyne, Bibliotheca Classica Batava, Supplementum, 159 (Leiden: E. J. Brill, 1996), 639. Richard Pervo also notes the "strong satiric features" of the Aesop romance in his article "A Nihilist Fabula: Introducing *The Life of Aesop*," in *Ancient Fiction and Early Christian Narrative*, ed. Ronald F. Hock, J. Bradley Chance, and Judith Perkins, SBL Symposium Series, ed. Gail R. O'Day, no. 6 (Atlanta: Scholars, 1998), 120.

[163] Lawrence Wills provides an English translation of the *Life of Aesop* in *The Quest of the Historical Gospel*, 180–215; as does Lloyd Daly, in *Aesop without Morals: The Famous Fables, and a Life of Aesop*, trans. and ed. Lloyd W. Daly, illustrated by Grace Muscarella (New York: Thomas Yoseloff, 1961), 29–90.

[164] Pervo, "A Nihilist Fabula," 116.

[165] On the Hippocratic letters, see *Hippocrates: Pseudepigraphic Writings*, ed., trans., with an introduction by Wesley D. Smith, Studies in Ancient Medicine, ed. John Scarborough, vol. 2. (Leiden: E. J. Brill, 1990). Quotations from the letters of Hippocrates are from this volume.

mocritus is not mad, but wise, for he laughs at human folly. Democritus explains:

> I laugh at one thing, humanity, brimming with ignorance, void of right action, childish in all aspirations, agonizing through useless woes for no benefit, traveling to the ends of the earth and her boundless depths with unmeasured desire, melting gold and silver, never stopping this acquisitiveness of theirs, ever in an uproar for more, so that they themselves can be less.[166]

Laughter and menippea are inseparable. The Menippean perspective on life sees the absurdity of human striving and claims that laughter is the only appropriate response.

In the *Life of Secundus*, this comic element is subdued, but detectable nonetheless.[167] Comic aspects are most evident in the account that explains why Secundus swore a vow of silence, albeit with tragic consequences for his mother. There is also the implicitly comic idea of a silent philosopher. What is more interesting for our purposes is the way the author pits Secundus against the reputedly wise and inquisitive emperor Hadrian. The learned emperor has only questions; the silent Secundus has answers.

In the preceding examples, an established literary genre has been modified under the influence of menippea. In each case, menippea uses the ideological tendency of the host genre and transforms it by bringing it into contact with the values of the immediate present. Thus, in the *Life of Aesop* and *Secundus the Silent Philosopher*, menippea subverts the conservative tendency of Greco-Roman biography by choosing humble subjects. It places these common heroes in dialogic contact with representatives of the dominant ideology in order to test that ideology. The action is set in the sphere of private experience rather than that of public political achievement. On the one hand, the kings and philosophers who represent the establishment are ideal types, who embody the values and knowledge that should give them success. On the other hand, the anti-heroes of Menippean biography embody everyday

---

[166] Letter 17.5.

[167] On the *Life of Secundus, see* Ben Edwin Perry, *Secundus the Silent Philosopher: The Greek Life of Secundus*, American Philological Association, Philological Monographs, no. 22 (Ithaca: American Philological Association, 1964); and Aune, "Greco-Roman Biography," 107–26.

values of simplicity and common sense, values shown to be superior to establishment values at coping with the prosaic demands of life. The Menippean hero may be ignorant of Greek philosophy and unable to master astronomical calculations, but he alone knows how to live.

In this connection, we must note the relationship between menippea and Cynic philosophy. Cynicism is the most important ideological influence in menippea. If Menippean satire is the literary manifestation of a concern for close contact with the present, Cynicism is its philosophical manifestation. Especially during the Second Sophistic, Cynicism represented a natural counter balance to an overweening Greek nationalism. Greek pride suffered a severe blow under Roman occupation. To a limited extent, Roman interest in Greek rhetoric and philosophy during the late first and early second centuries compensated for the loss of political autonomy. The Second Sophistic was symptomatic of this loss.[168] As a contemporary of the Second Sophistic, Lucian dissented from what seemed to him an unrestrained nostalgia for the Greek epic past.[169] Through his Menippean satires, Lucian argued that nostalgia for the epic past could not mitigate the harsh realities of Roman occupation and political disenfranchisement. By juxtaposing Cynic heroes such as Menippus and Diogenes with the poets, philosophers, and political leaders of the epic past, Lucian provided an important tonic for an overly romantic assessment of the Greek classical heritage. The past was not as great as it seemed, and the best way to cope with the present was to live simply and laugh at those who do not.

The fantastic temporal and spatial possibilities of the Menippean chronotope created wonderful opportunities for authors to bring epic traditions into direct contact with the present. In this dialogic encounter, menippea's loyalties clearly belonged to the latter. Menippea treated with utter disdain those who longed to resurrect the epic traditions and restore the glory days of ancient Greece. For menippea, the only hope for those living in turbulent times is a healthy dose of laughter. Everything else is just pretentious posturing.

---

[168] Bowie, "Greeks and Their Past in the Second Sophistic," 3–41.
[169] Branham, *Unruly Eloquence*, 7.

Conclusion

The breakdown of the epic chronotope brought about by the increased presence of polyglossia in the Hellenistic period created tremendous opportunities for literary creativity. Freed from the constraints of traditional literary genres, authors began to explore new ways to address the problems of life in their art. The authors of Greco-Roman biography preserved a traditional approach to the values of the past. By measuring the virtue of their heroes against the standards of the epic past, they tried to make a case for the enduring significance of those values. Romance and menippea elected to treat the threat of cultural instability in a more light-hearted and entertaining fashion. For its part, romance advocated bourgeois resignation while menippea adopted a more subversive and iconoclastic approach.

The Gospel of Mark was also written during this time of literary innovation. Given the polyglossic environment of Hellenism, it is possible that the author of the gospel was also engaged in a similar enterprise. In light of the gospel message, its author asks how the epic values of traditional Judaism measure up to the demands of the present. Scholars have suggested similarities between Mark and biography, romance, and Menippean satire. How would a Bakhtinian approach to the question of genre evaluate these comparisons? Would a chronotopic analysis support or overturn such comparisons? Even if direct influence between these genres and the Gospel of Mark proves unlikely, we might nevertheless gain some insight into the chronotopic characteristics of Mark's Gospel by means of such a comparison.

Chapter Four

THE GENRE OF MARK AND THE NOVELISTIC LITERATURE OF THE HELLENISTIC PERIOD

Recent biblical scholarship has generally come to acknowledge the creativity of the Markan author. The old form critical notion that Mark was merely a collector of traditions is no longer tenable. This new perspective has led to a profusion of literary investigations of Mark, which nevertheless tend to ignore the aesthetic dimensions of the gospel's story-world. To judge Mark's aesthetic achievement aright we must situate the gospel within the literary types of antiquity. In the preceding chapter, we surveyed three Greco-Roman narrative forms representative of popular literary activity in the first century: biography, romance, and Menippean satire. By analyzing these genres chronotopically, we exposed the essential characteristics of each one. Having done so, we are now in a position to take up the Gospel of Mark to see how it compares to these three Greco-Roman novelistic genres and, subsequently, how it compares to popular Jewish narratives of the same general period.

The Gospel of Mark and Greco-Roman Novelistic Literature

Bakhtin suggests that a properly conceived poetics must do two things. First, it must be able to describe the architectonic structure of the aesthetic work. To do so, it must understand how the aesthetic work refracts the values of its socio-historical environment. In other words, we must understand the literary work as an instance of spatially and temporally specific, value-laden perception. It is this perception that governs the overall, intentional structure of the aesthetic work. Second, a poetics that is adequate to its object must treat the text as an utterance, or an act of speech performance (*parole*). Not only is a text expressive of a particular perception of the world, it is an attempt to communicate that perception to others. This means that a poetics must account for the dialogic aspect of the text as a complex communicative event involving both author and reader.

Based upon Bakhtin's articulation of such a poetics, how does the Gospel of Mark compare to the novelistic literature of the first century? Does the Gospel of Mark perceive the world in the same way as Greco-Roman biography, romance, or menippea? More importantly, does the author of the gospel judge human activity, and especially the activity of the hero, in the same way as these literary genres? Put in a slightly different way, what we should ask is whether the Gospel of Mark is engaged in the same conversation as these other literary forms. Are they concerned with the same issues, and, if so, do they give similar answers?

Mark and Biography

Recent attempts to relate the Gospel of Mark to Greco-Roman biography are exemplary of the theoretism that Bakhtin opposed. Burridge, for example, defends the comparison between Mark and biography primarily based on what we can only describe as a mechanical and reductionistic procedure. He gives little or no consideration to the overarching purpose of the respective works. He virtually ignores the overall structure of the gospels in favor of a comparison with Greco-Roman biography based on their use of similar literary devices and linguistic conventions. Consequently, he leaves the Gospel of Mark's axiological orientation to life unexamined. The result is a superficially convincing comparison that leaves a lingering sense of dissatisfaction. The comparison with Greco-Roman biography seems to work, but only in an abstract way that is unrelated to the expressed values of the gospel. I believe dissatisfaction with the suggestion that the genre of the gospels derives from Greco-Roman biography is due largely to the use of the wrong methodological approach. The problem of genre is an aesthetic, literary problem and it cannot be resolved through the type of formalistic and reductionistic comparisons normally used to defend the connection with biography. As an aspect of literary criticism, genre is not about superficial taxonomical classification, but relates to the very essence, or quiddity, of literary works. Burridge seems to be aware of this;[1] nevertheless, the question is whether by positing a connection with Greco-Roman biography he has successfully identified the significant literary relations of the gospels. For Mark, the answer must be that he has not.

Whereas Greco-Roman biography focuses on a social space that emphasizes connections with family, clan, and *polis*, these elements are missing in Mark. Mark lacks any information about Jesus' ancestry, and his familial relationships are, for the purposes of Mark's story, relatively unimportant. The few oblique references to Jesus' family (3:21, 31–32) treat them largely as an impediment to his mission. Likewise, there is no mention of Jesus' lineage, birth, or childhood. The lineage that Mark emphasizes is Jesus' special relationship to God (1:11; 9:7). In the Gospel of Mark, Jesus' primary relationship is not social or familial, but theological. Jesus is God's specially appointed agent, commissioned to represent God, and the kingdom of God, to humankind.

As noted previously, both Bakhtin and Momigliano claim that ancient biography, at its most basic level, is the story of a whole life, from birth to death. If that is indeed the case, then the omission of information about Jesus' birth and childhood is one indication of Mark's deviation from the biographical norm. Birth and death serve a more important function than merely establishing the narrative boundaries of biography. Greco-Roman biography is fundamentally concerned with the exemplary life, and the natural boundaries of life are birth and death. By treating a person's life from birth to death, the author of biography provides a model of a whole life lived well, a model that readers can identify with and emulate. The Gospel of Mark does not present Jesus in this fashion. For the evangelist, Jesus is not exceptional because of his birth, or his superior virtue, or because he died well. Jesus is an important figure for Mark because of his divine calling (1:11; 9:7; 14:61–62; 15:39). No other person can aspire to this station. Jesus' calling is unique, a singular act of God at a particular place and time.

Greco-Roman biography recounts the public achievements of great men, who through their virtues, and often in spite of their vices,

---

[1] Burridge, *What are the Gospels?*, 33.

accomplished great things during their life. As a character in Mark's story, Jesus does not fit this model. If anything, when judged according to the standards of Greco-Roman biography, Jesus is an anti-hero. As a man of the first century, Jesus failed to accomplish anything of note during his lifetime, and, more importantly, as a Jew he failed to uphold the traditional Jewish standards of piety (2:7, 18, 24; 3:2; 7:2, 5).

This last point contrasts sharply with the conservative nature of Greco-Roman biography. Greco-Roman biography celebrated heroes from the past. These figures embodied the ethical and moral values that the authors of biography believed were essential to the demands of the present. Jesus, however, is no champion of traditional Pharisaic values. For Jesus, it is precisely the traditions of the elders that interfere with the realization of God's kingdom (3:1–6; 7:13). Although the characters of biography are representative members of traditional culture, Jesus' relationship with traditional first-century Judaism, at least as the Jewish leaders in Mark's Gospel represent it, is at the very least problematic.

One of the most significant indicators of the didactic interests of Greco-Roman biography is its diegetic narrative mode. The controlling voice of the narrator guides the reader's evaluation of the biographical hero. It is as if the narrator were constantly whispering in the reader's ear to ensure that the reader perceives the hero's virtues. When the hero is allowed to speak, it is only to illustrate the point already made by the narrator. In stark contrast to this diegetic technique, Mark opts for a mimetic narrative mode, making Jesus interact dialogically with others. In Mark, the narrator is almost mute, only occasionally interrupting the narrative to translate an Aramaic phrase (5:41; 7:34; 15:34), or to admonish the reader to pay attention (13:14). Completely absent is the guiding authorial voice uttering words of praise and approval. Praise and approval come indirectly from the characters in the story (e.g., 1:7–8, 27; 2:12; 7:37; 15:39), not from the narrator, and of these characters the most important is the voice from heaven (1:11; 9:7).

The presence of conflict is another indication of difference between Mark and Greco-Roman biography. Because of their public and political station in life, the characters of Greco-Roman biography are often engaged in conflict with others. For Greco-Roman biography, the precise details of these conflicts are less important than the hero's behavior under pressure. It is the special function of biography to show

how this behavior is consistent with the pattern of the hero's whole life. Conflict appears at decisive moments in Greco-Roman biography, but it does not govern the architectonic structure of the genre. The Gospel of Mark, on the other hand, depicts Jesus engaged in deadly conflict from the very beginning of the narrative (1:24). It is conflict, rather than the natural parameters of birth and death, that gives unity to the entire narrative of the gospel.[2] In this conflict, Jesus and the religious leaders are engaged in a battle over who has the authority to represent the will of God. From Mark's perspective, what is important in this conflict is not Jesus' behavior, but the success or failure of his mission.[3] Will God prevail in reestablishing his kingdom through his divinely appointed agent, or not? Thus, the Gospel of Mark is not about the illustration of character, as are the biographies, but about a fundamental conflict between God and those who infringe upon God's sovereignty.

As Burridge and others have demonstrated, there are biographical elements in Mark. Nevertheless, the more important question is whether it was the evangelist's intention to write a biography of Jesus. If our main interest is the evangelist's use of narrative devices, it might be useful to compare Mark with Greco-Roman biography. If, however, we are interested in authorial intention—what the author meant to express by composing this work and submitting it to public scrutiny—a comparison with Greco-Roman biography is less useful. The form-shaping ideology of the Gospel of Mark has very little in common with that of Greco-Roman biography. Mark did not compose his gospel simply because Jesus was a fascinating historical figure whose memory was worthy of preservation as a model for others. Instead, Mark wrote his gospel to show how God was at work in Jesus to achieve a decisive victory for the kingdom of God. Jesus is remarkable for Mark, not because he was a notable human being, but because in spite of, or perhaps as a direct result of, his apparent defeat at the hands of the Jewish leaders, God accomplished a marvelous thing through him.

---

[2] Jack Dean Kingsbury, *Conflict in Mark: Jesus, Authority, Disciples* (Minneapolis: Fortress, 1989), 28.

[3] Collins, "Genre and the Gospels," 244.

Mark and Romance

There are certainly chronotopic similarities between the Gospel of Mark and the Greek novel. Mark's loose temporal structure resembles the random contingency of the Greek novel. In Mark, scenes are often created by chance encounters with Jesus as he walks about the countryside. The breathless pace of Mark's narrative gives the impression of an almost unbroken series of events, yet an indeterminate amount of time often passes between events (e.g., 2:1, 23; 3:1; 4:1). Like the Greek novels, the Gospel of Mark rarely specifies precise temporal relationships, and the biographical time of the Markan story is amorphous. When it serves a specific purpose, Mark includes quotidian elements (6:35–36; 8:2), but these temporal indicators are used inconsistently. Thus, outside of the passion narrative, the reader rarely senses the regular, daily passage of time.[4]

Like Chariton's novel, the Gospel of Mark is set in a specific historical time. This is evident, for example, in the historically plausible roles played by figures such as Herod Antipas and Pilate. This historical setting is merely assumed, however, and nowhere does the evangelist attempt to verify it by giving precise dates or correlating it with external historical events. The most significant temporal feature of the gospel, and the one that most clearly distinguishes it from the Greek novel, is the sacred quality of its story time. From its opening lines, the Gospel of Mark emphasizes that its story is set in a time of eschatological fulfillment (1:15).[5] It is a special time, saturated with the activity of God; it is the time of the bridegroom (2:18–20), the time when the strong man is bound (3:27), and a special time of anointing (14:6–9).[6] In Mark's story, the earthly activity of Jesus does not define the limits of this sacred time. Markan time begins with the appearance of John the

---

[4] On the temporal flow of Mark's narrative, see Charles W. Hedrick, "What is a Gospel: Geography, Time and Narrative Structure," *Perspectives in Religious Studies* 10 (1983): 260–61.

[5] Joel Marcus, "'The Time has been Fulfilled!' (Mark 1:15)," in *Apocalyptic and the New Testament: Essays in Honor of J. Louis Martyn*, ed. J. Marcus and M. L. Soards, JSNTSup, 24 (Sheffield: JSOT, 1989), 49–68.

[6] Kingsbury (*Conflict*, 3) notes that Jesus' announcement in 1:15 indicates "a new epoch in history," a time that is "highly charged with meaning." Similarly, Collins notes that Mark is a story of prophetic fulfillment in a salvation historical mode (*Mark's Gospel*, 35).

Baptist (1:2–8) and tails off indefinitely with the account of the women at the tomb and the promise of a future appearance in Galilee. Thus, the Gospel of Mark evokes a time of fulfillment and imminent expectation (13:4–37; 14:62), which is to say it is an apocalyptic sense of time that extends beyond the temporal boundaries of the story in both directions.[7]

In Markan time, events unfold according to divine purpose; divine necessity surrounds the events that befall Jesus. Mark emphasizes this in several ways. First, the evangelist uses δεῖ to underscore the relentless flow of events in accordance with God's plan (8:31; 9:11; 13:7, 10). Second, in Mark, significant events unfold in a pattern of prediction and fulfillment. As a literary device, the use of prediction to foreshadow narrative events is not unique to Mark. The Greek novels often anticipate future events through dreams and portentous signs.[8] In Mark's Gospel, however, the evangelist uses these predictions to reinforce the sense of divine purpose surrounding Jesus' ministry and especially his death.

Regarding the spatial dimension of the gospel's chronotope, scholars have long recognized the importance of geographical location in Mark.[9] While they have often used the geography of Mark's story to explore the historical forces that produced the gospel, apart from recent literary critical works, the aesthetic quality of Markan space has received little attention. Like the Greek novel, Mark's Gospel is set in a hostile space. All sorts of dangerous forces are at work in the world of Mark's story: demonic forces (1:13, 23; 5:2–9), physical and meteorological forces (1:30–31, 40–42; 2:3–5, 4:37–38; 6:48), as well as human forces (3:6, 21–22; 12:12; 14:1). All these forces oppose Jesus in

---

[7] Collins, *Mark's Gospel*, 55, 63.

[8] Chariton, *Chaereas and Callirhoe* 1.12; 2.1, 9; and Xenophon, *An Ephesian Tale*, 1.13; 2.8; 5.8.

[9] Elizabeth Struthers Malbon surveys this theme in "Galilee and Jerusalem: History and Literature in Marcan Interpretation," *CBQ* 44 (1982): 242–55. Malbon later used the structuralism of Claude Lévi-Strauss to examine Markan space in *Narrative Space and Mythic Meaning in Mark*, New Voices in Biblical Studies (San Francisco: Harper & Row, 1986; reprint, Sheffield: JSOT, 1991). Bas van Iersel also applied structuralism to Markan space in "Locality, Structure and Meaning in Mark," *LB* 53 (1983): 45–54. Narrative critical works that briefly treat Mark's space include Kingsbury, *Conflict*, 1–4; and David Rhoads, Joanna Dewey, and Donald Michie, *Mark as Story: An Introduction to the Narrative of a Gospel*, 2d ed. (Minneapolis: Fortress, 1999), 63–72.

his divinely ordained mission. In fact, the hostility of Markan space is such that there is virtually no quiet space for private reflection. Multitudes of people crowd Mark's story, and while they are favorably disposed to Jesus, Mark characterizes the presence of the multitudes as an impediment to Jesus' activity. These crowds relentlessly follow Jesus and his disciples, allowing them little privacy (1:33; 2:1–2; 3:9, 20). The only time privacy is used to great effect in Mark is in the prayer at Gethsemane (14:32–42).[10] From his temptation in the wilderness to his death on the cross, Jesus is rarely alone in Mark's Gospel.

Jesus moves through this hostile world with authority and power. He casts out demons, heals the sick, calms storms, and bests his opponents in debate. God vests this power in Jesus as God's divinely appointed agent. A voice from heaven twice bestows this role on Jesus by declaring him God's "beloved Son" (1:11; 9:7). Jesus' capacity as God's specially appointed agent is underscored in the Parable of the Wicked Tenants (12:1–11), which indicates in an indirect but unmistakable way Jesus' role as God's special emissary.[11] As the "beloved Son," Jesus has come to reestablish God's sovereignty over the world.[12] It is this sense of mission that governs Jesus' movements in the gospel (1:38; 2:17; 10:32–34), rather than the irresistible whims of fate such as we find in Greco-Roman romance.

For purposes of comparison with the Gospel of Mark, the most important romances are those normally considered pre-sophistic, that is, those written apart from the influence of the Second Sophistic. These romances are important not because of the possibility of direct influence, but because they seem to have developed under similar social conditions.[13] When we place the Gospel of Mark next to the pre-

---

[10] On the similarities between Jesus' prayer and those of the Greek novel, see Mary Ann Tolbert, "The Gospel in Greco-Roman Culture," in *The Book and the Text: The Bible and Literary Theory*, ed. Regina M. Schwartz (Cambridge, Mass.: Basil Blackwell, 1990), 270–72; and Charles Hedrick, "Representing Prayer in Mark and Chariton's *Chaereas and Callirhoe*," *Perspectives in Religious Studies* 22 (1995): 239–57.

[11] Tolbert, *Sowing the Gospel*, 248–250.

[12] Collins, *Mark's Gospel*, 63–66; Kingsbury, *Conflict*, 56–58.

[13] Note, for example, Tomas Hägg's remark concerning the Acts of the Apostles: "The history of the birth of the novel was repeated once again: a new historical situation, with new demands, gave rise to a new literary form, which bor-

sophistic Greek romances, we can certainly point to important similarities. As in the romance, the hero of the Gospel of Mark is a historical figure whose life was nevertheless shrouded in obscurity. The evangelist, however, has used more traditional material in his story of Jesus than is typically the case in Greek romance. Nevertheless, the details of Jesus' life, the itinerary of his ministry, and especially the earliest events of his life, were apparently less well known. The evangelist has gathered the available materials and, much like the romance, arranged them by stringing events together in a loose chronological framework. Consequently, temporal duration is very difficult to measure in Mark, just as it is in the romance. Mark has a few references to the passage of time (1:13; 8:2; 9:2; 14:1), but not nearly enough to reconstruct specific day/night sequences. Instead, events are connected by means of vague temporal phrases, similar to those used by Chariton. This loose temporal organization allows the evangelist to expand and contract time at will, and, as in the romance, apart from the events of the passion narrative, the evangelist could have extended the gospel narrative almost indefinitely.

The Gospel of Mark also resembles the Greek romance in its use of the road as a structural device. In the Gospel of Mark, Jesus is on "the way," and on his journey, he encounters a number of colorful characters. In Mark, the road is a simple device that brings Jesus into contact with people. Because the road is an open and public space, Jesus meets a diverse cast of characters. In particular, the road is a place where Jesus can meet social and religious outcasts. On "the way," Jesus meets a leper (1:40), a man possessed by a legion of demons (5:2), a ritually unclean woman (5:25–34), and a blind beggar (10:46), to name just a few. These encounters are possible because the evangelist keeps Jesus in motion, moving about the land of ancient Palestine. In an interesting twist on a common motif of romance, there are also perilous voyages at sea in Mark, but they present more of a threat for the disciples than for Jesus. Indeed, whereas the characters of romance suffer many misfortunes on their journeys, Jesus rises above the perils of "the way." Even though Jesus also follows a path beset with dangers, at only one point does he appear to be overcome by fear and dread (14:34–36).

---

rowed freely from predecessors and contemporaries" (Hägg, *Novel in Antiquity*, 161).

Moreover, while the characters of romance travel their road led only by fate, Jesus chooses to follow his road out of a sense of divine compulsion.

In addition to the road, two other novelistic elements govern the composition of Mark's narrative. The first is that of conflict. While conflict in Greek romance centers on the hostility of the gods to the heroes of the story, in Mark the central conflict is between Jesus and the Jewish leaders.[14] This conflict, apparent from the third chapter of Mark right up to the tragic scene of Jesus' crucifixion, is what creates the main tension in the gospel's narrative. The second novelistic element is that of recognition and non-recognition. The failure of both the religious leaders and the disciples to recognize Jesus as God's messiah is sharply juxtaposed with the demonic recognition of Jesus' status as God's special envoy. As in Greek romance, the tension between recognition and non-recognition produces irony.[15] The reader of the gospel knows who Jesus is, since the evangelist states in the opening verses of the gospel that Jesus is "the Christ the Son of God."[16] In light of Jesus' special status as God's appointed agent, the opposition of the religious leaders, and the incomprehension of the disciples, is profoundly ironic.

In spite of their many similarities, the Gospel of Mark is not a Greek romance. Romance is essentially bourgeois entertainment. The emotional interiority of romance is quite unlike the public, dialogical chronotope of Mark's Gospel. Furthermore, Mark's apocalyptic time and space is distinct from the romance's preoccupation with the vicissitudes of fate. What the comparison indicates is the popular mode of the gospel narrative. The Gospel of Mark uses narrative techniques that are broadly attested in the popular literature of late Hellenism and the early Empire. As Tolbert correctly pointed out, Mark therefore belongs

---

[14] Kingsbury, *Conflict in Mark*, 63–88.

[15] On irony in ancient romance, see Perry, *Ancient Romances*, 143. On irony in Mark, see Jerry Camery-Hoggatt, *Irony in Mark's Gospel: Text and Subtext*, SNTSMS, ed. G. N. Stanton, 72 (Cambridge: Cambridge University Press, 1992).

[16] Even if we set aside the phrase "Son of God" as a textual variant, and discount Christ as a virtual surname, the same point could be made by pointing to 1:11, where the voice from heaven informs the reader that Jesus is God's beloved son. See Craig A. Evans, "Mark's Incipit and the Priene Calendar Inscription: From Jewish Gospel to Greco-Roman Gospel," *Journal of Greco-Roman Christianity and Judaism* 1 (2000), <http://www.jgrchj.com/page68> (September 4, 2000).

among the popular strata of ancient literature and not among the more sophisticated literature of the first century.

Mark and Menippea

In some respects, the Gospel of Mark is not at all like a Menippean satire. There are no talking animals or fantastic journeys to extraterrestrial locales. Mark does not have the slightest interest in the Greek philosophical tradition, which so interests menippea. Jesus is certainly no picaro, and the gospel lacks the crude vulgarity that often characterizes menippea. These differences notwithstanding, some aspects of the Gospel of Mark seem to invite a comparison to Menippean satire.

One point of contact between Mark and menippea is the importance of threshold events in the gospel. The first of these threshold events is the heavenly voice at Jesus' baptism (1:9–11). A voice rends the heavens asunder and pronounces divine favor on Jesus. This violation of the normal distance between divine and human space initiates Jesus' public ministry and is the only basis upon which Jesus has any claim to the titles of the opening verse in Mark's Gospel. The demonic recognitions constitute another example of threshold events in the gospel (1:24; 3:11; 5:7). The demonic recognitions are as close as Mark comes to the common Menippean theme of talking animals. Like the pig Gryllus, the demons possess a unique perspective on human events. They perceive a spiritual reality to which humans are blind. Like the voice from heaven, they breach the normal gulf that separates the human world from the demonic world. To this list of threshold events, we could also add the resurrection of dead persons and the resurrection of Jesus—the ultimate threshold event in the gospel.

Perhaps the best example of a threshold dialogue in the Gospel of Mark is the transfiguration of Jesus, although in comparison with Lucian the evangelist does very little with it. In the transfiguration, Jesus, like Menippus, talks to figures long since dead. These two figures are Moses and Elijah, the quintessential epic heroes of Israel's past. They appear in Mark's Gospel arrayed in splendor worthy of their dignity and station. Like Moses and Elijah, Jesus is temporarily transfigured, but elsewhere in the gospel, he never quite measures up to their accomplishments. Jesus never descends from Mt. Sinai, as Moses did, radiating the residual Shekinah glory from his encounter with God (Exod 34:29–35). Nor does he confront the king like Elijah and rain fire from heaven on the wicked (1 Kgs 18:17–40). In Mark's Gospel, Jesus is God's humble representative who brings the power of God to bear on everyday human suffering. The miracles Jesus performs are never spectacular, attention grabbing miracles like those of Moses (Exod 7:8–11:10; 14:21–29; 17:8–13) and Elijah (1 Kgs 17:1; 2 Kgs 1:9–15). Like Menippus, Jesus is a common person who lacks position and privilege. That Jesus is, for a fleeting moment, arrayed in epic splendor only increases the irony of his humble demeanor elsewhere in the gospel.

In their brief encounter with Jesus, Moses and Elijah "spoke together with Jesus" (ἦσαν συλλαλοῦντες τῷ 'Ιησοῦ), but unlike Menippean dialogues, where the content of the conversation is the central focus, the content of this conversation is never revealed. In the Gospel of Mark, the point of the transfiguration is not the dialogue with Moses and Elijah per se; it is the effect of the conversation on the three disciples. In the gospel, the emphasis rests on Jesus' dialogue with the disciples following the transfiguration rather than on the implied conversation between Jesus and the two great prophets.

The dialogic aspect of Mark's account of the transfiguration is perhaps the most important point of contact between Mark and menippea. Of the novelistic genres that we have considered so far, dialogue plays the most significant role in Menippean satire. In menippea, it is precisely the dialogic syncrisis and anacrisis of opposing ideas that carries the genre's ideological weight. Bakhtin writes that "the most important characteristic of the menippea" is

> the creation of *extraordinary situations* for the provoking and testing of a philosophical idea, a discourse, a *truth*, embodied in the image of a wise man, the seeker of this truth. . . . it is essential to emphasize once again that the issue is precisely the testing of an *idea*, of a *truth*, and not the testing of a particular human character.[17]

Menippea uses dialogue as an effective method for contrasting opposing ideas and subtly undermining dominant ideologies. Of course in Mark, dialogue centers on matters of religious devotion rather than philosophy, and the plot, unlike that of menippea, is devoid of adventure and the fantastic. Nevertheless, where we encounter dialogue, we en-

---

[17] Bakhtin, *PDP*, 114. Northrop Frye came to similar conclusions independently of Bakhtin (Frye, *Anatomy*, 310).

counter the juxtaposition of ideas, and in Mark, the conflict of ideas is what matters rather than the testing of Jesus' character. The dialogical idea in Mark concerns the nature of the divine will. Jesus and the other characters in Mark's Gospel engage one another in a debate over the nature of God's plan for the Jews. What should Judaism look like? How should Judaism respond to the physically, socially, and economically disadvantaged? When God's eschatological kingdom comes, what will divine deliverance look like? Disputes over ideas such as these are at the heart of Mark's Gospel rather than a demonstration of Jesus' exemplary moral character, as the comparison with Greco-Roman biography might suggest.

This fundamental conflict over the divine will expresses itself in the gospel through dialogic interaction, a narrative mode that, as we noted previously, is uncharacteristic of Greco-Roman biography. Unlike the biographies, the Gospel of Mark does not tell its story by simply summarizing Jesus' activities and quoting his most memorable sayings. Instead, it brings Jesus into dialogic contact with his contemporaries. This novelistic technique not only increases the gospel's popular appeal, but, more importantly, it creates a collision between ideas. Nor are these ideas monolithic. Mark pits Jesus against an array of ideas, ideas represented by the other characters in the gospel. We can consider these characters in three groups: the religious leaders, the disciples, and the minor characters.[18] Each group represents a distinctive idea within the dialogical purview of Mark's Gospel.

First, there are masses of people in the background of the Gospel of Mark who follow Jesus wherever he goes. Yet, the relationship between the crowds and Jesus is difficult to define. They are neither disciples nor opponents; sometimes they follow Jesus enthusiastically (2:2; 3:7–9; passim), but ultimately they reject him (15:13–15). Mark accents the plight of the crowds. The crowds are helpless, "like sheep without a shepherd" (6:34). Oppressed by diseases, demons, and onerous religious obligations, the crowds are desperately in need of deliverance. Out of the crowds, individual representatives of this physical,

---

[18] Rhoads, Dewey, and Michie, *Mark as Story*, 98–136; and Kingsbury, *Conflict in Mark*, 4–27. Kingsbury also distinguishes the Jewish crowd as a character in Mark's story alongside the minor characters. Because the crowd's relation to Jesus is somewhat ambivalent and since they are only vaguely characterized, I will consider them along with the minor characters.

spiritual and religious malaise come forward to seek assistance from Jesus. Of all the characters in the gospel, the minor characters are the ones who most often respond favorably to Jesus. As a group, their favorable response functions as a literary foil to accent the errors of the religious leaders and the imperceptivity of the disciples.[19] Often these characters represent outcast social groups: lepers, widows, gentiles, the demon possessed, and the physically handicapped. To these minor characters, Jesus announces words of deliverance and hope. He forgives their sins, casts out their demons, and heals their diseases. These are things the religious leaders are both unable and unwilling to perform for those in need.

Scenes of physical and spiritual deliverance are rare in menippea. Menippea emphasizes the Cynic message of simple living, wherein deliverance comes by adopting the right attitude to life. What Mark and the menippea have in common at this point is the attention they give to the predicament of common folk. Both view life from the bottom up. The trials and difficulties of everyday life assume center stage, while problems of intellectual abstraction, whether philosophical or theological, are set aside. In general, the Gospel of Mark and menippea agree that intellectual abstractions are of little or no help in addressing the plight of common folk. More often than not, these intellectual systems are only a hindrance and a burden that people must overcome.[20] Jesus, like the heroes of menippea, delivers the common folk from this burden by opposing those who represent the intellectual and religious establishment.

Thus, the idea represented by the crowds is that of simple faith welling up out of overwhelming spiritual and physical need. Unlike the disciples and the religious leaders, the crowds are passive representatives of this idea. The crowds do not present arguments for this idea; they embody the idea. Their response to Jesus is welcoming and enthusiastic, because they are in desperate need of deliverance. This need precludes any abstract theorizing about Jesus' identity, or reservations about his cavalier attitude toward the traditions of the elders. In Jesus,

---

[19] Rhoads, Dewey, and Michie, *Mark as Story*, 133.

[20] Note Northrop Frye's comment on Menippean satire: "Philosophies of life abstract from life, and an abstraction implies the leaving out of inconvenient data. The satirist brings up these inconvenient data, sometimes in the form of alternative and equally plausible theories" (Frye, *Anatomy of Criticism*, 229).

they find someone who brings the deliverance they long for. Ultimately, of course, this favorable response based upon desperate need is too shallow to support a lasting commitment to Jesus. In Jerusalem, the religious leaders easily sway the crowds and persuade them to turn against Jesus. Nevertheless, before the trial of Jesus, the crowds represent a simple, unreflective, wholehearted response to Jesus and his message.

Second, there are the Jewish religious leaders, who represent the traditional, pietistic ideals of the Jewish establishment. The Gospel of Mark challenges the legitimacy of Judaism's reigning religious ideology by opposing those who defend it. Mark consistently portrays those who preserved and maintained the traditions of the Jewish religion as Jesus' most determined enemies.[21] Almost from the beginning of the gospel, the Jewish religious leaders conclude that Jesus must be killed (3:11). This decision reflects their disagreement with Jesus over the best way to demonstrate one's loyalty to God. In this conflict, the Jewish leaders adopt an essentially defensive, or conservative, posture. They defend the traditional interpretations of the institutions and prescriptions of the Jewish faith. Although Mark's Jesus is no religious anarchist—Jesus respects the traditions of Torah and encourages others to do so (1:44; 10:19; 12:29–31)—he will not allow religious traditions and regulations to interfere with the purposes of God's kingdom. In an important scene that sets the tone for the rest of Mark's story (3:1–6), Jesus asks the Pharisees: "Is it lawful on the sabbath to do good or to do harm, to save life or to kill?" Jesus' subsequent actions make it clear that it is always right to do what is good, even when doing so infringes on traditional religious practice. As this scene illustrates, whenever the observance of religious tradition conflicts with the present experience of God's kingdom, Mark's Jesus opts for the latter. In this sense, Jesus' attitude toward Jewish religious traditions is essentially iconoclastic. More often than not, Jesus sees the religious traditions of the Jewish authorities as an impediment to the eschatological realization of God's kingdom.

Like a Menippean hero, Jesus uses penetrating questions and clever responses to subvert the authority of those who represent the religious establishment. Jesus refuses to trump the religious leaders with

---

[21] Kingsbury, *Conflict in Mark*, 14.

displays of divine power or heavenly glory (8:11–12). Instead, he bests them at their own game. Jesus uses the heteroglossic power of words to defeat the religious authorities, the official arbiters of religious words. For example, Jesus raises such "ultimate" issues as what it means to forgive sins (2:9) and what constitutes good and evil (3:4). When the Sadducees try to discredit Jesus' understanding of Scripture, Jesus shows them that they do not even understand Scripture well enough to ask the right question (12:18–27, 35–37). Jesus' speech renders the religious leaders inarticulate and silent: wordless. They are completely incapable of responding to Jesus' dialogic challenges (3:4; 11:33; 12:34).

Like menippea, the Gospel of Mark incorporates a variety of speech genres such as parables (4:3–9, 26–29, 30–32), sayings (2:17b; 4:24b; 10:11b–12), and inserted stories (6:14–29; 14:66–72). The novelistic flavor of the Gospel of Mark derives in large measure from its eclectic use of speech genres. One of the more noticeable aspects of this eclecticism is the frequency with which Mark quotes the Old Testament.[22] Mark maintains a strong connection with Judaism by using the Hebrew Scriptures, but, in ironic fashion, he appropriates these passages in surprising ways. Mark depicts Jesus using Scripture against the Scripture experts by giving its meaning new and surprising twists. Much as menippea often quotes Homer and mimics Homeric themes and tropes to lampoon them, Mark uses Scripture as an authority but not in the standard manner. In citing passages from the Hebrew Scriptures, the evangelist reinterprets them. Mark appropriates the literature of the dominant ideology of his immediate context (first century Judaism) and uses it to support his own position. Nevertheless, unlike menippea, which often treats epic traditions with satirical disrespect, Mark always quotes Scripture reverently. There is no attempt to replace sacred Scripture with a new canon. In the gospel, the battle is over who may rightfully claim the authoritative tradition of Scripture. On the narrative plane, this means that Jesus and the religious leaders are engaged in a battle over the proper interpretation of Jewish Scripture.

---

[22] Joel Marcus and Adela Yarbro Collins explore this phenomenon in a recent collection of essays. See Joel Marcus, "Scripture and Tradition in Mark 7," in *The Scriptures in the Gospels*, ed. C. M. Tuckett, BETL, 131 (Leuven: Leuven University Press, 1997), 177–95; and Adela Yarbro Collins, "The Appropriation of the Psalms of Individual Lament by Mark," ibid., 223–41.

Although in relation to menippea the comic element in Mark is less prevalent, the gospel certainly has a comic dimension. This is most evident in Jesus' dialogic exchanges with the religious leaders.[23] According to Bakhtin, laughter and polyglossia are closely related. By laughter, Bakhtin means nothing more than "the ridiculing of another's language and another's direct discourse."[24] In menippea, when a person appropriates another's language, he or she exposes that language's underlying assumptions by using it in unexpected ways. This exposes the deficiencies of the other's language, its inability to finalize the world of experience. The result is parody or laughter. In Mark, Jesus appropriates the language of the religious leaders and draws their discourse into close contact with the prosaic realities of the present (3:1–6; 7:9–13; 10:17–22). Just as menippea rejects the sophistries of philosophical speculation, Jesus rejects the theological and legal musings of the religious leaders that ignore immediate human need. Jesus never allows himself to be drawn into lengthy conversations about the details of the Jewish legal code. He merely deflects questions of this sort (12:13–17, 18–27). Like the Greek philosophers parodied by menippea, in the Gospel of Mark the religious leaders are so preoccupied with abstract distinctions and legal minutiae that their vast learning is, at best, of no practical use and, at worst, a bane to those who need it most. Not only does their erudition blind them to the presence of the messiah, it also impedes the present reality of God's kingdom. As we noted above, Mark accents the failure of the religious leaders by pointing to the dire circumstances of the Jewish people. In the Gospel of Mark, the very people for whom the religious leaders are responsible wander aimlessly about the countryside like lost sheep (6:34).[25]

---

[23] Dan O. Via has also observed the comic, or serio-comic, dimension of Mark's narrative in his book *Kerygma and Comedy in the New Testament: A Structuralist Approach to Hermeneutic* (Philadelphia: Fortress, 1975). However, under the influence of structuralism, he developed it in a much different way.

[24] Bakhtin, "Prehistory of Novelistic Discourse," 50.

[25] For the purposes of literary analysis, the normally valid historical question of whether Mark has represented the Jewish leaders fairly is moot, since we are only interested in how the religious leaders function as characters within the Markan story world. The Gospel of Mark portrays the religious leaders in this way to set its characterization of Jesus in sharper relief. See for example, Petri Merenlahti and Raimo Hakola, "Reconceiving Narrative Criticism," in *Characterization in the Gospels: Reconceiving Narrative Criticism*, ed. David Rhoads and Kari

Third, there are the disciples, Jesus' constant companions right up to the end of the gospel. The obtuseness of the disciples creates opportunities for Jesus to present the positive side of his message. Menippean satires, as well as Socratic dialogues, often make use of secondary characters for similar reasons.[26] These characters act as friendly foils, lobbing questions to the main character and giving the hero a chance to expand on his theme. In Mark, this technique creates opportunities for Jesus to elaborate on topics left intentionally ambiguous when broached with his opponents.[27] The disciples, however, are more than literary foils. As characters, they bear a mistaken notion of who Jesus is, or should be. They believe that Jesus is a political messiah, come to deliver the Jews from political bondage.[28] The disciples expect Jesus to assume a position of power and glory when he enters Jerusalem. For example, such an expectation lies behind the request of James and John (10:37), as well as the royal overtones of the entry into Jerusalem (11:7–10). The rich irony of the acclamation of Jesus as King of the Jews during the crucifixion scene also turns on this assumption (15:2–32). The disciples therefore find it inconceivable that Jesus should suffer and die a humiliating death (8:32; 9:32). The finest example of this dialogical conflict is Peter's identification of Jesus as the Christ in 8:27–38.

When Peter declares that Jesus is the Christ, he merely confirms what we, as readers, have known since the first verse of the gospel. Je-

---

Syreeni, JSNTSup, vol. 184 (Sheffield: Sheffield Academic, 1999), 42–43, where they comment on Matthew's negative portrayal of the Jewish leaders.

[26] The Greek romance also uses secondary characters as companions. However, in romance their role never involves instruction or correction. The secondary characters in romance function primarily as proxies for the main character when it is important for the main character to remain passive. Occasionally, the disciples also function in this capacity in Mark, as they do when they retrieve the colt (11:1–6) and secure the upper room (14:12–16).

[27] Rhoads, Dewey, and Michie, *Mark as Story*, 124.

[28] The precise nature of messianic expectation in the first century is problematic. There are, however, indications that such a mood was current. For a recent survey of the evidence see Gerbern S. Oegema, *The Anointed and His People: Messianic Expectations from the Maccabees to Bar Kochba*, JSP Supplement Series, ed. Lester L. Grabbe and James H. Charlesworth, 27 (Sheffield: Sheffield Academic Press, 1998), especially chapter 4. For the purposes of the present discussion, the first century historical details are less important than the presupposition of such an expectation in Mark's narrative.

sus is indeed God's own anointed servant (1:11), the messiah foretold by the prophets (1:2–3). It is rather shocking, then, that Jesus immediately rebukes the disciples (ἐπετίμησεν αὐτοῖς) and charges them to keep this information to themselves (8:30). Elsewhere in Mark, Jesus uses ἐπιτιμάω only to rebuke demons and natural elements (1:25; 3:12; 4:36; 9:25). In each case, he uses this word in the context of hostile confrontations. In relation to Peter's apparently proper identification of Jesus as the Christ, the term ἐπιτιμάω seems strangely out of place. Jesus, however, admonishes Peter and the disciples because the term "Christ" has inappropriate overtones. Their notion of Christ is not the same as Jesus', a point the gospel vividly illustrates in the following verses. In the first passion prediction (8:31), Jesus informs the disciples "the Son of Man must undergo great suffering, and be rejected by the elders, the chief priests, and the scribes, and be killed, and after three days rise again." This does not conform to the disciples' notion of what it means to be the Christ, and Peter rebukes (ἐπιτιμᾶν) Jesus for his scandalous remark (8:32). This in turn prompts Jesus to rebuke (ἐπετίμησεν) Peter in front of the gathered disciples (8:33). In the Gospel of Mark, the term Christ can only be used conditionally, or with what Bakhtin calls "intonational quotation marks."[29] For Mark's Jesus, the term Christ is a bit too grandiose, its triumphalistic overtones too pronounced. Thus, there is a reticence within Mark's Gospel to use the term Christ without qualification. True, Jesus is the "Christ"— God's anointed—but in a very different sense than the disciples expected.[30]

The hesitancy of the Gospel of Mark to use glorified titles for Jesus is roughly parallel to menippea's opposition to the dominant philosophical agendas of its day. Menippea satirizes philosophical schools because they propound dogmatic solutions to life's prosaic problems. Menippea is too familiar with the everyday complexity of life to settle for artificially simplistic solutions. Thus, as Northrop Frye has observed, for menippea "philosophical pedantry becomes, as every target of satire eventually does, a form of romanticism or the imposing of over-simplified ideals on experience."[31] Although in the Gospel of Mark the issues are religio-political rather than philosophical, the disci-

---

[29] Bakhtin, "Prehistory of Novelistic Discourse," 76.

[30] Kingsbury, *Conflict in Mark*, 43–44; idem, *The Christology of Mark's Gospel* (Philadelphia: Fortress, 1983), 136–37.

[31] Frye, *Anatomy*, 231.

ples are nevertheless badly out of touch with the realities of Jesus' ministry. They can think only of abstract notions of glorification and triumphant splendor (9:5, 34; 10:37). Their own hopes and ambitions obscure their vision of Jesus' ministry, and they cannot accept the harsh reality that awaits Jesus in Jerusalem.

Jesus steadfastly opposes the disciples' idea of glorification and political triumph. He repeatedly reminds the disciples that the path of obedience lies through sacrifice and service to others (8:31, 34–38; 9:31–32, 35–37; 10:33–34, 43–45). Being first in the kingdom of God means being last on earth, and future exaltation depends on present humiliation. This inverted sense of values resonates strongly with menippea. For example, in the *Life of Aesop,* it is not the great philosopher Xanthos who is wise, but his deformed slave Aesop. Likewise, in Lucian, the comical and unsophisticated Menippus is the only one who knows how to face life's ultimate problems with dignity and grace. Like menippea, the Gospel of Mark delights in the knowledge that things are not always as they seem. In Mark, as in menippea, outward displays of piety are a poor indication of a person's religious devotion. More often than not, outward appearances only mask a secret hypocrisy (12:38–40). In the ideological world of the Gospel of Mark, a poor woman who tithes her last penny is more generous than the prosperous folk who make larger donations (12:41–44). Similarly, those blessed with great wealth do not necessarily enter heaven ahead of those who renounce their earthly possessions for the sake of the gospel (10:23–30).

This point is explicit in Jesus' admonition that the greatest person in the kingdom "must be last of all and servant of all" (9:35; also 10:31, 43–44). Of course, Jesus is himself the crowning example of this inversion of values. The man whom God ordained to be the messiah is a lowly Galilean of unknown extraction with little regard for Jewish traditions. Jesus is neither a political nor a religious leader. Instead, he leads a band of common folk around the countryside until the Jewish religious leaders deliver him to the Romans for crucifixion on trumped up charges. For Mark, the ultimate irony is that the scandalous death of this otherwise insignificant person is not a defeat, but a triumphant victory for God's kingdom.

By comparing Mark to Menippean satire, I do not intend to suggest a direct connection between the two. Their similarities are, it seems to me, striking and suggestive, but there can be no question of direct dependence. Mark never quotes or alludes to a Menippean source, nor is he preoccupied with the same philosophical questions. If there is an ideological similarity, it stems from the similar cultural conditions surrounding their composition. Menippean satire and the Gospel of Mark were both written under the influence of polyglossia, the intermingling of languages and ideological perspectives that characterized the late Hellenistic and early Roman imperial period. Polyglossia provided a fertile environment for the Gospel of Mark to challenge the dominant, "epic" traditions of Judaism. Under the influence of polyglossia, the Markan author adopted a natural literary strategy, to subvert the authoritative structures of Judaism by means of a serio-comic, dialogical composition. The similarity between the Gospel of Mark and menippea lies in their common function as popular, iconoclastic forms of literature. Under the influence of a common polyglossia, both are intent on loosening the hegemony of their culture's reigning ideological powers. The polyglossic instability of Hellenism led the Greek authors of menippea to reconsider their attachment to the epic past with its distinguished philosophical heritage. For its part, the Gospel of Mark questions the dominant understanding of the traditions of Jewish identity and, with them, the true nature of devotion to God.

The cultural instability of the first and second centuries also triggered reactions that were more interested in conserving traditional values. In Greece, nostalgia for the past expressed itself in the Second Sophistic. In Jewish circles, militant nationalism fed by a longing for the glory days of the Davidic kingdom led to a series of revolts and ultimately to open warfare with Rome. The ideological instability within Judaism that underlies this period of unrest is at least partially responsible for the appearance of the Gospel of Mark. Under the influence of polyglossia, Mark and menippea responded to the nationalistic nostalgia of their contemporaries in similar ways. They used new language forms and ideological perspectives to subvert those hopes. In their own way, both argue that it is necessary to reassess the national epic traditions in light of present circumstances. Thus, they both drag their respective epic traditions into contact with the prosaic realities of the present. In contrast to menippea, the issues for Mark are religious rather than political or philosophical, although it would be unwise to draw such distinctions too sharply. Mark casts the Christian experience of

Jesus such that it also forces a reassessment of Jewish hopes for political independence from Rome (12:17). The Gospel of Mark maintains that it is not God's intention to restore the throne of David as the seat of political power. By juxtaposing the discourse of the Jewish *status quo* with the prophetic discourse of Jesus, the Markan author seeks to subvert the former. The net result is that devotion to God is no longer a matter of temple ritual and religious observance, but a matter of individual commitment and sacrifice (8:34–35; 9:35; 10:43–44). Consequently, it was not only Jewish political hopes that were in need of reassessment but religious convictions as well.

Summary

Judaism was not immune to the ideological instability of the early empire. Self-rule eluded the Jews and the lure of Hellenistic culture placed additional pressure on their religious and cultural purity. In the context of this instability, and perhaps as a reflection of it, Christianity emerged from within Judaism. At about the time Mark was written, Christians were starting to search for their own identity apart from Judaism. Quite naturally, there was a variety of ways to articulate this new identity. If the author of Mark had wished to preserve the continuity between Christianity and Judaism, he might naturally have chosen biography as a vehicle for his message. Biography would have allowed him to present Jesus as a model of the ancient virtues: a leader blessed by God, a victorious leader and king, whose opponents would no doubt have been the foreign oppressors. If, however, Mark wished to distance himself from the practices of Judaism, he needed a genre capable of destabilizing the authority of the dominant religious paradigm.

Biography would have been an infelicitous vehicle for such a message. It lacked the sharp, satirical edge that Mark required for his critique of Judaism. The romance, it would seem, lacked the requisite seriousness. Menippea would have better suited his ideological purposes. As a genre, it provided the necessary tools for a satirical broadside against the Jewish religious leaders. By casting the Pharisees in a negative light and having Jesus best them at their own game, Mark could subvert their authority and simultaneously lay claim to a reinterpreted Judaism. The presentation of Jesus in the Gospel of Mark shows that God's salvation does not come through traditional means, but through radical and surprising means. A triumphalistic presentation more in line with the practices of Greco-Roman biography would have undermined Mark's claim that salvation comes through humble and sacrificial obedience rather than through legal observance and piety.

Therefore, biography is the wrong genre for Mark, in no small measure because of its conservative and traditional ideological orientation. Greco-Roman biography was ill-suited to the kind of hostile, dialogic interaction characteristic of Jesus' relationship with the religious leaders in Mark. The subject of a Greco-Roman biography often faces opposition, but he succeeds by venerating and embodying the traditions and values of the past. When the hero of biography abandons traditional values, his decline is imminent. The hero of Greco-Roman biography is never a counter-cultural figure. This contrasts markedly with Jesus, whom the Gospel of Mark depicts as a counter-cultural, and in some respects iconoclastic, figure in the context of first century Judaism. Mark's Jesus more closely resembles a Menippean hero. He is a religious interloper, a common man who boldly challenges the religious hegemony of the Jewish leaders. In doing so, he makes them look foolish and desperate. Nevertheless, they are too blinded by their own pretensions to see that force cannot defeat Jesus. God has chosen Jesus and his eventual victory is therefore certain. The irony is, of course, that from God's perspective Jesus is neither counter-cultural nor a religious interloper, but the authoritative representative of God's kingdom. Indeed, the religious leaders are the ones guilty of interloping upon God's kingdom (12:1–12).

The chronotope of Mark's Gospel is therefore quite different from both the adventure chronotope of Greek romance and the ethical paraenetic chronotope of Greco-Roman biography. Although Mark and menippea are similar, their similarities are due more to a broadly shared literary strategy than to direct or even indirect dependence. In particular, the apocalyptic and theological chronotope of the gospel make it very different from menippea. In the past, an emphasis on the gospel's kerygmatic qualities was often used to defend the uniqueness of the gospel genre. Before we draw such a conclusion, however, we should look for chronotopically similar works within Jewish narrative literature.

Jewish Novelistic Literature

Scholars who have examined Mark's genre and its relation to ancient literature have only occasionally suggested Jewish narratives as worthy of comparison.[32] The main objection has been that Jewish literature produced few biographical works.[33] The claim is typically that the Gospel of Mark is a self-contained narrative that focuses on the career of a single individual. Since Jewish literature lacks works of this kind, the influences must lie elsewhere. The resulting concentration on Greco-Roman parallels is somewhat puzzling given Mark's obvious and frequent use of the Septuagint. Nevertheless, if we look beyond narrowly biographical works, there are Jewish narratives of moderate length chronotopically similar to Mark's Gospel. These "Jewish novels," as Lawrence Wills calls them, were all produced, or received their final form, in the late Hellenistic period.[34] In this category, Wills includes Greek Daniel, Tobit, Greek Esther, Judith, *Joseph and Aseneth*, and a few other Jewish "historical novels." To one degree or another, each story represents a self-contained narrative of a Jewish hero in difficult circumstances. As Wills suggests, these stories may provide a more fruitful comparison with the gospels than do the pre-Sophistic Greek novels.[35] If nothing else, Mark is a gifted story-teller, and it is perhaps to the tradition of Jewish storytelling that we should turn if we wish to understand the generic heritage of Mark's Gospel.

---

[32] Collins (*Mark's Gospel*, 46–62) suggests a comparison with historical and apocalyptic narratives. See also George W. E. Nickelsburg, "The Genre and Function of the Markan Passion Narrative," *HTR* 73 (1980): 155; Robbins, "Mark as Genre," 390; Klaus Baltzer, *Die Biographie der Propheten* (Neukirchen-Vluyn: Neukirchener, 1975), 187–189.

[33] Tolbert, *Sowing the Gospel*, 55–56; Burridge, *What are the Gospels?* 25, 53–54; Aune, "The Gospels: Biography or Theology?," 19–20; and Bryan, *Preface to Mark*, 22–25.

[34] Wills, *Jewish Novel*, 10. For a compact survey of the narrative literature of the Hellenistic period, see G. W. E. Nickelsburg, "Stories of Biblical and Early Post-Biblical Times," in *Jewish Writings of the Second Temple Period: Apocrypha, Pseudepigrapha, Qumran Sectarian Writings, Philo, Josephus*, CRINT 2.2 (Assen: Van Gorcum and Philadelphia: Fortress, 1984), 33–87.

[35] Wills, *Jewish Novel*, 29, n. 53.

Jewish Novelistic Literature in the Hellenistic Period

Just as Cynicism represented a well-established déclassé philosophical tradition within Greek culture, official Israelite religion also had a counter tradition in the Hebrew prophets. Since the time of the Davidic monarchy, the Hebrew prophets represented the voice of divine opposition to pretentious religious institutions and syncretistic practices. The Gospel of Mark seems to have drawn deeply from this tradition; however, the prophetic tradition never produced a narrative genre quite like that of Mark. There are narrative passages in the prophetic literature that preserve historical details and recount specific events in the life of the prophet. Nevertheless, these narrative passages never constitute an independent literary form, and dialogue is almost incidental to the main thrust of prophetic narrative.[36] Prophetic texts make their point not by juxtaposing dialogical positions, but by proclaiming the utterly monological words of God.

In the Hellenistic period, Jewish literature developed in a new novelistic direction, drawing upon the experiences of the exile to interpret the challenges of foreign rule under the Ptolemies and Seleucids. Jewish writers began to compose narratives about the heroic acts of rather ordinary, although remarkably pious, individuals. Jewish fiction pits these ordinary heroes against oppressive foreign rulers. Thus, Jewish narrative fiction displays a decidedly subversive and "nationalistic" flavor.[37] By illustrating the superiority of Jewish practices and vindicating divine concern in the eyes of those who felt abandoned, the authors of Jewish fiction engaged in a defensive action designed to reinforce Jewish faith in the face of unpromising external circumstances. Thus, Daniel and Esther, for example, stress the possibility of Jewish faithfulness, and even prosperity, within the confines of foreign rule.[38]

In addressing the needs of a community under duress, the authors of Jewish narrative fiction created engaging and entertaining stories designed to capture the attention of their Jewish audience. Their narrative techniques no doubt reflect widespread practices of oriental story tell-

---

[36] Thomas Jemielity, *Satire and the Hebrew Prophets*, Literary Currents in Biblical Interpretation, ed. Danna Nolan Fewell and David M. Gunn (Louisville, Ky.: Westminster/John Knox, 1992), 63.

[37] Braun, *History & Romance*, 26.

[38] W. Lee Humphreys, "A Life-Style for Diaspora: A Study of the Tales of Esther and Daniel," *JBL* 92 (1973): 211–223.

ing, although the precise nature of this connection lies beyond the boundaries of this study. Of greater relevance is the fact that Jewish authors responded to these challenging circumstances by producing self-contained tales of common heroes engaged in conflicts wherein they represent the interests of God against hostile human forces. These conflicts are explicitly dialogical, involving a hero who matches wits with a foreign king or courtier. In a manner designed to delight Jewish audiences, the hero manifests in his or her behavior the superiority of traditional Jewish practices and invariably triumphs over the king, making him look foolish and weak.[39] In this fashion, Jewish authors subtly subverted the pretensions of their foreign masters by celebrating the superiority of their own traditions.

In tracing the development of the Jewish novel, Wills finds that the earliest books—Daniel, Esther, and Tobit—are composite works that have undergone a long process of transmission. In each case, an author has gathered disparate traditions related to a heroic figure and woven them into a unified narrative. Although these Jewish novels presumably treat historical figures, there is no discernible attempt to produce strictly biographical accounts. The stories begin with a threat to God's people, and they conclude with the elimination of that threat. Similarly, although the narrative framework is realistic and alludes to historical events, historical accuracy is not a major concern. The Jewish novels display a careless, almost playful attitude toward historical accuracy.[40] The events that comprise these narratives all relate directly to the successful resolution of a particular moment of crisis. The goal of the narrative is to recount, in an engaging way, the story of God's provision of deliverance and the subjugation of God's enemies. Therefore, we might loosely describe the earliest Jewish novels as heroic stories, based on historical persons, set in realistic but fictive worlds.

In the course of the genre's development, the early Jewish novels gave way to later works with an even more attenuated connection with historical events and persons. Both Judith and *Joseph and Aseneth* strive for a sense of historical verisimilitude, but they are nevertheless clearly imaginative works. *Joseph and Aseneth* is a legendary expan-

---

[39] Ze'ev Weisman, *Political Satire in the Bible*, SBLSS, ed. Vincent L. Wimbush, no. 32 (Atlanta: Scholars, 1998), 161.

[40] On the cavalier treatment of historical 'facts' in the novels, see Wills, *Jewish Novel*, 217–24.

sion of a Joseph tradition (Gen 41:45–50; 46:20), and Judith has no direct connection to known historical events. The heightened role of authorial creativity in both books is apparent in their more refined literary style; both are carefully constructed, artistic narratives.[41] The relative absence of the theme of religious persecution and the corresponding emphasis on romantic love and introspection suggest that with *Joseph and Aseneth* the Jewish novel began to fall under the influence of the Greek novel.[42] Since Judith is unaffected by this influence, it may be the best representative of the strictly Jewish form of the novel.

The Jewish novel is invariably set in a time of crisis. The crisis arises when hostile forces make threats of physical violence against God's people and challenge their allegiance to God's kingdom. The antagonist in this drama is the foreign king, or one of his representatives, who, unwittingly or intentionally, usurps God's sovereignty over his people. This creates a crisis of decision for God's people; will they capitulate and ally themselves with the usurper, or will they place themselves in jeopardy and remain loyal to God? Their response to this moment of crisis is the central concern of the narrative. The crisis is resolved through a pious human who acts as God's agent. This agent, against overwhelming odds and in spite of her apparent weakness, secures victory for God's people and thereby protects the integrity of God's kingdom.[43]

As one of the earliest Jewish novels, the narrative structure of the first six chapters of Daniel is only imperfectly realized. Instead of a co-

---

[41] For a clear and persuasive demonstration of Judith's literary accomplishment, see Toni Craven, *Artistry and Faith in the Book of Judith*, SBLDS 70 (Chico, Calif.: Scholars, 1983); and the abbreviated version bearing the same title in *Semeia* 8 (1977): 75–101. Luis Alonso-Schökel also explored literary aspects of Judith in *Narrative Structures in the Book of Judith*, Center for Hermeneutical Studies, Protocol Series of the Colloquies, 11 (Berkeley: The Center for Hermeneutical Studies in Hellenistic and Modern Culture, 1974).

[42] In addition to Wills (*Jewish Novel*, 170–84), see Richard I. Pervo, "*Joseph and Aseneth* and the Greek Novel," *SBLSP* 10, ed. George MacRae (Missoula: Scholars, 1976), 171–81; and Howard C. Kee, "The Socio-Religious Setting and Aims of '*Joseph and Aseneth*,'" in ibid., 183–92; as well as idem, "The Socio-Cultural Setting of *Joseph and Aseneth*," *NTS* 29 (1983): 394–413.

[43] As Ze'ev Weisman notes, both Esther and Judith "effect a 'miracle' of national salvation," by exploiting their "physical beauty, cunning and . . . quick tongue" (*Political Satire*, 150).

herent plot line, the book of Daniel contains a number of loosely connected vignettes centering on the person of Daniel and in one case on his companions. Nevertheless, in the narrative portions of the book, Daniel and his companions defend the sovereignty of God by repeatedly resisting the encroachments of the foreign king. As exiles in a foreign land, Daniel and his companions are powerless against the machinations of their enemies. Their only recourse is steadfast confidence in their God, which they express through their pietistic devotion to the Jewish law.

The story of Susanna develops this theme in a slightly different way. Daniel's wise intervention in a case of perverted justice vindicates Susanna's piety and virtue. Although the threat to Susanna's virtue comes from her own countrymen and not from the foreign king, the message is similar to the other stories in the book of Daniel: God will save those who remain steadfast and pious in the face of oppression. Unlike the other stories in Daniel, salvation comes to Susanna not through divine intervention, but through the agency of a pious, but otherwise powerless, individual. Daniel, who is only a young man, boldly defends Susanna's honor in spite of his youth (Sus 45) and thereby thwarts the evil intentions of the two elders. As in the narrative sections of the book of Daniel, God's salvation does not come through the normal channels of justice, but through a marginal hero who is nevertheless devoted to God.

One of the more remarkable features of the Daniel narratives is the veneration of God by the foreign king. Although such devotion is historically improbable, it underscores the ironic and subversive intention of the book of Daniel. The book of Daniel characterizes the foreign king as the unwitting puppet of his advisors, who conspire against Daniel and his companions. Furthermore, the foreign king is overtly characterized at several points, not merely as incompetent, but as incapacitated by debilitating madness. The burden of these passages is the vindication of the sovereignty of God in the face of the false pretensions of the foreign court. This is apparent in the refrain that the king must learn that "the Most High rules the kingdom of men, and gives it to whom he wills" (Dan 4:25, 32; 5:21).

The first characteristic of the chronotope of Daniel is, therefore, conflict. Daniel, as well as Susanna and the three young men, all find their lives threatened because of their loyalty to God. These conflicts arise because the characters find themselves in an alien space. As exiles in a foreign land, exotic foods and harsh legislation challenge their devotion to the God of Israel. Even though the story of Susanna appears to be an exception, Susanna is nevertheless an alien in the patriarchal space of her Jewish judges, and, like her male counterparts, her choice is between death and devotion to God. Thus, in general, the Jewish novels are concerned with a conflict between God and human authority. The protagonists of the Jewish novel find themselves in the midst of this conflict and must decide where to place their loyalty.

Should they choose to remain loyal to God, these pious heroes must stand firm against overwhelming odds. In every case, they are outmaneuvered and powerless against the forces arrayed against them. Their only hope is divine deliverance. The second characteristic of the chronotope of Daniel is, therefore, the expectation of imminent divine salvation. For Daniel and his companions, salvation is not an abstract hope projected into the future, but the expectation of immediate deliverance from hostile forces in the present. Divine salvation serves not only to save the lives of Daniel and his companions, but also to vindicate God's sovereignty over all creation. In the book of Daniel, God's sovereignty is made manifest in the miraculous deliverance of the righteous who confidently call upon the name of God.

The threat against the Jews is more pronounced and widespread in Esther than in Daniel. The critical moment in the plot occurs when Mordecai, Esther's cousin and adoptive father, refuses to bow in homage before the king's viceroy Haman (Esth 3:2), a situation already familiar to readers of Daniel (Dan 3:8–12). Like Daniel, the Greek additions to the book of Esther make it clear that Mordecai's refusal to acknowledge Haman's position relates directly to his devotion to God (Esth 13:14). Mordecai's piety piques Haman's wrath and inadvertently jeopardizes not only his own life, but also the life of the entire Jewish nation.

Like Daniel, Esther is a pious Jew who holds a prominent position in the court of the foreign king. Esther's position as queen in the king's harem does not, however, give her free access to the king such that she might plead the cause of her kinsman before the king's throne. We know from the opening chapter that Ahasuerus is contemptuous of strong-willed women. Queen Vashti loses her position in the king's harem simply for refusing to pander to the desires of a room full of drunken men. Esther's insolence in entering the king's throne room is a much more serious matter (Esth 4:11). Only by risking her own life can Esther approach the king on behalf of the Jews. She prepares for her task by requesting the prayers of others and through her private acts of humility and supplication. For three days, Esther prays for the deliverance of God's people. In her prayers, she declares her piety and devotion to God, confessing that she despises her position as the king's concubine, as well as the bounty and splendor of his court. Having appealed to God for the salvation of her people, Esther then dresses in her finest apparel and sets out to outwit the evil Haman.

Of course, Esther's plan succeeds. Her beauty captivates Ahasuerus and he spares her life in spite of her impertinence in approaching his throne. In the scenes that follow, the narrative is rich with irony. At the king's direction, Haman must parade his enemy Mordecai through the city proclaiming him the beneficiary of the king's favor. For the reader, this is a clear indication that God favors Mordecai, which bodes ill for Haman. Haman, however, is blind to his impending doom, even though his family and friends warn him that Mordecai is destined to prevail. Haman has no chance to repent of his evil intentions toward Mordecai. While he bemoans the honor the king has bestowed upon Mordecai, he is summoned to dine for the second time with Esther and the king. Blinded by his own vanity, Haman revels in Esther's invitation. Since only Mordecai knows Esther's Jewish heritage, when Esther reveals her ethnic identity to the king, Haman suddenly discovers that he has been unmade. Then, in a comical *coup de grâce*, the king misinterprets Haman's groveling before Esther as a brazen assault on the queen's virtue and has Haman dispatched on the gallows once intended for Mordecai.

Like Daniel, crisis and the expectation of divine deliverance are the most prominent features of the chronotope of Esther. The most notable difference is that in Esther, God's deliverance comes not through direct divine intervention but indirectly through the actions of a human agent. A less likely champion would be difficult to imagine. Nevertheless, in spite of her powerlessness, God uses Esther's wit and courage to secure salvation for the Jewish people. In the process, the court of the foreign king is ridiculed and Jewish piety is celebrated. Thus, as in Daniel, an ironic and subversive space characterizes the chronotope of Esther.

In Judith, the characteristic crisis of the Jewish novel takes the superficial shape of a military threat. On a deeper level, however, the central conflict is between Nebuchadnezzar and God. In Judith's story-world, the conflict between Nebuchadnezzar and God is not resolved directly through open confrontation, but indirectly through their representative agents. Nebuchadnezzar commissions Holofernes to execute his judgment against the people of the western provinces and provides him with ample resources to carry out this commission. God's agent is Judith (Jdt 13:14), whom God sends to oppose Holofernes. Judith is also well armed, not with weapons of war, but with piety and beauty (Jdt 8:7). In this apparently lopsided battle, God is victorious. The God of the Jews defeats the vast army of Nebuchadnezzar with only a single woman prepared to defend his honor. The irony of this unexpected victory is lost on neither the Jews (Jdt 13:15; 16:6–10) nor the "Assyrians" (Jdt 14:18).

The conflict between God and Nebuchadnezzar, acted out by their respective agents, draws attention to the special quality of space in Judith. In this world, as in the other Jewish novels, there is no sharp distinction between the heavenly realm and the earthly realm. Because these realms overlap, it is inevitable that conflict will erupt between their respective sovereigns. In this hostile atmosphere, Judith risks her life and pious reputation in a dangerous game of deception. Judith's radiant appearance and the audacity of her plan lull the "Assyrians" into a false sense of security. Holofernes finds Judith's beauty especially beguiling, and he is therefore unable to sense the mendacity of her words. Consequently, Judith emerges victorious, unscathed from her confrontation with Holofernes, her virtuous reputation intact. In this conflict, the use of irony abounds, not only in Judith's words, but also in the entire arrangement of the events of the story. In the ironic space of Judith's story-world, appearances are deceiving. Words do not always mean what they seem to mean, and vulnerability is frequently the position of greatest strength.

Like Esther, the book of Judith opens with what appears to be a conventional historical reference. Nevertheless, when we learn that Nebuchadnezzar is "King of the Assyrians" seated on his throne in Nineveh, in a story characterized as post-exilic (Jdt 4:3), this impression proves mistaken. These anachronisms suggest that the time of Judith's narrative is therefore not historical, but intentionally pseudo-historical.

Within this fictive story-world, the author carefully accounts for the entire extent of the story-time of the narrative by indicating either iterative-durative action (Jdt 2:28; 4:1), or day-and-night phases. The latter are particularly noticeable in passages where the author retards time to draw attention to specific actions; for example, the siege of Bethulia (Jdt 7:1, 6) and Judith's infiltration of Holofernes' camp (Jdt 12:7, 10; 13:1; 14:11). Thus, in spite of its overt anachronisms, the overall effect is one of historical verisimilitude.

The chronotope of the Jewish novel reflects a world open to divine intervention. Nevertheless, direct divine intervention is rare. God more often acts by sending a faithful and pious emissary. In the Jewish novel, divine deliverance is characteristically accomplished by means of weakness, or passive obedience. Women representatives, like Esther and Judith, achieve victory on God's behalf in spite of their inferior position as women in a patriarchal culture.[44] Men like Daniel are passive in the face of opposition. These pious heroes risk their lives in obedience to God's call. Their complete dependence upon God only serves to add greater emphasis to God's unassailable sovereignty and power.

A time of crisis and a hostile and ironic space characterize the chronotope of the Jewish novel. Within this chronotope, human and divine interests overlap, yet, for the most part, God refrains from acting directly in human affairs. Instead, God brings about the salvation of the Jewish people, not through overwhelming divine force, but through the faithfulness and vulnerability of a single individual. The expectation of imminent divine intervention that these heroes embody, in turn, creates a story-world filled with surprising reversals and topsy-turvy values. The sovereignty of God undermines all human authority and manifests itself in unexpected ways for those who trust in God's deliverance. In this sense, the Jewish novels possess an awareness of the immediacy of divine sovereignty similar to that of apocalyptic literature. God can and will break into human time and space to assert the divine will and save those loyal to God's kingdom. However, unlike more overtly apocalyptic works, the time and space of the Jewish novel is realistic, and thus we might characterize the chronotope of the Jewish novel as realistic-

---

[44] That God defeats Holofernes by the hand of a woman is, for example, an irony that Judith's author exploits to great effect (Jdt 13:15; 14:18; 16:6–7).

apocalyptic: the anticipation of divine deliverance and the actualization of divine sovereignty within a realistic time and space.

The Genre of Mark and the Jewish Novel

Following Bakhtin, I have argued that genre is primarily about how an author shapes narrative time and space in conversation with preceding works of literature. By configuring time and space in a particular way, the author creates a space specifically to accommodate the meaningful activity of the hero. The axiological possibilities of distinct chronotopes are not interchangeable. A particular chronotope creates a field of activity for the hero that is different from the possibilities that might exist in another chronotope. Therefore, the elucidation of a work's genre is primarily a matter of charting its literary history in relation to other works chronotopically configured in similar ways.

I propose that the chronotope of the Gospel of Mark most closely resembles that of the Jewish novels. This is not to deny other influences on the composition of the gospel. It does mean, however, that the Gospel of Mark shares its most important literary relationship with the Jewish novels rather than some other type of Greco-Roman literature. The following comparison of Mark with the Jewish novels intends to elucidate the similarities that exist within this literary continuum and the way in which the second evangelist has applied this chronotope to his own circumstances.

Like the Jewish novels, an expectation of divine deliverance permeates Markan time and space. In both Mark and the Jewish novel, faithful human agency is the means by which divine deliverance from forces opposed to God's rule is achieved. Readers of Mark's Gospel familiar with the Jewish literature of the Hellenistic period would have recognized this pattern of divine deliverance achieved through human agency. The Old Testament contains many stories of divine deliverance accomplished by loyal human agents, and, in light of Mark's frequent allusions the Old Testament, it is all but certain that Mark is familiar with this venerable tradition. Nevertheless, Mark presents a more compact and self-contained account of divine deliverance in which God plays a less active part. Unlike the stories embedded in the larger "historical" works of the Old Testament, God remains in the background in Mark, speaking only twice, and even then only briefly. In this respect, Mark also closely resembles the Jewish novels.

The Gospel of Mark also shares the Jewish "novelistic" perspective on the world. Just as the Jewish novels were the product of the cultural instability of early Hellenism, Mark was also produced during a period of cultural upheaval. In words that could also apply to the Jewish novel, Günther Bornkamm observed that in the first century Judaism was caught between the past and the future, between what they once were and what God would make of them in the future.[45] The Gospel of Mark echoes this sense of time. Mark draws upon the ancient prophecies that predicted the coming of God's messiah who would restore the kingdom of God (1:2–3). For Mark, Jesus is that messiah, the man who inaugurated the restoration of God's kingdom. The hopes of the disciples, who expected Jesus to restore the throne of David, were also deeply rooted in Judaism's epic past. For them, salvation meant a return to the glory of the Davidic kingdom. Although Jesus brings the kingdom near through his proclamation of the gospel (4:11) and his mediation of divine power (1:27; 2:10; 5:30), the consummation of God's kingdom nevertheless lies in a more distant future (13:32–37; 14:62). Jesus announces the future return of the son of man, but the apocalyptic message that accompanies this return is one of judgment and not restoration (13:24–27).

Both Mark and the Jewish novel respond to this interim sense of time by drawing it into contact with present concerns.[46] The Jewish novel does not bemoan the collapse of the Davidic monarchy, nor does it project its longings for the restoration of the monarchy into the future. Instead, it addressed the immediate needs of a people under duress. Mark, likewise, focuses on the needs of the immediate present. Everywhere Jesus goes in the gospel, he sees people in need, people in need of compassion (6:34; 8:2) and deliverance (1:25, 32–33, 39; 3:9–10; 5:8). The restoration of the Jewish state in some far off time was too remote and abstract to address their needs. Jesus brought the kingdom of God near, in part by meeting the needs of these desperate people. Therefore, the chronotope of Mark's Gospel lies between Israel's

---

[45] Günther Bornkamm, *Jesus of Nazareth*, trans. Irene and Fraser McLuskey with James M. Robinson (New York: Harper & Brothers, 1960), 55.

[46] Note Bornkamm's observation: "The immediate present is the hallmark of all the words of Jesus, of his appearance and his actions, in a world which as we said, had lost the present, because it lived between the past and the future" (*Jesus of Nazareth*, 58).

epic past and its eschatological future. Mark's narrative is set squarely in the present moment between these two distant points. It is a special time of prophetic fulfillment, a time for the accomplishment of divine purposes.[47]

Unlike the Greek novel, where divine actions are arbitrary and mercurial, in both Mark and the Jewish novels, God has a benevolent plan for those who serve him. Nevertheless, God carries out this divine plan on the terrestrial plane through human characters acting as divine agents. God's activity in the Markan narrative is more overt than in Judith or Esther. Nevertheless, in all three, divine intervention is at the center of the action. God alone saves, and God's salvific plan is not subject to human manipulation or interference. Just as the elders of Bethulia learn that their attempts to place conditions on God's will are futile (Jdt 8:15–17), so also in Mark we learn that it is not Jesus' will but God's that is determinative of future events (Mark 14:35–36, cf. 8:33). In both Mark and the Jewish novel, God's will is comprehensive and sovereign.

The world of Mark's Gospel is filled with the presence of God. Nevertheless, there are few ostentatious displays of unmediated divine power. Instead, the power of God is displayed through the human agency of Jesus, God's own beloved son. When Jesus displays the power granted to him by God, it is to deliver people from oppression and suffering. He never uses divine power to compel obedience to God's kingdom. As God's agent, Jesus comes to serve rather than be served (10:45), and it is precisely through this service that God will achieve victory. In Mark's upside-down world, Jesus secures victory for the kingdom of God through faithful obedience to God (14:36). Jesus' obedience to God never wanes, and it is through his sacrifice that the kingdom of God triumphs over those who would oppose it.

In Mark's story, the sovereignty of God permeates the entire narrative. Temporally, the story-world of Mark is charged with divine significance rather than historical or biographical importance. The gospel opens with the announcement that "the time is fulfilled, and the kingdom of God is at hand" (1:15). This time of fulfillment and expectation is temporally suspended between Old Testament prophecy (1:2–3) and

---

[47] Brenda Deen Schildgen, *Crisis and Continuity: Time in the Gospel of Mark*, JSNTSS, 159 (Sheffield: Sheffield Academic, 1998), 17–20.

eschatological consummation (14:62). These temporal reference points give weight to the narrative time of the gospel. Through Jesus, God is in the process of achieving a decisive victory for the kingdom of God. Thus, Mark depicts the time of Jesus' ministry as a time for repentance and decision, a time to choose sides. Even the progression of events in the gospel is controlled by divine necessity (8:31; 9:31; 10:33–34). The gospel is propelled toward its conclusion not by chronological or biographical concerns, but by the purposes of God. Therefore, in its most significant aspects, God's redemptive acts order the time of Mark's Gospel.

In the Jewish novel, foreign leaders who encroach upon the sovereignty of God threaten God's people. Their laws punish those who observe the law of God, and they demand obeisance from a people who must bow only to the one God. As I noted previously, this creates a moment of crisis for characters of the Jewish novel. Likewise, in Mark, the Jewish people face a crisis of decision. Will people accept Jesus as the divinely appointed agent of God and observe the law of God, or will they follow the religious leaders and observe "human tradition" (Mark 7:8)? As in the Jewish novels, Jesus' dialogic interaction with his antagonists circles around this central issue. The heroes of the Jewish novels debate the superiority of God and God's laws with those who would urge otherwise (Dan 1:8–16; 3:16; Bel 3–9; 23–26). Jesus, likewise, debates the merits of obeying God's law with the religious leaders who advocate observance of the "traditions of men" (Mark 7:1–13). This dialogic juxtaposition of ideas is the primary manifestation of the gospel's "novelistic" character.

As God's agent, Jesus enters a world rife with conflict. In Mark, conflict is the center around which the whole gospel is organized. Jesus no sooner announces the gospel of the kingdom of God (1:15) than he encounters opposition in the synagogue at Capernaum (1:23–26). This scene, along with the other demonic encounters in the first half of Mark (3:11–12; 5:1–13), establishes demonic oppression and opposition to the kingdom of God as a major theme in Mark's Gospel. Jesus' statement about the necessity of binding the strong man (3:23–27) brings additional focus to this theme. Jesus, in his capacity as divine agent, has come to bind the demonic forces of oppression and liberate those who are suffering. In this mission, Jesus is opposed both by demonic forces and by the religious leaders. The religious leaders believe that the divine deliverance announced by Jesus infringes upon their traditional religious practices (2:6–7, 16, 18, 24; 3:2). Ultimately, their perception of Jesus as disrespectful toward traditional religious practices leads them to reject Jesus' indirect claim to be God's divinely appointed agent. Thus, Mark depicts a story-world in which people are oppressed by both inimical demonic forces and misguided religious forces. Both of these forces conspire against Jesus and his message and are therefore, within the Markan story-world, enemies of God and the kingdom of God.

Within the Jewish novel's chronotope of crisis and expectation, the heroes function primarily as conduits of divine deliverance. They are conduits in the sense that victory for God's kingdom is achieved through them, in spite of their apparent weakness. Because the chronotope of the Jewish novel is dominated by the presence of a sovereign God who alone can save, a powerful hero who brings victory through personal charisma and military prowess is impossible. Such a hero would draw too much glory to himself. Instead, the chronotope of the Jewish novel demands a weak and vulnerable hero, a hero who will not detract from the glory due the sovereign God.

In many respects, Jesus is this kind of hero. Although Jesus mediates the power of God to those in need, he is in other respects unremarkable. He has no official position in society, nor does he belong to an important family. He is simply an itinerant layman who dares to challenge the authority of the religious leaders. Nor does Jesus tap into the lines of power through his association with others. Those with whom he associates are marginal members of Jewish society and frequently social outcasts. These relationships make Jesus' claims suspect in the eyes of the religious authorities (2:16), even though his actions bring praise not to himself but to God (2:12). Whatever praise does accrue to Jesus is ultimately short lived. In the end, Jesus achieves victory for God's kingdom only through an act of self-renunciation, abandoned by all who once followed him. Only by placing his trust completely in God and laying his life down for others, can Jesus inaugurate the kingdom of God (10:45; 14:36).

The temporal aspect of Mark's chronotope is somewhat different from that of the Jewish novel. Mark projects a realistic, historical time, while the Jewish novels, and in particular Judith, project a realistic, pseudo-historical time. Nevertheless, what they share is a common emphasis on a time of physical and spiritual crisis. In this time of crisis, God acts to accomplish God's will. Unlike the Greek romance, where things revert to their original state at the end of the story, in both Mark and the Jewish novel events in the narrative radically alter the *status quo*. In Judith, the Jews throw off their overlord and plunder his wealth (Jdt 5:11). Likewise, Esther secures the salvation of the Jewish nation in exile (Add Esth 10:4–9). In Mark, the change is even more dramatic. Jesus not only delivers many people from sickness and demonic bondage, but through the death and resurrection of the "beloved Son" God also inaugurates a new eschatological age of salvation (Mark 13).[48] The significance of Mark's temporal modification of the Jewish salvation story is that he concretizes it. Mark's story of divine salvation is no longer set in an amorphous pseudo-historical time, but in a specific historical time and place; and the change is not merely the alleviation of a momentary temporal crisis, but the dawning of a new eschatological age.

The most striking difference between Mark and the Jewish novels is apparent in Mark's attitude toward Jewish piety. The Jewish novels emphasize the importance of kashruth, the pious observance of Jewish dietary laws and ritual observance. The heroes of the Jewish novel are eligible for divine service precisely because they are scrupulous in their observance of the Jewish law. Jesus, however, downplays the importance of ritual observance. His own religious observance is casual to the point of drawing criticism: he "works" on the Sabbath (2:24; 3:2), he consorts with the ritually unclean (2:15), he touches the sick (1:41; 7:33). In his encounters with the religious leaders, he shows how legal observance is often little more than an onerous burden that interferes with the work of God. By his actions, Jesus echoes the cries of the Hebrew prophets who called for mercy and justice rather than ritual and regulation (Jer 7:4–5; Amos 5:21–24; Mic 6:6–8). In Mark's story, Jesus forces the Pharisees—who traffic in problems of legal interpretation abstracted from life—to confront the immediate needs of the present (3:1–6). In doing so, Mark, like menippea, strips away the abstract to deal with immediate reality. According to Mark, the salvation that God has wrought through Jesus makes the immediacy of the kingdom relevant to everyone. It combats the impracticality of a pharisaic pietism

---

[48] Collins, *Mark's Gospel*, 35–36.

prone to religious elitism and makes the service of God accessible and practical for all. In this respect, then, the Gospel of Mark subverts one of the main features of the Jewish novel.

The chronotope of the Gospel of Mark is therefore most like that of the Jewish novel. They are both engaged in a similar conversation about the nature of divine presence and action in the midst of crisis. Both are convinced that God can and will save those who trust in God's compassion and mercy. They differ somewhat on the nature of the crisis confronting God's people. For Mark, the conflict is no longer one of political sovereignty and potential genocide as it is in the Jewish novel. Instead, the crisis depicted in the pages of Mark is one of physical and spiritual oppression at the hands of a religious system that has lost its bearings. The piety that served the heroes of the Jewish novel so well becomes, in Mark's story-world, the very source of bondage for God's people. Using the same subversive strategy employed so effectively in the Jewish novel, Mark challenges this religious tradition by bring it into immediate contact with the polyglossic present. In so doing, the gospel exposes the careless cruelty of an overwrought and misguided piety, while at the same time celebrating divine deliverance achieved through obedience and weakness.

Conclusion

In certain respects, it would be problematic to conclude that Mark should be included among the Jewish novels. The episodic structure of chapters 1–10 is uncharacteristic of the Jewish novels, which, overall, present more tightly formulated plots. The introduction of significant amounts of *chreia* and anecdote also distinguishes Mark from the Jewish novel. Yet, these are superficial differences. What establishes a generic connection between Mark and the Jewish novel is their use of a realistic-apocalyptic chronotope. Mark and the Jewish novel create narrative worlds characterized by a conflict between divine and human sovereignty. God's response to this conflict is immediate and dramatic. By means of vulnerable human agents, God's sovereign authority is reestablished. Ultimately these divinely appointed agents prevail, not through their own resources, but through the power of God.

According to the Gospel of Mark, God made Jesus, who never knew royal status on earth and who died the death of a criminal, to be messiah. Mark's challenge as an author is to make a case for this deeply ironic Christian claim. To do so, he draws from a Jewish narrative tradition that celebrated the adventures and victories of God's appointed agents. These heroes, or more often heroines, were noted for their piety, beauty, and wisdom, but were otherwise weak and powerless. Through their simple obedience to God's call, they achieved great victories for his kingdom and deliverance for God's people. Jesus is this kind of hero in the Gospel of Mark. The gospel emphasizes Jesus' humble obedience to the call of God, and it is his obedience, rather than power and prestige, that secures victory for God's kingdom. Nevertheless, in an ironic twist, Mark at the same time subverts the celebration of Jewish piety that is so characteristic of the Jewish novels.

Considered chronotopically, the Gospel of Mark is a story of divine deliverance accomplished through human agency, set in an eschatologically charged time. The gospel configures its time and space to highlight the presence and activity of God among a people in crisis. In the gospel, Jesus is the locus of this divine activity. The strong correlation between the chronotope of the gospel and that of the Jewish novel establishes a secure generic link between them. This of course is not to deny other possible influences, nor is it to claim that Mark has followed the chronotopic pattern of the Jewish novel slavishly. The importance of relating the genre of Mark to the Jewish novel is that it provides an important and hermeneutically significant connection between the Gospel of Mark and its literary antecedents. The Gospel of Mark is part of a literary tradition that celebrates the salvific acts of God. Thus, while God's presence in the gospel is subdued, a generic connection with the Jewish novel suggests that God is nevertheless the central character in the Markan narrative. Jesus is the hero of the gospel story for no other reason than that he is the agent sent by God to announce in word and deed the presence and power of the kingdom of God.

Chapter Five

CONCLUSION

This dissertation began with a question: What kind of book is the Gospel according to Mark? For a literary critic this question demands an answer, yet over the years, it has resisted a satisfactory solution. In a recent posting to an Internet listserve, a well-known Markan scholar, who has published his own conclusions about the genre of the Gospel of Mark, wrote that he is "still trying to find a good definition of Mark's genre." For my part, I have claimed that a chronotopic investigation of the genre of the Gospel of Mark supports a connection with Jewish novelistic literature of the Hellenistic period. Whatever differences there might be between Mark and the Jewish novels, I maintain that they both compose their stories along similar ideological lines. In support of that claim, I examined the chronotopic patterns of Greco-Roman biography, ancient romance, and Menippean satire. This examination demonstrated that while the Gospel of Mark is similar, in certain respects, to these Greco-Roman genres, there are also significant differences. I then compared the Gospel of Mark with Jewish narrative literature of the late Hellenistic period and found that they shared strong chronotopic similarities. In light of the differences with Greco-Roman genres and the similarities with Jewish genres, I propose that the chronotope of Jewish novelistic literature provides a more fruitful point of comparison.

I have argued that these claims are warranted by Bakhtin's identification of chronotope as the most important indication of literary genre. Those inclined to a more formalistic approach to the problem of

161

genre may be unpersuaded by the argument presented here. They would no doubt point to the absence in the Jewish novels of themes like martyrdom, and literary forms like parable and aphorism. Following Bakhtin, however, I claim that similar themes, motifs, and literary forms are insufficient to establish a generic connection. Generic relationships rest rather on the chronotopic similarity between works of literature. Therefore, in rejecting Greco-Roman biography as an appropriate description of the genre of the Gospel of Mark, I maintain that previous attempts to do so are mistaken, not because they have been poorly executed, but because they are theoretically inadequate. The evidence they appeal to in support of their claim is insufficient to establish a meaningful generic connection between Mark and Greco-Roman biography, since it does not address the essence of literary genre.

One conclusion to be drawn from this exploration into the genre of the Gospel of Mark is that one's choice of method has profound effects on one's conclusions. The theoretical justification of method is therefore crucial in the debate over genre. In drawing attention to this fact, I do not claim that Bakhtin has solved all the problems surrounding genres and their formation. I believe, however, that Bakhtin's approach is a more theoretically sound alternative than those previously used to explore the genre of the Gospel of Mark. No doubt the debate over genre will continue. I have not assumed the task of defending Bakhtin's literary theory against competing theories. I have simply presented Bakhtin's theoretical approach to genre as an example of a consistent and unified poetics capable of further illuminating the genre of Mark's Gospel.

A theoretically valid approach to genre ought to produce interesting and defensible observations about how the literary work in question relates to its predecessors. I have argued that these relations must be more than superficial. For purposes of interpretation, these relations must be founded upon what is essential to the literary work as a creative act of communication. Apart from its theoretical coherence and plausibility, I believe Bakhtin's approach to genre provides interesting avenues of interpretation, as I have tried to demonstrate. Analyzing a work's chronotope exposes what is most essential to the work as an aesthetic creation. Chronotope governs the architectonic structure of the literary work as a whole and thereby reveals its form-shaping ideology. By laying bare the axiological orientation of the work's perception of time and space, we can isolate a defensible, and instructive, point of comparison with other literary works.

The argument I have presented here does not provide an exhaustive explanation of the historical influences that led to the creation of Mark's Gospel. Other genres may have influenced the composition of the Gospel of Mark. In the context of the first century, it would not be surprising to find that Mark, to one degree or another, borrowed from both Greek and Jewish literary forms. An exhaustive account of the influences that led to the gospel's production would involve a more comprehensive investigation of ancient genres, both Greco-Roman and Jewish. However, if correct, my analysis of Mark's chronotope suggests that it would be wrong to focus our attention solely on biographical genres. Although Jesus is clearly the main character in Mark's narrative, the gospel is not interested in Jesus simply as a model human or a great teacher. Mark presents Jesus as God's agent of salvation. Mark's story is not so much about Jesus' exemplary piety as it is about what God accomplishes through Jesus. The apocalyptic and subversive quality of the gospel's chronotope argues against a successful comparison with Greco-Roman biography. Instead, Mark's story belongs with other popular Jewish stories of divine deliverance mediated through human agency.

The importance of Mark's apocalyptic understanding of time and space as it relates to matters of genre has not yet received the attention that it deserves. Mikhail Bakhtin's conceptualization of genre underscores the critical nature of this oversight. A chronotopic approach to Markan genre allows us to move beyond a limited comparison of the gospels with ancient "biographical" genres. If we no longer focus solely on similarities of form and content, we can consider other popular narrative genres and test the validity of those comparisons according to their chronotopic similarities. I believe a chronotopic analysis demonstrates that the Jewish novel provides the most plausible literary genre for the Gospel according to Mark. In contrast to those who compare Mark with Greco-Roman biography, I have argued that Mark does not present Jesus merely as an ethical role model, but as the divinely appointed agent of God. Like the protagonists of the Jewish novels, Jesus is the agent of God who defeats the enemies of the kingdom, not by force, but by faithful and sacrificial obedience. What matters most for Mark is that God calls Jesus, and Jesus is obedient to that call. It is this dynamic that animates the gospel and not the portrayal of Jesus as a teacher of virtue. The comparison of Mark with the Jewish novel is therefore warranted not by formal similarities, but by mutual dependence upon a common axiological orientation to the world. Thus, a comparison with the Jewish novel clarifies the literary heritage and illuminates the ideological interests of the Markan author better than a comparison with Greco-Roman literary types.

BIBLIOGRAPHY

Abrams, M. H. "The Transformation of English Studies: 1930–1995." *Daedalus* 126 (1997): 105–31.

———. *A Glossary of Literary Terms*, 5th ed. Fort Worth: Holt, Rinehart & Winston, 1988.

Achtemeier, Paul J. "Gospel Miracle Tradition and the Divine Man." *Int* 26 (1972): 174–97.

Adrados, Francisco R. "The Life of Aesop and the Origin of Novel in Antiquity." *Quaderni Urbinati di Cultura Classica* 30 (1979): 93–112.

Agassiz, Louis. *Essay on Classification*. Edited by Edward Lurie, John Harvard Library, ed. Bernard Bailyn. Cambridge: Harvard University Press, Belknap Press, 1962.

Alexander, Philip S. "Rabbinic Biography and the Biography of Jesus: A Survey of the Evidence." In *Synoptic Studies: The Ampleforth Conferences of 1982 and 1983*, edited by C. M. Tuckett, JSNTSup, ed. David J. A. Clines, 7, 19–50. Sheffield: JSOT, 1984.

Alonso-Schökel, Luis. *Narrative Structures in the Book of Judith*. Center for Hermeneutical Studies, Protocol Series of the Colloquies, ed. W. Wuellner, 11. Berkeley: The Center for Hermeneutical Studies in Hellenistic and Modern Culture, 1974.

Amphoux, Christian-B. "Quelques remarques sur la formation, le genre littéraire et la composition de l'Évangile de Marc." *Filologia Neotestamentaria* 10 (1997): 5–34.

Anderson, Graham. *Eros Sophistes: Ancient Novelists at Play*. American Classical Studies, ed. Deborah Samuel, no. 9. Chico, Calif.: Scholars, 1982.

———. *Ancient Fiction: The Novel in the Graeco-Roman World*. London: Croom Helm; Totowa, N.J.: Barnes & Noble, 1984.

———. *The Second Sophistic: A Cultural Phenomenon in the Roman Empire*. London: Routledge, 1993.

Angenot, Marc. "Bakhtine, sa critique de Saussure et la recherche contemporaine." *Études françaises* 20 (1984): 7–19.

Aristotle. *The Complete Works of Aristotle: The Revised Oxford Translation*, 2 vols. Edited by Jonathan Barnes, Bollingen, vol. 71, no. 2. Princeton: Princeton University Press, 1984.

Atkins, J. W. H. *Literary Criticism in Antiquity: A Sketch of Its Development,* 2 vols. Cambridge: Cambridge University Press, 1934. Reprint, Gloucester, Mass.: Peter Smith, 1961.

Auerbach, Eric. *Mimesis: The Representation of Reality in Western Literature*. Translated by Willard R. Trask. Princeton: Princeton University Press, 1953.

Aune, David E. "Septum sapientium convivium (Moralia 146B–164D)." In *Plutarch's Ethical Writings and Early Christian Literature*, edited by Hans Dieter Betz, SCHNT, ed. H. D. Betz, G. Delling, and W. C. van Unnik, vol. 4, 51–105. Leiden: E. J. Brill, 1978.

———. "The Problem of the Genre of the Gospels: A Critique of C. H. Talbert's *What is a Gospel?*" In *Gospel Perspectives: Studies of History and Tradition in the Four Gospels*, edited by R. T. France and D. Wenham, 2:9–60. Sheffield: JSOT, 1981.

———. *The New Testament in Its Literary Environment*. Library of Early Christianity, ed. Wayne A. Meeks, vol. 8. Philadelphia: Westminster, 1987.

———. "The Gospels as Hellenistic Biography." *Mosaic* 20, no. 4 (1987): 1–10.

———. "Greco-Roman Biography." In *Greco-Roman Literature and the New Testament: Selected Forms and Genres*, edited by David E. Aune, SBLSBS, ed. Bernard Brandon Scott, no. 21, 107–26. Atlanta: Scholars, 1988.

———. "The Gospels: Biography or Theology?" *Bible Review* 6, no. 1 (1990): 14–21.

Austin, J. L. *How to Do Things with Words*, 2d ed. Edited by J. O. Urmson and Marina Sbisa. Cambridge: Harvard University Press, 1975.

Averintsev, Sergei, and Vadim Kozinov. "The World of Mikhail Bakhtin." *Soviet Literature* 1, no. 346 (1977): 143–51.

Bailey, James L., and Lyle D. Vander Broek. *Literary Forms in the New Testament: A Handbook.* Louisville: Westminster/John Knox, 1992.

Baird, J. Arthur. "Genre Analysis as a Method of Historical Criticism." In *SBLSP*, edited by Lane C. McGaughy, 2:385–411. N.p.: Society of Biblical Literature, 1972.

———. *A Comparative Analysis of the Gospel Genre: The Synoptic Mode and Its Uniqueness.* Studies in the Bible and Early Christianity, vol. 24. Lewiston, N.Y.: Edwin Mellen, 1991.

Baker, Aelred. "Form and the Gospels." *Downside Review* 88 (1970): 14–26.

Bakhtin Centre. "Analytical Database." May 19, 2000. <http://www.shef.ac.uk/uni /academic/A-C/bakh/dbase.html> (June 6, 2000).

Bakhtin, M. M. *Rabelais and His World* (1965). Translated by Hélène Iswolsky. Cambridge, MIT Press, 1968. Reprint, Bloomington: Indiana University Press (Midland Book), 1984.

———. "The Art of the Word and the Culture of Folk Humor (Rabelais and Gogol')" (1940). In *Semiotics and Structuralism: Readings from the Soviet Union*, edited with an introduction by Henryk Baran, 284–96. White Plains, N. Y.: International Arts and Sciences, 1976.

———. *The Dialogic Imagination: Four Essays by M. M. Bakhtin.* Edited by Michael Holquist, translated by Caryl Emerson and Michael Holquist, UTPSS, ed. Michael Holquist, no. 1. Austin: University of Texas Press, 1981.

———. "Epic and Novel: Toward a Methodology for the Study of the Novel" (1941). In *DI*, 3–40.

———. "From the Prehistory of Novelistic Discourse" (1940). In *DI*, 41–83.

———. "Forms of Time and of the Chronotope in the Novel: Notes toward a Historical Poetics" (1937–38). In *DI*, 84–258.

———. "Discourse in the Novel" (1934–35). In *DI*, 259–422.

———. *Problems of Dostoevsky's Poetics* (1963). Edited and translated by Caryl Emerson, with an introduction by Wayne C. Booth, THL, ed. Wlad Godzich and Jochen Schulte-Sasse, vol. 8. Minneapolis: University of Minnesota Press, 1984.

———. "Three Fragments from the 1929 Edition, *Problems of Dostoevsky's Art* (1979)." In *PDP*, 275–82.

———. "Toward a Reworking of the Dostoevsky Book" (1961). In *PDP*, 283–302.

————. *Speech Genres and Other Late Essays*. Edited by Caryl Emerson and Michael Holquist, translated by Vern W. McGee, UTPSS, ed. Michael Holquist, no. 9. Austin: University of Texas Press, 1986.

————. "From Notes Made in 1970–71." In *SpG*, 132–58.

————. "Response to a Question from the Novy Mir Editorial Staff" (1970). In *SpG*, 1–9.

————. "The Bildungsroman and Its Significance in the History of Realism (Toward a Historical Typology of the Novel)" (1936–38). In *SpG*, 10–59.

————. "The Problem of Speech Genres" (1952–53). In *SpG*, 60–102.

————. "The Problem of the Text in Linguistics, Philology, and the Human Sciences: An Experiment in Philosophical Analysis" (1959–61). In *SpG*, 103–31.

————. "Toward a Methodology for the Human Sciences" (1974). In *SpG*, 159–72.

————. *Art and Answerability: Early Philosophical Essays by M. M. Bakhtin*. Edited by Michael Holquist and Vadim Liapunov, translated with notes by Vadim Liapunov, supplement translated by Kenneth Brostrom, UTPSS, ed. Michael Holquist, no. 9. Austin: University of Texas Press, 1990.

————. "Art and Answerability" (1919). In *A&A*, 1–3.

————. "Author and Hero in Aesthetic Activity" (ca. 1920). In *A&A*, 4–256.

————. "The Problem of Content, Material, and Form in Verbal Art" (1924). In *A&A*, 257–325.

————. *Toward a Philosophy of the Act* (ca. 1920). Edited by Vadim Liapunov and Michael Holquist, translated with notes by Vadim Liapunov, UTPSS, ed. Michael Holquist, no. 10. Austin: University of Texas Press, 1993.

Bakhtin, M. M. / P. N. Medvedev. *The Formal Method in Literary Scholarship: A Critical Introduction to Sociological Poetics* (1928). Translated by Albert J. Wehrle. Baltimore: Johns Hopkins University Press, 1978.

Baldwin, B. "Biography at Rome." In *Studies in Latin Literature and Roman History*, vol. 1, edited by Carl Deroux, Collection Latomus, vol. 164, 100–18. Brussels: Latomus, 1979.

Baltzer, Klaus. *Die Biographie der Propheten*. Neukirchen-Vluyn: Neukirchener, 1975.

Barns, John Wintour Baldwin. "Egypt and the Greek Romance." In *Akten des VIII. Internationalen Kongresses für Papyrologie: Wein 1955*, Mitteilungen aus der Papyrussammlung der Österreichischen Nationalbibliothek (Papyrus Erzherzog Rainer), n.Ser., hrsg. Hans Gerstinger, 5. F., 29–36. Vienna: Rudolf M. Rohrer, 1956.

Barr, David Lawrence. "Toward a Definition of the Gospel Genre: A Generic Analysis and Comparison of the Synoptic Gospels and the Socratic Dialogues by Means of Aristotle's Theory of Tragedy." Ph.D. diss., Florida State University, 1974.

Bartoňková, Dagmar. "Prosimetrum, the Mixed Style, in Ancient Literature." *Eirene* 14 (1976): 65–92.

Batto, Bernard F. *Slaying the Dragon: Mythmaking in the Biblical Tradition*. Louisville: Westminster/John Knox, 1992.

Beach, Curtis. *The Gospel of Mark: Its Making and Meaning*. New York: Harper & Brothers, 1959.

Beardslee, William A. *Literary Criticism of the New Testament*. GBS, ed. Dan O. Via, Jr. Philadelphia: Fortress, 1969.

Benda, Frederick Joseph. "The Tradition of Menippean Satire in Varro, Lucian, Seneca and Erasmus." Ph.D. diss., University of Texas at Austin, 1979.

Benjamin, David Eugene. "The Identification of the Genre 'Gospel' and its Hermeneutical Significance for the Canonical Gospels." Ph.D. diss., Southwestern Baptist Theological Seminary, 1995.

Berg, Sandra Beth. *The Book of Esther: Motifs, Themes and Structure*. SBLDS, ed. Howard C. Kee and Douglas A. Knight, no. 44. Missoula, Mont.: Scholars, 1979.

Berger, Klaus. "Hellenistische Gattungen im Neuen Testament." In *ANRW*, hrsg. H. Temporini and W. Haase, 2.25.2, 1031–432. Berlin: Walter de Gruyter, 1984.

————. "Zur Diskussion um die Gattung Evangelium: Formgeschichtliche Beiträge aus Beobachtungen an Plutarchs *Leben der Zehn Redners*." In *The Four Gospels 1992: Festschrift Frans Neirynck*, edited by F. Van Segbroeck et al. BETL, 100, 1:121–27. Leuven: Leuven University Press/Peeters, 1992.

Berger, Peter L., and Thomas Luckmann. *The Social Construction of Reality: A Treatise in the Sociology of Knowledge*. New York: Doubleday, 1966; Anchor Books, 1967.

Bernard-Donals, Michael F. *Mikhail Bakhtin: Between Phenomenology and Marxism*. Literature, Culture, Theory, ed. Richard Macksey and Michael Sprinker, 11. Cambridge: Cambridge University Press, 1994.

Betz, Hans Dieter. "Jesus as Divine Man." In *Jesus and the Historian [Festschrift for Ernest Cadman Colwell]*, edited by F. Thomas Trotter, 114–33. Philadelphia: Westminster, 1968.

Betz, Otto. "The Concept of the so-called 'Divine Man' in Mark's Christology." In *Studies in New Testament and Early Christian Literature [Festschrift Allen P. Wilkgren]*, edited by David Edward Aune, 229–40. Leiden: E. J. Brill, 1972.

Bialostosky, Don. "Bakhtin versus Chatman on Narrative: The Habilitation of the Hero." *University of Ottawa Quarterly* 53, no. 1 (1983): 109–16.

———. "Booth's Rhetoric, Bakhtin's Dialogics and the Future of Novel Criticism." *Novel* 18 (1985): 209–16.

———. "Dialogic, Pragmatic, and Hermeneutic Conversation: Bakhtin, Rorty, and Gadamer." *Critical Studies* 1 (1989): 107–19.

———. "Dialogics, Narratology, and the Virtual Space of Discourse." *Journal of Narrative Technique* 19 (1989): 167–73.

Bilezikian, Gilbert G. *The Liberated Gospel: A Comparison of the Gospel of Mark and Greek Tragedy*. Baker Biblical Monograph. Grand Rapids: Baker, 1977.

Blackburn, Barry. *Theios Aner and the Markan Miracle Tradition: A Critique of the Theios Aner Concept as an Interpretative Background of the Miracle Traditions Used by Mark*. WUNT, vol. 2, no. 40. Tübingen: J. C. B. Mohr (Paul Siebeck), 1991.

Bloor, David. *Knowledge and Social Imagery*. London: Routledge & Kegan Paul, 1976.

Bocharov, Sergey. "Conversations with Bakhtin." *PMLA* 105 (1994): 1009–24.

———. "The Event of Being: On Mikhail Mikhailovich Bakhtin." In *Critical Essays on Mikhail Bakhtin*, edited by Caryl Emerson, Critical Essays on World Literature, ed. Robert Lecker, 29–44. New York: G. K. Hall, 1999.

Bolongaro, Eugenio. "From Literariness to Genre: Establishing the Foundations for a Theory of Literary Genres." *Genre* 25 (1992): 277–313.

Booth, Wayne C. *The Rhetoric of Fiction*. Chicago: University of Chicago Press, 1983.

————. Introduction to *Problems of Dostoevsky's Poetics*, by Mikhail Bakhtin. Minnesota: University of Minnesota Press, 1984.

Borgen, Peter. "Philo of Alexandria." In *Jewish Writings of the Second Temple Period: Apocrypha, Pseudepigrapha, Qumran Sectarian Writings, Philo, Josephus*, edited by Michael E. Stone, CRINT, sec. 2, vol. 2., 233–82. Philadelphia: Fortress, 1984.

Boring, M. Eugene. "Mark 1:1–15 and the Beginning of the Gospel." *Semeia* 52 (1990): 43–81.

Bornkamm, Günther. *Jesus of Nazareth*, Translated by Irene McLuskey and Fraser McLuskey with James M. Robinson. New York: Harper & Brothers, 1960.

Bowersock, G. W. *Fiction as History: Nero to Julian*. Sather Classical Lectures, vol. 37. Berkeley: University of California Press, 1994.

Bowersock, G. W., and E. L. Bowie. "Between Philosophy and Rhetoric." In *CHCL*, vol. 1, pt. 4, *The Hellenistic Period and the Empire*, edited by P. E. Easterling and B. M. W. Knox, 105–23. Cambridge: Cambridge University Press, 1989.

Bowie, E. L. "Greeks and Their Past in the Second Sophistic." *Past and Present* 46 (1970): 3–41.

————. "The Greek Novel." In *CHCL*, vol. 1, pt. 4, *The Hellenistic Period and the Empire*, edited by P. E. Easterling and B. M. W. Knox, 123–39. Cambridge: Cambridge University Press, 1989.

Boyd-Taylor, C. "Esther's Great Adventure: Reading the LXX Version of the Book of Esther in Light of its Assimilation to the Conventions of the Greek Romantic Novel." *BIOSCS* 30 (1997): 81–113.

Branham, R. Bracht. "Inventing the Novel." In *Bakhtin in Contexts: Across the Disciplines*, edited by Amy Mandelker and Caryl Emerson, Rethinking Theory, 79–87. Evanston, Ill.: Northwestern University Press, 1995.

————. *Unruly Eloquence: Lucian and the Comedy of Traditions*. Revealing Antiquity, ed. G. W. Bowersock, 2. Cambridge: Harvard University Press, 1989.

Braun, Martin. *History and Romance in Graeco-Oriental Literature*. Preface by Arnold Toynbee, Ancient Greek Literature, ed. Leonardo Tarán. Oxford: Basil Blackwell, 1938. Reprint, New York: Garland, 1987.

Brenk, Frederick E. *In Mist Apparelled: Religious Themes in Plutarch's Moralia and Lives*. Mnemosyne, Bibliotheca Classica Batava, Supplementum, ed. W. den Boer et al., 48. Leiden: E. J. Brill, 1977.

Brewer, Derek. "The Gospels and the Laws of Folktale." *Folklore* 90 (1979): 37–52.

Brichto, Herbert Chanan. *Toward a Grammar of Biblical Poetics: Tales of the Prophets*. New York: Oxford University Press, 1992.

Brown, P. "The Rise and Function of the Holy Man in Late Antiquity." *JRS* 61 (1971): 80–101.

Bruce, F. F. "When is a Gospel not a Gospel?" *BJRL* 45 (1962–63): 319–39.

Bryan, Christopher. *A Preface to Mark: Notes on the Gospel in Its Literary and Cultural Settings*. Oxford: Oxford University Press, 1993.

Bultmann, Rudolf. *History of the Synoptic Tradition*, rev. ed. Translated by John Marsh. New York: Harper & Row, 1963.

———. "The Gospels (Form)." In *Twentieth Century Theology in the Making*, vol. 1, *Themes of Biblical Theology*, edited by J. Pelikan, translated by R. A. Wilson, Fontana Library Theology and Philosophy, 12/6, 86–92. New York: Harper & Row, 1969.

Burch, Ernest W. "Tragic Action in the Second Gospel: A Study in the Narrative of Mark." *JR* 11 (1931): 346–58.

Burkert, Walter. *The Orientalizing Revolution: The Near Eastern Influence on Greek Culture in the Early Archaic Age*. Translated by Margaret E. Pinder and Walter Burkert, Revealing Antiquity, ed. G. W. Bowersock, 5. Cambridge: Harvard University Press, 1992.

Burridge, Richard A. *What Are the Gospels? A Comparison with Graeco-Roman Biography*. SNTSMS, ed. G. N. Stanton, 70. Cambridge: Cambridge University Press, 1992.

———. "Biography." In *Handbook of Classical Rhetoric in the Hellenistic Period (330 B.C.–A.D. 400)*, edited by Stanley Porter, 371–91. Leiden: E. J. Brill, 1997.

———. "The Gospels and Acts." In *Handbook of Classical Rhetoric in the Hellenistic Period (330 B.C.–A.D. 400)*, edited by Stanley Porter, 507–32. Leiden: E. J. Brill, 1997.

———. "About People, by People, for People: Gospel Genre and Audiences." In *The Gospels for All Christians: Rethinking the Gospel Audiences*, edited by Richard Bauckham, 113–45. Grand Rapids: Eerdmans, 1998.

Butts, James R. "The 'Progymnasmata' of Theon: A New Text with Translation and Commentary." Ph.D. diss., Claremont Graduate School, 1983.

Cairns, Francis. *Generic Composition in Greek and Roman Poetry*. Edinburgh: Edinburgh University Press, 1972.

Camery-Hoggatt, Jerry. *Irony in Mark's Gospel: Text and Subtext*. SNTSMS, ed. G. N. Stanton, 72. Cambridge: Cambridge University Press, 1992.

Cancik, Hubert. "Die Gattung Evangelium: Markus im Rahmen der antiken Historiographie." In *Markus-Philologie: Historische, literargeschichtliche und stilistische Untersuchungen zum zweiten Evangelium*, hrsg. Hubert Cancik, WUNT, hrsg. Martin Hengel and Otfried Hofius, 33, 85–113. Tübingen: J. C. B. Mohr (Paul Siebeck), 1984.

———. "Bios und Logos: Formgeschichtliche Untersuchungen zu Lukians 'Demonax'." In *Markus-Philologie: Historische, literargeschichtliche und stilistische Untersuchungen zum zweiten Evangelium*, hrsg. Hubert Cancik, WUNT, hrsg. Martin Hengel and Otfried Hofius, 33, 115–30. Tübingen: J. C. B. Mohr (Paul Siebeck), 1984.

Canevet, Mariette. "Remarques sur l'utilisation du genre littéraire historique par Philon d'Alexandrie dans la *Vita Moysis*, ou Moïse général en chef-prophète." *RevScRel* 60 (1986): 189–206.

Carré, Henry Beach. "The Literary Structure of the Gospel of Mark." In *Studies in Early Christianity*, edited by Shirley Jackson Case, 105–26. New York: Century, 1928.

Cassirer, Ernst. *The Philosophy of Symbolic Forms*, 3 vols. Translated by Ralph Manheim, preface and introduction by Charles W. Hendel. New Haven: Yale University Press, 1953–57.

Ceserani, Remo. "Genre Theory, Literary History, and the Fantastic." In *Literary Theory and Criticism: Festschrift Presented to René Wellek in Honor of His Eightieth Birthday*, Part I: *Theory*, edited by Joseph P. Strelka, 2. Aufl. 121–38. New York: Peter Lang, 1985.

Chance, J. Bradley. "Fiction in Ancient Biography: An Approach to a Sensitive Issue in Gospel Interpretation." *Perspectives in Religious Studies* 18 (1991): 125–42.

Chatman, Seymour. "On Defining 'Form'." *New Literary History* 2 (1971): 217–28.

———. *Story and Discourse: Narrative Structure in Fiction and Film*. Ithaca: Cornell University Press, 1978.

Chion of Heraclea: A Novel in Letters. Edited with introduction and commentary by Ingemar Düring, Acta Universitatis Gotoburgensis, Göteborgs högskolas

Årsskrift, bd. 57, no. 5. Göteborg: Wettergren & Kerbers, 1951. Reprint, New York: Arno, 1979.

Clark, Katerina, and Michael Holquist. *Mikhail Bakhtin*. Cambridge: Harvard University Press, 1984.

———. "A Continuing Dialogue." *Slavic and East European Journal* 30 (1986): 96–102.

Cobley, Evelyn. "Mikhail Bakhtin's Place in Genre Theory." *Genre* 21 (1988): 321–38.

Collins, Adela Yarbro. "Narrative, History, and Gospel: A General Response." *Semeia* 43 (1988): 145–53.

———. *Is Mark's Gospel a Life of Jesus? The Question of Genre*. The Père Marquette Lecture in Theology. Milwaukee: Marquette University Press, 1990.

———. *The Beginning of the Gospel: Probings of Mark in Context*. Minneapolis: Fortress, 1992.

———. "Genre and the Gospels." *JR* 75 (1995): 239–46.

———. "The Appropriation of the Psalms of Individual Lament by Mark." In *The Scriptures in the Gospels*, edited by C. M. Tuckett, BETL 131, 223–41. Leuven: Leuven University Press, 1997.

Conte, Gian Biagio. *Latin Literature: A History*. Translated by Joseph B Solodow, revised by Don Fowler and Glenn W. Most. Baltimore: Johns Hopkins University Press, 1994.

Cox, Patricia. *Biography in Late Antiquity: A Quest for the Holy Man*. Transformation of the Classical Heritage, ed. Peter Brown, 5. Berkeley: University of California Press, 1983.

Craig, Kenneth M., Jr. *Reading Esther: A Case for the Literary Carnivalesque*. Literary Currents in Biblical Interpretation, ed. Danna Nolan Fewell and David M. Gunn. Louisville: Westminster/John Knox, 1995.

Craven, Toni. *Artistry and Faith in the Book of Judith*. SBLDS, ed. Robert R. Wilson, no. 70. Chico, Calif.: Scholars, 1983.

Cuddon, J. A. *A Dictionary of Literary Terms and Literary Theory*, 3rd ed. Oxford: Blackwell Reference, 1991.

Daly, Lloyd W. *Aesop without Morals: The Famous Fables, and a Life of Aesop*. Translated and edited by Lloyd W. Daly, illustrated by Grace Muscarella. New York: Thomas Yoseloff, 1961.

Damrosch, David. *The Narrative Covenant: Transformations of Genre in the Growth of Biblical Literature.* Ithaca: Cornell University, 1987.

Dancy, J. C., with W. J. Fuerst, and R. J. Hammer. *The Shorter Books of the Apocrypha: Tobit, Judith, Rest of Esther, Baruch, Letter of Jeremiah, Additions to Daniel, and Prayer of Manasseh.* Cambridge Bible Commentary, ed. P. R. Ackroyd, A. R. C. Leaney, and J. W. Packer. Cambridge: Cambridge University Press, 1972.

Dibelius, Martin. *From Tradition to Gospel.* Translated by Bertram Lee Woolf. Greenwood, S.C.: Attic, 1982.

Dihle, Albrecht. "The Gospels and Greek Biography." In *The Gospel and the Gospels*, edited by P. Stuhlmacher, translated by John Vriend, 361–86. Grand Rapids: Eerdmans, 1991.

———. *Die Entstehung der historischen Biographie.* SHAW, 3. Heidelberg: Winter, 1987.

———. *Greek and Latin Literature of the Roman Empire: From Augustus to Justinian.* Translated by Manfred Malzahn. London: Routledge, 1994.

———. *History of Greek Literature: From Homer to the Hellenistic Period.* London: Routledge, 1994.

———. *Studien zur griechischen Biographie.* Abhandlungen der Akademie der Wissenschaften in Göttingen, Philologisch-Historische Klasse, 3. Folge, Nr. 37. Göttingen: Vandenhoeck & Ruprecht, 1956.

Dodd, C. H. *The Apostolic Preaching and Its Developments.* New York: Harper & Brothers, 1962.

Dormeyer, Detlev. "Die Kompositionsmetapher 'Evangelium Jesu Christi, des Sohnes Gottes' Mk 1:1: Ihre theologische und literarische Aufgabe in der Jesus-biographie des Markus." *NTS* 33 (1987): 452–68.

———. *Evangelium als literarische und theologische Gattung.* ErFor, Bd. 263. Darmstadt: Wissenschaftliche Buchgesellschaft, 1989.

———. "Mk 1:1–15 als Prolog des ersten Idealbiographischen Evangeliums von Jesus Christus." *Biblical Interpretation* 5 (1997): 181–211.

———. *The New Testament among the Writings of Antiquity.* Translated by Rosmarie Kossov, translation edited by Stanley E. Porter, Biblical Seminar, 55. Sheffield: Sheffield Academic, 1998.

Dormeyer, Detlev, and Hubert Frankemölle. "Evangelium als literarische Gattung und als theologischer Begriff: Tendenzen und Aufgaben der Evangelienforschung im 20. Jahrhundert, mit einer Untersuchung des Markus-evangeliums in seinem Verhältnis zur antiken Biographie." In *ANRW* 2.25.2, hrsg. H. Temporini and W. Haase, 1543–704. Berlin: Walter de Gruyter, 1984.

Dorothy, Charles V. *The Book of Esther: Structure, Genre and Textual Integrity.* JSOTSupS, ed. David J. A. Clines and Philip R. Davies, 187. Sheffield: Sheffield Academic, 1997.

Dorst, John D. "Neck-riddle as a Dialogue of Genres: Applying Bakhtin's Genre Theory." *Journal of American Folklore* 96 (1983): 413–33.

Doty, William G. "The Concept of Genre in Literary Analysis." In *SBLSP*, edited by Lane C. McGaughy, 2:413–48. N.p: Society of Biblical Literature, 1972.

Dowd, Sharyn E. "The Gospel of Mark as Ancient Novel." *LTQ* 26 (1991): 53–59.

Downing, F. Gerald. "Contemporary Analogies to the Gospels and Acts: 'Genres' or 'Motifs'?" In *Synoptic Studies: The Ampleforth Conferences of 1982 and 1983*, edited by C. M. Tuckett, JSNTSup, ed. David J. A. Clines, 7, 51–65. Sheffield: JSOT, 1984.

———. "A bas les aristos: The Relevance of Higher Literature for the Understanding of the Earliest Christian Writings." *NovT* 30 (1988): 212–30.

Droge, Arthur J. "Call Stories in Greek Biography and the Gospels." In *SBLSP*, edited by Kent Harold Richards, 245–57. Chico, Calif.: Scholars, 1983.

Dubrow, Heather. *Genre.* Critical Idiom, ed. John D. Jump, 42. London: Methuen, 1982.

Ducrot, Oswald, and Tzvetan Todorov. *Encyclopedic Dictionary of the Sciences of Language.* Translated by Catherine Porter. Baltimore: Johns Hopkins University Press, 1979.

Duff, J. Wight. *Roman Satire: Its Outlook on Social Life.* Sather Classical Lectures, vol. 12. Berkeley: University of California Press, 1936.

Duff, Tim. *Plutarch's "Lives": Exploring Virtue and Vice.* Oxford: Clarendon, 1999.

Edwards, Mark. "Biography and the Biographic." In *Portraits: Biographical Representation in the Greek and Latin Literature of the Roman Empire*, edited by M. J. Edwards and Simon Swain, 227–34. Oxford: Clarendon, 1997.

Elliott, Robert C. "The Definition of Satire: A Note on Method." *Yearbook of Comparative and General Literature* 11, supp. (1962): 19–23.

Elsom, Helen. "The New Testament and Greco-Roman Writing." In *The Literary Guide to the Bible*, edited by Robert Alter and Frank Kermode, 561–78. Cambridge: Harvard University Press, 1987.

Emerson, Caryl. "Bakhtin and Intergeneric Shift: The Case of Boris Godunov." *Studies in Twentieth Century Literature* 9 (1984): 145–67.

———. "Problems with Baxtin's Poetics." *Slavic and East European Journal* 32 (1988): 503–26.

———. "Russian Orthodoxy and the Early Bakhtin." *Religion and Literature* 22, nos. 2–3 (1990): 109–31.

———. "Irreverent Bakhtin and the Imperturbable Classics." *Arethusa* 26 (1993): 123–39.

———. "Keeping the Self Intact During the Culture Wars: A Centennial Essay for Mikhail Bakhtin." *New Literary History* 27 (1996): 107–26.

———. *The First Hundred Years of Mikhail Bakhtin*. Princeton: Princeton University Press, 1997.

Evans, Craig A. "Mark's Incipit and the Priene Calendar Inscription: From Jewish Gospel to Greco-Roman Gospel." *Journal of Greco-Roman Christianity and Judaism* 1 (2000), <http://www.jgrchj.com/> (September 4, 2000).

Fairweather, Janet. "Fiction in the Biographies of Ancient Writers." *Ancient Society* 5 (1974): 231–75.

Falconer, Rachel. "Bakhtin and the Epic Chronotope." In *Face to Face: Bakhtin in Russia and the West*, edited by Carol Adlam et al., 254–72. Sheffield: Sheffield Academic Press, 1997.

Fantham, Elaine. *Roman Literary Culture: From Cicero to Apuleius*. Baltimore: Johns Hopkins University Press, 1996.

Farmer, William R. "Jesus and the Gospels: A Form-critical and Theological Essay." *PSTJ* 28 (1975): 1–62.

———. *Jesus and the Gospels: Tradition, Scripture, and Canon*. Philadelphia: Fortress, 1982.

Fee, Gordon. "The Genre of New Testament Literature and Biblical Hermeneutics." In *Interpreting the Word of God: Festschrift in Honor of Steven Barnabas*, edited by S. J. Schultz and M. A. Inch, 105–27. Chicago: Moody, 1976.

Fendler, Folkert. *Studien zum Markusevangelium: Zur Gattung, Chronologie, Messiasgeheimnistheorie und Überlieferung des zweiten Evangeliums.* GTA, hrsg. Georg Strecker, Bd. 49. Göttingen: Vandenhoeck & Ruprecht, 1991.

Finkelberg, Margalit. *The Birth of Literary Fiction in Ancient Greece.* Oxford: Clarendon, 1998.

Fishelov, David. *Metaphors of Genre: The Role of Analogies in Genre Theory.* University Park: Pennsylvania State University Press, 1993.

Fitzgerald, John. "The Ancient Lives of Aristotle and the Modern Debate about the Genre of the Gospels." *ResQ* 36 no. 4 (1994): 209–21.

Foley, Joe. "Form Criticism and Genre Theory." *Language and Literature* 4 (1995): 173–91.

Fowler, Alastair. "The Life and Death of Literary Forms." *New Literary History* 2 (1971): 199–216.

———. *Kinds of Literature: An Introduction to the Theory of Genres and Modes.* Cambridge: Harvard University Press, 1982.

———. "The Future of Genre Theory: Functions and Constructional Types." In *The Future of Literary Theory*, edited by Ralph Cohen, 291–303. New York: Routledge, 1989.

Fox, Michael V. *Character and Ideology in the Book of Esther.* Studies on Personalities of the Old Testament, ed. James L. Crenshaw. Columbia, S.C.: University of South Carolina Press, 1991.

Frankemölle, Hubert. *Evangelium—Begriff und Gattung: Ein Forschungsbericht.* SBB, hrsg. Hubert Frankemölle and Frank-Lothar Hossfeld, 15. Stuttgart: Katholisches Bibelwerk, 1988.

Frickenschmidt, Dirk. *Evangelium als Biographie: Die vier Evangelien im Rahmen antiker Erzählkunst.* Téxte und Arbeiten zum neutestamentlichen Zeitalter, hrsg. Klaus Berger et al., 22. Tübingen: Francke, 1997.

Frye, Northrop. *Anatomy of Criticism: Four Essays.* Princeton: Princeton University Press, 1957.

Frye, Roland Mushat. "The Jesus of the Gospels: Approaches through Narrative Structure." In *From Faith to Faith: Essays in Honor of Donald G. Miller on his Seventieth Birthday*, edited by Dikran Y. Hadidian, PTMS, 31, 75–89. Pittsburgh: Pickwick, 1979.

Fusillo, Massimo. "Modern Critical Theories and the Ancient Novel." In *The Novel in the Ancient World*, edited by Gareth Schmeling, Mnemosyne, Bibliotheca Classica Batava, Supplementum, ed. J. M. Bremer et al., 159, 277–305. Leiden: E. J. Brill, 1996.

Gardiner, Michael. *The Dialogics of Critique: M. M. Bakhtin and the Theory of Ideology.* London: Routledge, 1992.

Gasparov, M. L. "M. M. Bakhtin in Russian Culture of the Twentieth Century: Translation, Notes and Commentary by Ann Shukman." *Studies in Twentieth Century Literature* 9 (1984): 169–76.

Geiger, J. *Cornelius Nepos and Ancient Political Biography.* Historia Einzelschr., 47 Stuttgart: Steiner, 1985.

Genette, Gérard. *The Architext: An Introduction.* Translated by Jane E. Lewin, forward by Robert Scholes. Berkeley: University of California Press, 1992.

Gentili, Bruno, and Giovanni Cerri. *History and Biography in Ancient Thought.* London Studies in Classical Philology, ed. Giuseppe Giangrande, vol. 20. Amsterdam: J. C. Gieben, 1988.

Georgi, Dieter. "The Records of Jesus in the Light of Ancient Accounts of Revered Men." In *SBLSP*, edited by Lane C. McGaughy, 2:527–42. N.p.: Society of Biblical Literature, 1972.

Gera, Deborah Levine. *Xenophon's "Cyropaedia": Style, Genre, and Literary Technique.* Oxford Classical Monographs. Oxford: Clarendon, 1993.

Gerhart, Mary. "Generic Studies: Their Renewed Importance in Religious and Literary Interpretation." *JAAR* 45 (1977): 309–25.

———. "The Dilemma of the Text: How to Belong to a Genre." *Poetics* 18 (1989): 355–73.

———. "Generic Competence in Biblical Hermeneutics." *Semeia* 43 (1988): 29–44.

Giangrande, G. "On the Origins of the Greek Romance." *Eranos* 60 (1962): 132–59.

Giangrande, Lawrence. *The Use of "Spoudaiogeloion" in Greek and Roman Literature.* Studies in Classical Literature, 6. Hague: Mouton, 1972.

Gill, Christopher. "The Question of Character Development: Plutarch and Tacitus." *CQ* 33 (1983): 469–87.

————. "The Character-Personality Distinction." In *Characterization and Individuality in Greek Literature*, edited by Christopher Pelling, 1–31. Oxford: Clarendon Press, 1990.

Godzich, Wlad. "Correcting Kant: Bakhtin and Intercultural Interactions." *Boundary 2* 18 (1991): 5–17.

Gold, Barbara K. "A Question of Genre: Plato's *Symposium* as Novel." *MLN* 95 (1980): 1353–59.

Goodyear, F. R. D. "Prose Satire." In *CHCL*, vol. 2, pt. 4, *The Early Principate*, edited by E. J. Kenney, 137–42. Cambridge: Cambridge University Press, 1982.

————. "History and Biography." In *CHCL*, vol. 2, pt. 4, *The Early Principate*, edited by E. J. Kenney, 143–70. Cambridge: Cambridge University Press, 1982.

Gossage, A. J. "Plutarch." In *Latin Biography*, edited by T. A. Dorey, Studies in Latin Literature and Its Influence, 45–77. London: Routledge & Kegan Paul, 1967.

Green, Barbara. *Mikhail Bakhtin and Biblical Scholarship: An Introduction.* SBLSS, ed. Danna Nolan Fewell, vol. 38. Atlanta: Society of Biblical Literature, 2000.

Grottanelli, Cristiano. "The Ancient Novel and Biblical Narrative." *Quaderni Urbinati di Cultura Classica* 27 (1987): 7–34.

Grube, G. M. A. *The Greek and Roman Critics.* Toronto: Toronto University Press, 1965. Reprint, Indianapolis: Hackett, 1995.

Grübel, Rainer. "The Problem of Value and Evaluation in Bachtin's Writing." *Russian Literature* 26 (1989): 131–66.

Gruen, Erich S. *Heritage and Hellenism: The Reinvention of Jewish Tradition.* Hellenistic Culture and Society, ed. Anthony W. Bulloch et al., 30. Berkeley: University of California Press, 1998.

Guelich, Robert A. "The Gospels: Portraits of Jesus and His Ministry." *JETS* 24 (1981): 117–25.

————. "The Gospel Genre." In *The Gospel and the Gospels*, edited by P. Stuhlmacher, 173–208. Grand Rapids: Eerdmans, 1991.

Guillén, Claudio. *Literature as System: Essays toward the Theory of Literary History.* Princeton: Princeton University Press, 1971.

Gundry, Robert H. "Recent Investigations into the Literary Genre 'Gospel'." In *New Dimensions in New Testament Study*, edited by Richard N. Longenecker and Merrill C. Tenney, 97–114. Grand Rapids: Zondervan, 1974.

———. "ΕΥΑΓΓΕΛΙΟΝ: How Soon a Book?" *JBL* 115 (1996): 321–25.

Güttgemanns, Erhardt. *Candid Questions concerning Gospel Form Criticism: A Methodological Sketch of the Fundamental Problematics of Form and Redaction Criticism*. Translated by William G. Doty, PTMS, ed. Dikran Y. Hadidian, no. 26. Pittsburgh: Pickwick, 1979.

Hack, R. K. "The Doctrine of Literary Forms." *Harv. Stud.* 27 (1916): 1–65.

Hadas, Moses. *A History of Greek Literature*. New York: Columbia University Press, 1950.

Hadas, Moses, and Morton Smith. *Heroes and Gods: Spiritual Biographies in Antiquity*. Religious Perspectives, ed. Ruth Nanda Anshen, vol. 13. New York: Harper & Row, 1965.

Hägg, Tomas. *Narrative Technique in Ancient Greek Romances: Studies in Chariton, Xenophon Ephesius, and Achilles Tatius*. Skrifter utgivna av Svenska Institutet i Athen 8°, 8. Stockholm: Svenska Institutet i Athen, 1971.

———. *The Novel in Antiquity*. Berkeley: University of California Press, 1983.

Haight, Elizabeth Hazelton. "Oriental Stories in Classical Prose Literature." In *Essays on Ancient Fiction*, 1–45. New York: Longmans, 1936.

Halliwell, Stephen. "Traditional Greek Conceptions of Character." In *Characterization and Individuality in Greek Literature*, edited by Christopher Pelling, 32–59. Oxford: Clarendon Press, 1990.

Hamburger, Käte. *The Logic of Literature*, 2nd rev. ed. Translated by Marilynn J. Rose. Bloomington: Indiana University Press, 1993.

Hanhart, Karel. *The Open Tomb: A New Approach, Mark's Passover Haggadah (+/- 72 C.E.)*. Collegeville, Md.: Michael Glazier, 1994.

Hare, D. R. A. "The Lives of the Prophets." In *The Old Testament Pseudepigrapha*, vol. 2, *Expansions of the "Old Testament" and Legends, Wisdom and Philosophical Literature, Prayers, Psalms, and Odes, Fragments of Lost Judeo-Hellenistic Works*, edited by James H. Charlesworth, 379–99. Garden City, N.Y.: Doubleday, 1985.

Hartman, Lars. "Some Reflections on the Problem of the Literary Genre of the Gospels." In *Text-Centered New Testament Studies: Text-Theoretical Es-*

says on Early Jewish and Early Christian Literature, edited by David Hellholm, 3–23. Tübingen: Mohr Siebeck, 1997.

Hauptmeier, Helmut. "Sketches of Theories of Genre." *Poetics* 16 (1987): 397–430.

Hawtrey, R. S. W. "On Bion the Borysthenite." *Prudentia* 9 (1977): 63–80.

Hedrick, Charles W. "What is a Gospel: Geography, Time and Narrative Structure." *Perspectives in Religious Studies* 10 (Fall 1983): 255–68.

———. "What is a Gospel: Geography, Time and Narrative Structure." *Perspectives in Religious Studies* 10 (Fall 1983): 255–68.

Heiserman, Arthur. *The Novel before the Novel: Essays and Discussion about the Beginnings of Prose Fiction in the West*. Chicago: University of Chicago Press, 1977.

Helm, Rudolf. *Der Antike Roman*. Göttingen: Vandenhoeck & Ruprecht, 1956.

Hengel, Martin. "Literary, Theological, and Historical Problems in the Gospel of Mark." In *The Gospel and the Gospels*, edited by P. Stuhlmacher, translated by John Bowden, 209–51. Grand Rapids: Eerdmans, 1991.

Hernadi, Paul. *Beyond Genre: New Directions in Literary Classification*. Ithaca: Cornell University Press, 1972.

———. "The Scope and Mood of Literary Works: Toward a Poetics beyond Genre." In *Language, Logic, and Genre: Papers from the Poetics and Literary Theory Section, Modern Language Association*, edited by Wallace Martin, 44–54. Lewisburg: Bucknell University Press, 1974.

Hiller, Barbara. "Anmerkungen zu Bachtins Chronotopos-Theorie." In *Roman und Gesellschaft: Internationales Michail Bachtin Colloquium*, herausgeben Hans-Günter Hilbert, 117–21. Jena: Friedrich Schiller Universität, 1984.

Hippocrates (Pseud.). *Hippocrates: Pseudepigraphic Writings*. Edited, translated, with an introduction by Wesley D. Smith, Studies in Ancient Medicine, ed. John Scarborough, vol. 2. Leiden: E. J. Brill, 1990.

Hirsch, E. D., Jr. *Validity in Interpretation*. New Haven: Yale University Press, 1967.

———. *The Aims of Interpretation*. Chicago: University of Chicago Press, 1976.

Hirschkop, Ken, and David Shepherd, eds. *Bakhtin and Cultural Theory*. Manchester: Manchester University Press, 1989.

Hock, Ronald F. "The Greek Novel." In *Greco-Roman Literature and the New Testament: Selected Forms and Genres*, edited by David E. Aune, SBLSBS, ed. Bernard Brandon Scott, no. 21, 127–46. Atlanta: Scholars, 1988.

———. "The Rhetoric of Romance." In *Handbook of Classical Rhetoric in the Hellenistic Period (330 B.C.–A.D. 400)*, edited by Stanley Porter, 445–65. Leiden: E. J. Brill, 1997.

Holland, Phillip Hoyt. "Robert Burton's *Anatomy of Melancholy* and Menippean Satire, Humanist and English." Ph.D. diss., University College London, 1979.

Holquist, Michael. "Answering as Authoring: Mikhail Bakhtin's Trans-Linguistics." In *Bakhtin: Essays and Dialogues on His Work*, edited by Gary Saul Morson, 59–71. Chicago: University of Chicago Press, 1986.

———. *Dialogism: Bakhtin and his World*. New Accents. London: Routledge, 1990.

Holquist, James M., and Katarina Clark. "The Influence of Kant in the Early Work of M. M. Bakhtin." In *Literary Theory and Criticism: Festschrift Presented to René Wellek in Honor of His Eightieth Birthday*, Part I: *Theory*, Edited by Joseph P. Strelka, 2. Aufl., 299–313. New York: Peter Lang, 1985.

Holzberg, Niklas. "A Lesser Known 'Picaresque' Novel of Greek Origin: The *Aesop Romance* and Its Influences." In *Groningen Colloquia on the Novel*, vol. 5, edited by H. Hofmann, 1–16. Groningen: Egbert Forsten, 1993.

———. "Der griechische Briefroman: Versuch einer Gattungstypologie." In *Der griechische Briefroman: Gattungstypologie und Textanalyse*, hrsg. Niklas Holzberg with the assistance of Andreas Beschorner and Stefan Merkle, Classica Monacensia, Münchener Studien zur Klassischen Philologie, hrsg. Hellmut Flashar and Niklas Holzberg, Bd. 8, 1–52. Tübingen: Gunter Narr, 1994.

———. *The Ancient Novel: An Introduction*. Translated by Christine Jackson-Holzberg. London: Routledge, 1995.

———. "The Genre: Novels Proper and the Fringe." In *The Novel in the Ancient World*, edited by Gareth Schmeling, Mnemosyne, Bibliotheca Classica Batava, Supplementum, ed. J. M. Bremer et al., 159, 11–28. Leiden: E. J. Brill, 1996.

———. "Novel-Like Works of Extended Prose Fiction II." In *The Novel in the Ancient World*, edited by Gareth Schmeling, Mnemosyne, Bibliotheca Classica Batava, Supplementum, ed. J. M. Bremer et al., 159, 619–53. Leiden: E. J. Brill, 1996.

Holzberg, Niklas, with assistance from Andreas Beschorner and Stefan Merkle, Hrsg. *Der Äsop-Roman: Motivgeschichte und Erzählstruktur*. Classica Monacensia, Münchener Studien zur Klassischen Philologie, hrsg. Hellmut Flashar and Niklas Holzberg, Bd. 6. Tübingen: Gunter Narr, 1992.

Humphreys, W. Lee. "A Life-Style for Diaspora: A Study of the Tales of Esther and Daniel." *JBL* 92 (1973): 211–23.

————. "Novella." In *Saga, Legend, Fable, Tale, Novella: Narrative Forms in Old Testament Literature*, edited by George W. Coats, JSOTSup, ed. David J. A. Clines and Philip R. Davies, 35, 82–96. Sheffield: JSOT, 1985.

————. "The Story of Esther and Mordecai: An Early Jewish Novella." In *Saga, Legend, Fable, Tale, Novella: Narrative Forms in Old Testament Literature*, edited by George W. Coats, JSOTSup, ed. David J. A. Clines and Philip R. Davies, 35, 97–113. Sheffield: JSOT, 1985.

Iersel, Bas van. "Locality, Structure, and Meaning in Mark." *LB* 53 (1983): 45–54.

Isocrates. *Isocrates*. Translated by George Norlin and La Rue Van Hook, LCL, 3 vols. London: Heinemann; New York: G. P. Putnam's Sons, 1928–45.

Jakobson, Roman. "Linguistics and Poetics." In *Language and Literature*, edited by Krystyna Pomorska and Stephen Rudy, 62–94. Cambridge: Belknap, 1987.

Jemielity, Thomas. *Satire and the Hebrew Prophets*. Literary Currents in Biblical Interpretation, ed. Danna Nolan Fewell and David M. Gunn. Louisville, Ky.: Westminster/John Knox, 1992.

Jenkinson, Edna. "Nepos—An Introduction to Latin Biography." In *Latin Biography*, edited by T. A. Dorey, Studies in Latin Literature and Its Influence, 1–15. London: Routledge & Kegan Paul, 1967.

Julian. *The Works of the Emperor Julian*. Translated by Wilmer Cave Wright. LCL, 3 vols. London: Heinemann; New York: Macmillan, 1913–23.

Kaiser, Mark. "P. N. Medvedev's 'The Collapse of Formalism'." In *Language and Literary Theory: In Honor of Ladislav Matejka*, edited by Benjamin A. Stolz, I. R. Titunik, Lubomír Doležel, Papers in Slavic Philology, vol. 5, 405–41. Ann Arbor: University of Michigan, Department of Slavic Languages and Literatures, 1984.

Kant, Immanuel. *Critique of Pure Reason*. Translated by F. Max Müller. New York: MacMillan, 1915.

Kea, Perry V. "New Testament Literary Genres." *Fourth R* 6, no. 4 (July/August 1993): 10–16.

Keck, Leander E. "Mark 3:7–12 and Mark's Christology." *JBL* 84 (1965): 341–51.

Kee, Howard C. "Aretalogy and Gospel." *JBL* 92 (1973): 402–22.

———. *Aretalogies, Hellenistic "Lives," and the Sources of Mark.* Center for Hermeneutical Studies, Protocol series of the Colloquies, ed. W. Wuellner, 12. Berkeley: The Center for Hermeneutical Studies in Hellenistic and Modern Culture, 1975.

———. "The Socio-Religious Setting and Aims of 'Joseph and Aseneth'." In *SBLSP*, ed. George MacRae, 183–92. Missoula, Mont.: Scholars, 1976.

———. *Community of the New Age: Studies in Mark's Gospel.* Philadelphia: Westminster, 1977. Reprinted with corrections, Macon, Ga.: Mercer University Press, 1983.

———. "The Socio-Cultural Setting of Joseph and Aseneth." *NTS* 29 (1983): 394–413.

Kelber, Werner H. *The Oral and the Written Gospel: The Hermeneutics of Speaking and Writing in the Synoptic Tradition, Mark, Paul, and Q.* Philadelphia: Fortress, 1983.

———. "Apostolic Tradition and the Form of the Gospel." In *Discipleship in the New Testament*, edited by with an introduction by Fernando F. Segovia, 24–46. Philadelphia: Fortress, 1985.

———. "Narrative as Interpretation and Interpretation of Narrative: Hermeneutical Reflections on the Gospels." *Semeia* 39 (1987): 107–33.

Kelly, Aileen M. "The Flesh of Time: Mikhail Bakhtin." In *Views from the Other Shore: Essays on Herzen, Chekhov, and Bakhtin*, Russian Literature and Thought, ed. Gary Saul Morson. New Haven: Yale University Press, 1999.

Kennedy, George A. "The Evolution of a Theory of Artistic Prose." In *The Cambridge History of Literary Criticism*, vol. 1, *Classical Criticism*, edited by George A. Kennedy, 184–99. Cambridge: Cambridge University Press, 1989.

Kent, Thomas. *Interpretation and Genre: The Role of Generic Perception in the Study of Narrative Texts.* Lewisburg: Bucknell University Press; London: Associated University Presses, 1986.

———. "Hermeneutics and Genre: Bakhtin and the Problem of Communicative Interaction." In *The Interpretive Turn: Philosophy, Science, and Culture*, edited by David R. Hiley, James F. Bohman, Richard Shusterman, 282–303. Ithaca: Cornell University Press, 1991.

Kerényi, K. *Die Grieschisch-Orientalische Romanliteratur in religions– geschichtlicher Beleuchtung: Ein Versuch.* Tübingen: Mohr, 1927. Reprint, Darmstadt: n.p., 1962.

———. *Die antike Roman: Einführung und Textauswahl.* Darmstadt: Wissen– schaftliche Buchgesellschaft, 1971.

Kermode, Frank. *The Genesis of Secrecy: On the Interpretation of Narrative.* Cam– bridge: Harvard University Press, 1979.

Kindstrand, Jan Fredrik. *Bion of Borysthenes: A Collection of the Fragments with Introduction and Commentary.* Acta Universitatis Upsaliensis, Studia Grae– ca Upsaliensia, 11. Stockholm: Almqvist & Wiksell, 1976.

Kingsbury, Jack Dean. "The 'Divine Man' as the Key to Mark's Christology: The End of an Era?" *Int* 35 (1981): 243–57.

———. *The Christology of Mark's Gospel.* Philadelphia: Fortress, 1983.

———. *Conflict in Mark: Jesus, Authorities, Disciples.* Minneapolis: Fortress, 1989.

Kirk, Eugene P. *Menippean Satire: An Annotated Catalogue of Texts and Criti– cism.* Garland Reference Library of the Humanities, vol. 191. New York: Garland, 1980.

Kline, Meredith G. "The Old Testament Origins of the Gospel Genre." *WTJ* 38 (1975–76): 1–27.

Knight, Douglas A. "The Understanding of "Sitz im Leben" in Form Criticism." In *SBLSP*, edited by George MacRae, 1:105–25. Cambridge, Mass.: Society of Biblical Literature, 1974.

Knorpp, William Max. "What Relativism Isn't." *Philosophy* 73 (1998): 277–300.

Koester, Helmut. "One Jesus and Four Primitive Gospels." In *Trajectories through Early Christianity*, edited by James M. Robinson and Helmut Koester. Philadelphia: Fortress, 1971.

———. "Apocryphal and Canonical Gospels." *HTR* 73 (1980): 105–30.

———. "From the Kerygma-Gospel to Written Gospels." *NTS* 35 (1989): 361–81.

———. *Ancient Christian Gospels: Their History and Development.* London: SCM; Philadelphia: Trinity, 1990.

Konstan, David. "The Invention of Fiction." In *Ancient Fiction and Early Christian Narrative*, edited by Ronald F. Hock, J. Bradley Chance, and Judith Per–

kins, SBL Symposium Series, ed. Gail R. O'Day, no. 6, 3–17. Atlanta: Scholars, 1998.

Konstantinovic, Zoran. "Bachtins Begriff des 'Chronotopos': Ein Beitrag zum Verhältnis Zeit-Raum in der Theorie des Romans." In *Roman und Gesellschaft: Internationales Michail Bachtin Colloquium*, hrsg. Hans-Günter Hilbert, 109–16. Jena: Friedrich Schiller Universität, 1984.

Kowalski, Edward. "Michail Bakhtins Beitrag zur Entwicklung einer Poetik der literarischen Genres (dargestellt am Beispielseiner romantheoretischen Ansichten)." In *Roman und Gesellschaft: Internationales Michail Bachtin Colloquium*, hrsg. Hans-Günter Hilbert, 25–32. Jena: Friedrich Schiller Universität, 1984.

Kozhinov, Vadim. "Bakhtin and His Readers." In *Critical Essays on Mikhail Bakhtin*, edited by Caryl Emerson, Critical Essays on World Literature, ed. Robert Lecker, 67–80. New York: G. K. Hall, 1999.

Krischer, T. "Die Stellung der Biographie in der griechischen Literatur." *Hermes* 110 (1982): 51–64.

Kristeva, Julia. "The Ruin of a Poetics." In *Russian Formalism: A Collection of Articles and Texts in Translation*, edited by Stephen Bann and John E. Bowlt, 20th Century Studies, 102–19. New York: Barnes & Noble, 1973.

———. "Word, Dialogue, and Novel." In *Desire in Language: A Semiotic Approach to Literature and Art*, edited by Leon S. Roudiez, translated by Thomas Gora, Alice Jardine, and Leon S. Roudiez, 64–91. New York: Columbia University Press, 1980.

Kürzinger, Joseph. "Die Aussage des Papias von Hierapolis zur literarischen Form des Markusevangeliums." *BZ* 21 (1977): 245–64.

Ladin, Jay. "Fleshing Out the Chronotope." In *Critical Essays on Mikhail Bakhtin*, edited by Caryl Emerson, Critical Essays on World Literature, ed. Robert Lecker, 212–36. New York: G. K. Hall, 1999.

Lang, Friedrich Gustav. "Kompositionsanalyse des Markusevangeliums." *ZTK* 74 (1977): 1–24.

Langleben, Maria. "M. Bachtin's Notions of Time and Textanalysis." *Russian Literature* 26 (1989): 167–90.

Lee, Charles Marston. "Varro's Menippean Satires." Ph.D. diss., University of Pittsburgh, 1937.

Lefkowitz, Mary R. "Fictions in Literary Biography: The New Poem and the Archilochus Legend." *Arethusa* 9 (1976): 181–89.

————. "The Poet as Hero: Fifth-century Autobiography and Subsequent Biographical Fiction." *CQ* 28 (1978): 459–69.

————. *The Lives of the Greek Poets*. Baltimore: Johns Hopkins University Press, 1981.

Lejeune, Philippe. "The Autobiographical Contract." In *French Literary Theory Today: A Reader*, edited by Tzvetan Todorov, translated by R. Carter, 192–222. Cambridge: Cambridge University Press; Paris: Éditions de la Maison des Sciences de l'Homme, 1982.

Leo, Friedrich. *Die griechisch-römische Biographie nach ihrer literarischen Form*. Leipzig: Teubner, 1901. Reprint, Hildesheim: Georg Olms, 1990.

Létoublon, Françoise. *Les Lieux Communs du Roman: Stéréotypes Grecs d'Aventure et d'Amour*. Mnemosyne, Bibliotheca Classica Batava, Supplement, ed. A. D. Leeman, C. J. Ruijgh, and H. W. Pleket, 123. Leiden: E. J. Brill, 1993.

Lewis, C. S. *A Preface to Paradise Lost*, revised and enlarged ed. Oxford: Oxford University Press, 1942.

Liefeld, Walter L. "The Hellenistic 'Divine Man' and the Figure of Jesus in the Gospels." *JETS* 16 (1973): 195–205.

Lindsey, William D. "'The Problem of Great Time:' A Bakhtinian Ethics of Discourse." *JR* 73 (1993): 311–28.

Lloyd, Charles S. "An Investigation of Greco-Roman Literary Forms: A Possible Solution to the Question of Gospel Genre." Ph.D. diss., Southwestern Baptist Theological Seminary, 1976.

Lucian of Samosata. *Lucian*. Translated by A. M. Harmon et al., LCL, 8 vols. Cambridge, Ma. : Harvard University Press, 1968–79.

Lührmann, Dieter. "Biographie des Gerechten als Evangelium: Vorstellungen zu einem Markus-Kommentar." *WD* 14 (1977): 25–50.

————. *Das Markusevangelium*. HNT, hrsg. Andreas Lindemann, 3. Tübingen: J. C. B. Mohr (Paul Siebeck), 1987.

MacDonald, Dennis R. *The Homeric Epics and the Gospel of Mark*. New Haven: Yale University Press, 2000.

Major, Wilfred E. "Menander in a Macedonian World." *GRBS* 38 (1997): 41–73.

Malbon, Elizabeth Struthers. "Galilee and Jerusalem: History and Literature in Marcan Interpretation." *CBQ* 44 (1982): 242–55.

————. *Narrative Space and Mythic Meaning in Mark.* New Voices in Biblical Studies. San Francisco: Harper & Row, 1986; reprint, Sheffield: JSOT, 1991.

Mannheim, Karl. *Essays on the Sociology of Knowledge.* Edited by Paul Kecskemeti. New York: Oxford University Press, 1952.

Marcus, Joel. "'The Time has been Fulfilled!' (Mark 1:15)." *Apocalyptic and the New Testament: Essays in Honor of J. Louis Martyn.* Edited by J. Marcus and M. L. Soards, JSNTSup 24, 49–68. Sheffield: JSOT, 1989.

————. "Scripture and Tradition in Mark 7." In *The Scriptures in the Gospels*, edited by C. M. Tuckett, BETL 131, 177–95. Leuven: Leuven University Press, 1997.

————. *Mark 1–8: A New Translation with Introduction and Commentary.* AB 27. New York: Doubleday, 2000.

Mare, W. Harold. "Genre Criticism and the Gospels." In *The Gospels Today: A Guide to Some Recent Developments*, edited by Malcolm J. Robertson, III and William L. Lane, New Testament Student, ed. John H. Skilton, 6, 82–101. Philadelphia: Skilton House, The Sowers, 1990.

Margolin, Uri. "Historical Literary Genre: Its Concept and Its Uses." *Comparative Literature Studies* 10 (1973): 51–59.

Marincola, John. "Genre, Convention, and Innovation in Greco-Roman Historiography." In *The Limits of Historiography: Genre and Narrative in Ancient Historical Texts*, edited by Christina Shuttleworth Kraus, 281–324. Leiden: E. J. Brill, 1999.

Marxsen, Willi. "Bemerkungen zur "Form" der sogenannten synoptischen Evangelien." *TLZ* 81 (1956): cols. 345–48.

————. *Mark the Evangelist: Studies in the Redaction History of the Gospel.* Translated by James Boyce et al. Nashville: Abingdon, 1969.

Mason, H. J. "Romance in a Limestone Landscape." *Classical Philology* 90 (1995): 263–66.

Matzov, Anna. "The Idea of Time in the Works of Bachtin." *Russian Literature* 26 (1989): 209–17.

McCarthy, Carmel, and William Riley. *The Old Testament Short Story.* Message of Biblical Spirituality, ed. Carolyn Osiek, vol. 7. Wilmington, Del.: Michael Glazier, 1986.

————. *The Scandal of the Gospels: Jesus, Story, and Offense*. New York: Oxford University Press, 1994.

Medvedev, P. N. *The Formal Method in Literary Scholarship: A Critical Introduction to Sociological Poetics*. See entry under Bakhtin, M. M., / P. N. Medvedev.

————. "The Formal (Morphological) Method, or Scholarly Salieri-ism" (1925). In Ann Shukman, ed., *Bakhtin School Papers*, translated by Ann Shukman, 51–65.

Mellor, Ronald. "Roman Historiography and Biography." In *Civilization of the Ancient Mediterranean: Greece and Rome*, vol. 3, edited by Michael Grant and Rachel Kitzinger, 1541–62. New York: Charles Scribner's Sons, 1988.

Merenlahti, Petri, and Raimo Hakola. "Reconceiving Narrative Criticism." In *Characterization in the Gospels: Reconceiving Narrative Criticism*, edited by David Rhoads and Kari Syreeni. JSNTSup, vol. 184, 13–48. Sheffield: Sheffield Academic, 1999.

Merkelbach, R. *Roman und Mysterium in der Antike*. Munich: Beck, 1962.

————. "Novel and Aretalogy." In *The Search for the Ancient Novel*, edited by James Tatum, 283–95. Baltimore: Johns Hopkins University Press, 1994.

Mihailovic, Alexander. *Corporeal Words: Mikhail Bakhtin's Theology of Discourse*. Northwestern University Press Studies in Russian Literature and Theory, ed. Caryl Emerson. Evanston, Ill.: Northwestern University Press, 1997.

Moessner, David P. "And Once Again, What Sort of 'Essence'? A Response to Charles Talbert." *Semeia* 43 (1988): 75–84.

Momigliano, Arnaldo. *The Development of Greek Biography*, expanded ed. Cambridge: Harvard University Press, 1993.

————. "History and Biography." In *The Legacy of Greece: A New Appraisal*, edited by M. I. Finley, 155–83. Oxford: Oxford University Press, 1984.

————. "Greek Culture and the Jews." In *The Legacy of Greece: A New Appraisal*, edited by M. I. Finley, 325–46. Oxford: Oxford University Press, 1984.

————. "Ancient Biography and the Study of Religion in the Roman Empire." In *Poikilia: Études offertes à Jean-Pierre Vernant*, Recherches d'histoire et de sciences sociales, 26, 33–48. Paris: École des Hautes Études en Sciences Sociales, 1987.

Moore, Stephen D. "Are the Gospels Unified Narratives?" In *SBLSP*, edited by Kent Harold Richards, 443–58. Atlanta: Scholars, 1987.

Morgan, J. R. "The Greek Novel: Towards a Sociology of Production and Reception." In *The Greek World*, edited by Anton Powell, 130–52. London: Routledge, 1995.

———. "Make-believe and Make Believe: The Fictionality of the Greek Novels." In *Lies and Fiction in the Ancient World,* edited by Christopher Gill and T. P. Wiseman, 175–229. Austin: University of Texas Press, 1993.

Morgan, J. R., and Richard Stoneman, eds. *Greek Fiction: The Greek Novel in Context*. London: Routledge, 1994.

Morson, Gary Saul. "The Heresiarch of *Meta*." *PTL* 3 (1978): 407–27.

———. *The Boundaries of Genre: Dostoevsky's "Diary of a Writer" and the Traditions of Literary Utopia*. Evanston, Ill.: Northwestern University Press, 1981.

———. "The Baxtin Industry." *Slavic and East European Journal* 30 (1986): 81–90.

———. "Prosaics: An Approach to the Humanities." *American Scholar* (autumn, 1988): 515–28.

———. "Prosaics, Criticism, and Ethics." *Formations* 5, no. 2 (1989): 77–95.

———. "Bakhtin, Genres, and Temporality." *New Literary History* 22 (1991): 1071–92.

———. "Prosaic Bakhtin: *Landmarks*, Anti-intelligentsialism, and the Russian Countertradition." In *Bakhtin in Contexts: Across the Disciplines*, edited by Amy Mandelker and Caryl Emerson, Rethinking Theory, 33–78. Evanston, Ill.: Northwestern University Press, 1995.

———. "Prosaics Evolving." *Slavic and East European Journal* 41 (1997): 57–73.

———, ed. *Bakhtin: Essays and Dialogues on His Work*. Chicago: University of Chicago Press, 1986.

Morson, Gary Saul, and Caryl Emerson, eds. *Rethinking Bakhtin: Extensions and Challenges*. Northwestern University Press Series in Russian Literature and Theory, edited by Gary Saul Morson. Evanston, Ill.: Northwestern University Press, 1989.

———. *Mikhail Bakhtin: Creation of a Prosaics*. Stanford: Stanford University Press, 1990.

————. "Extracts from a *Heteroglossary*." In *Dialogue and Critical Discourse: Language, Culture, Critical Theory*, edited by Michael Macovski, 256–72. New York: Oxford University Press, 1997.

Murphy, Nancey. "Textual Relativism, Philosophy of Language, and the Baptist Vision." In *Theology Without Foundations: Religious Practice and the Future of Theological Truth*, edited by Stanley Hauerwas, Nancey Murphy and Mark Nation, 245–70. Nashville: Abingdon, 1994.

Newsome, Carol A. "Bakhtin, the Bible, and Dialogic Truth." *JR* 76 (1996): 290–306.

Nickelsburg, George W. E. "The Genre and Function of the Markan Passion Narrative." *HTR* 73 (1980): 153–84.

————. "Stories of Biblical and Early Post-Biblical Times." In *Jewish Writings of the Second Temple Period: Apocrypha, Pseudepigrapha, Qumran Sectarian Writings, Philo, Josephus*, edited by Michael E. Stone, CRINT, sec. 2, vol. 2, 33–87. Philadelphia: Fortress, 1984.

Oegema, Gerbern S. *The Anointed and His People: Messianic Expectations from the Maccabees to Bar Kochba*. JSP Supplement Series, ed. Lester L. Grabbe and James H. Charlesworth, 27. Sheffield: Sheffield Academic Press, 1998.

O'Sullivan, James N. *Xenophon of Ephesus: His Compositional Technique and the Birth of the Novel*. Untersuchungen zur antiken Literatur und Geschichte, Bd. 44. Berlin: Walter de Gruyter, 1995.

O'Toole, L. M., and Ann Shukman. *Formalism: History, Comparison, Genre*. Russian Poetics in Translation, ed. Anne Shukman, vol. 5. Oxford: University of Essex and Holdan Books, 1978.

Pabst, Bernhard. *Prosimetrum: Tradition und Wandel einer Literaturform Zwischen Spätantike und Spätmittelalter*. Hrsg. Ulrich Ernst and Christel Meier. ORDO: Studien Zur Literatur und Gesellschaft des Mittelalters und der Frühen Neuzeit, Band 4/1. Köln: Böhlau, 1994.

Patterson, David. "Bakhtin on Word and Spirit: The Religiosity of Responsibility." *Cross Currents* 41 (Spring 1991): 33–51.

————. "The Religious Aspect of Bakhtin's Aesthetics." *Renascence* 46 (1993): 55–71.

Peradotto, John. "Texts and Unrefracted Facts: Philology, Hermeneutics and Semiotics." *Arethusa* 16 (1983): 15–33.

Peradotto, John, Paul Allen Miller, and Charles Platter, eds. *Bakhtin and Ancient Studies: Dialogues and Dialogics*." *Arethusa* 26 (1993): 117–216.

Paterson, Gail Anne. "The Divine Man in Hellenistic Popular Religion." Ph.D. diss., Drew University, 1983.

Pelling, C. B. R. "Truth and Fiction in Plutarch's *Lives*." In *Antonine Literature*, edited by D. A. Russell, 19–52. Oxford: Clarendon, 1990.

———. "Childhood and Personality in Greek Biography." In *Characterization and Individuality in Greek Literature*, edited by Christopher Pelling, 213–44. Oxford: Clarendon Press, 1990.

———. "Is Death the End? Closure in Plutarch's *Lives*." In *Classical Closure: Reading the End in Greek and Latin Literature*, edited by Deborah H. Roberts, Francis M. Dunn, and Don Fowler, 228–50. Princeton: Princeton University Press, 1997.

Perlina, Nina. "Bakhtin-Medvedev-Voloshinov: An Apple of Discourse." *University of Ottawa Quarterly* 53, no. 1 (1983): 35–47.

———. "Bakhtin and Buber: Problems of Dialogic Imagination." *Studies in Twentieth Century Literature* 9 (1984): 13–28.

———. *Funny Things are Happening on the Way to the Bakhtin Forum*. Kennan Institute Occasional Paper, no. 231. Washington, D.C.: Wilson Center, 1989.

Perrin, Norman. *What is Redaction Criticism?* GBS, ed. Dan O. Via, Jr. Philadelphia: Fortress, 1969.

———. "The Literary *Gattung* 'Gospel'—Some Observations." *ExpT* 82 (1970–71): 4–7.

Perry, B. E. "Chariton and His Romance from a Literary-Historical Point of View." *American Journal of Philology* 51 (1930): 93–134.

———. *Secundus the Silent Philosopher: The Greek Life of Secundus*. American Philological Association, Philological Monographs, no. 22. Ithaca: American Philological Association, 1964.

———. *The Ancient Romances: A Literary-Historical Account of Their Origins*. Sather Classical Lectures, vol. 37. Berkeley: University of California Press, 1967.

Pervo, Richard I. "Joseph and Aseneth and the Greek Novel." In *SBLSP*, ed. George MacRae, 171–81. Missoula, Mont.: Scholars, 1976.

———. "A Nihilist Fabula: Introducing *The Life of Aesop*." In *Ancient Fiction and Early Christian Narrative*, edited by Ronald F. Hock, J. Bradley Chance, and Judith Perkins, SBL Symposium Series, ed. Gail R. O'Day, no. 6, 77–120. Atlanta: Scholars, 1998.

Petersen, Norman. "Can One Speak of a Gospel Genre?" *Neot* 28, no. 3 (1994): 137–58.

Philo. *Philo*. Translated by F. H. Colson and G. H. Whitaker, LCL, 10 vols. Cambridge, Mass.: Harvard University Press; London: Heinemann, 1968–81.

Philostratus. *Flavii Philostrati opera*. Hrsg. C. L. Kayser, 2 vols. Leipzig: Teubner, 1870. Reprint, Hildesheim: Olms, 1964.

Pinault, Jody Rubin. *Hippocratic Lives and Legends*. Studies in Ancient Medicine, ed. John Scarborough, vol. 4. Leiden: E. J. Brill, 1992.

Plutarch, *Moralia*, Translated by Frank Cole Babbitt et al., LCL, 15 vols. London: Heinemann; Cambridge: Harvard University Press, 1927–76.

Pokorný, Petr. "Die Bedeutung des Markusevangeliums für die Entstehung der christlichen Bibel." In *Texts and Contexts: Biblical Texts in Their Textual and Situational Contexts (Essays in Honor of Lars Hartman)*, edited by Tord Fornberg and David Hellholm, with Christer D. Hellholm, 409–27. Oslo: Scandinavian University Press, 1995.

Ponzio, Augusto, and Angela Biancofiore. "Dialogue et altérité dans les genres littéraires." In *Dialoganalyse 2: Referate der 2. Arbeitstagung Bochum 1988*, Bd. 2., hrsg. Edda Weigand and Hundsnurscher, 163–72. Tübingen: Niemeyer, 1989.

Quasten, Johannes. *Patrology*. Vol. 1, *The Beginnings of Patristic Literature*. Utrecht: Spectrum, 1950. Reprint, Westminster, Md.: Christian Classics, 1986.

Quintilian. *Institutio Oratoria*. Translated by H. E. Butler, LCL, 4 vols. Cambridge, Mass.: Harvard University Press, 1920–22.

Reardon, B. P. "The Greek Novel." *Phoenix* 23 (1969): 291–309.

———. *Courants Littéraires Grecs des IIe et IIIe Siècles Après J.-C.* Paris: Les Belles Lettres, 1971.

———. "The Second Sophistic and the Novel." In *Approaches to the Second Sophistic: Papers Presented at the 105th Annual Meeting of The American Philological Association*, edited by G. W. Bowersock, 23–29. University Park, Penn.: American Philological Association, 1974.

———. "Aspects of the Greek Novel." *GR* 23 (1976): 118–31.

————. "Theme, Structure, and Narrative in Chariton." In *Later Greek Literature*, edited by John J. Winkler and Gordon Williams, YClS, vol. 27, 1–17. Cambridge: Cambridge University Press, 1982.

————. *The Form of Greek Romance*. Princeton: Princeton University Press, 1991.

————. "Chariton." In *The Novel in the Ancient World*, edited by Gareth Schmeling, Mnemosyne, Bibliotheca Classica Batava, Supplementum, ed. J. M. Bremer et al., 159, 309–35. Leiden: E. J. Brill, 1996.

Reardon, B. P., ed. *Collected Ancient Greek Novels*. Berkeley: University of California Press, 1989.

Reed, Walter L. *Dialogues of the Word: The Bible as Literature According to Bakhtin*. New York: Oxford University Press, 1993.

Reiser, Marius. "Der Alexanderroman und das Markusevangelium." In *Markus-Philologie: Historische, literargeschicht-liche und stilistische Untersuchungen zum zweiten Evangelium*, hrsg. Hubert Cancik, WUNT, hrsg. Martin Hengel and Otfried Hofius, 33, 131–63. Tübingen: J. C. B. Mohr (Paul Siebeck), 1984.

————. *Syntax und Stil des Markusevangeliums im Licht der hellenistischen Volksliteratur*. WUNT 2.11. Tübingen: J. C. B. Mohr (Paul Siebeck), 1984.

————. "Die Stellung der Evangelien in der antiken Literaturgeschichte." *ZNW* 90 (1999): 1–27.

Relihan, Joel C. "On the Origin of 'Menippean Satire' as the Name of a Literary Genre." *Classical Philology* 79 (1984): 226–29.

————. *Ancient Menippean Satire*. Baltimore: Johns Hopkins University Press, 1993.

————. "Menippus in Antiquity and the Renaissance." In *The Cynics: The Cynic Movement in Antiquity and Its Legacy*, edited by R. Bracht Branham and Marie-Odile Goulet-Cazé. Berkeley: University of California Press, 1996.

Rhoads, David, Joanna Dewey, and Donald Michie. *Mark as Story: An Introduction to the Narrative of a Gospel*, 2nd ed. Minneapolis: Fortress, 1999.

Riikonen, H. K. *Menippean Satire as a Literary Genre: With Special Reference to Seneca's Apocolocyntosis*. Commentationes Humanarum Litterarum, ed. Holger Thesleff, 83. Helsinki: Finnish Society of Sciences and Letters (Societas Scientiarum Fennica), 1987.

Robbins, Vernon K. "Mark as Genre." In *SBLSP*, edited by Paul J. Achtemeier, 371–99. Chico, Calif.: Scholars, 1980.

————. *Jesus the Teacher: A Socio-Rhetorical Interpretation of Mark.* Philadelphia: Fortress, 1984.

————. "Interpreting the Gospel of Mark as a Jewish Document in a Graeco-Roman World." In *New Perspectives on Ancient Judaism*, edited by Paul V. M. Flesher, 47–72. Lanham, N.Y.: University Press of America, 1990. Reprinted by the author under the same title in, *New Boundaries in Old Territory: Form and Social Rhetoric in Mark.* Emory Studies in Early Christianity, ed. David B. Gowler, 3, 219–42. New York: Peter Lang, 1994.

————. "Text and Context in Recent Studies of the Gospel of Mark." *RelSRev* 17 (1991): 16–23.

Robinson, James M. *The Problem of History in Mark.* Studies in Biblical Theology, no. 21. London: SCM, 1957. Reprinted in *The Problem of History in Mark: And other Marcan Studies*, 55–133. Philadelphia: Fortress, 1982.

————. "The Problem of History in Mark, Reconsidered." *USQR* 20 (1965): 131–47.

————. "On the *Gattung* of Mark (and John)." In *Jesus and Man's Hope*, edited by David G. Buttrick, 1:99–129. Pittsburgh: Pittsburgh Theological Seminary, 1970. Reprinted in *The Problem of History in Mark: And Other Marcan Studies*, 11–39. Philadelphia: Fortress, 1982.

————. "The Gospel as Narrative." In *The Bible and the Narrative Tradition*, edited by Frank McConnell, 97–112. Oxford: Oxford University Press, 1986.

Rohde, Erwin. *Der griechische Roman und seine Vorläufer*, 3. Aufl. Leipzig: Teubner, 1914.

Rosenmeyer, Thomas G. "Ancient Literary Genres: A Mirage?" *Yearbook of Comparative and General Literature* 34 (1985): 74–84.

Ruf, Frederick J. "The Consequences of Genre: Narrative, Lyric, and Dramatic Intelligibility." *JAAR* 62 (1994): 799–818.

Russell, D. A. "On Reading Plutarch's *Lives*." *GR* 13 (1966): 139–54.

————. *Criticism in Antiquity.* Berkeley: University of California, 1981.

Russell, D. A., and M. Winterbottom, eds. *Ancient Literary Criticism: The Principle Texts in New Translations.* Oxford: Oxford University Press, 1972.

Rzhevsky, Nicholas. "Kozhinov on Bakhtin." *New Literary History* 25 (1994): 429–44.

Sandmel, Samuel. "Prolegomena to a Commentary on Mark." In *Two Living Traditions: Essays on Religion and the Bible*, 147–57. Detroit: Wayne State University Press, 1972.

Sandy, Gerald N. "Recent Scholarship on the Prose Fiction of Classical Antiquity." *CW* 67 (1974): 321–59.

Saussure, Ferdinand de. *Course in General Linguistics*. Edited by Charles Bally and Albert Sechehaye, in collaboration with Albert Riedlinger, translated with introduction and notes by Wade Baskin. New York: McGraw Hill, 1966.

Schaeffer, Jean-Marie. *Qu'est-ce qu'un genre littéraire?* Poétique, ed. Gérard Genette. Paris: Éditions du Seuil, 1989.

———. "Literary Genres and Textual Genericity." In *The Future of Literary Theory*, edited by Ralph Cohen, 167–87. New York: Routledge, 1989.

Scheler, Max. *Problems of a Sociology of Knowledge*. Edited with an introduction by Kenneth W. Stikkers, translated by Manfred S. Frings, International Library of Sociology. London, Routledge & Kegan Paul, 1980.

Schildgen, Brenda Deen. "A Blind Promise: Mark's Retrieval of Esther." *Poetics Today* 15 (1994): 115–31.

———. *Crisis and Continuity: Time in the Gospel of Mark*. JSNTSS, ed. Stanley E. Porter, 159. Sheffield: Sheffield Academic, 1998.

Schmeling, Gareth, ed. *The Novel in the Ancient World*. Mnemosyne, Bibliotheca Classica Batava, Supplementum, ed. J. M. Bremer et al., 159. Leiden: E. J. Brill, 1996.

Schmidt, Karl Ludwig. "Die Stellung der Evangelien in der allgemeinen Literaturgeschichte." In *ΕΥΧΑΡΙΣΤΗΡΙΟΝ: Studien zur Religion und Literature des Alten und Neuen Testaments*, hrsg. Hermann Gunkel and Hans Schmidt, FRLANT, vol. 2, 50–134. Göttingen: Vandenhoeck & Ruprecht, 1923. Reprinted in, *Neues Testament Judentum Kirche: Kleine Schriften*, hrsg. Gerhard Sauter, 37–130. Munich: Chr. Kaiser, 1981.

Schneemelcher, Wilhelm. "Introduction: Gospels." In *New Testament Apocrypha*, rev. ed., edited by E. Hennecke and W. Schneemelcher, translated by R. McL. Wilson, 1:77–87. Cambridge: James Clarke; Louisville: Westminster/John Knox, 1991.

Schniewind, Julius. "Zur Synoptiker-Exegese." *TRu* n.F. 2 (1930): 129–89.

Scholz, Bernard F. "Bakhtin's Concept of 'Chronotope': The Kantian Connection." In *The Contexts of Bakhtin: Philosophy, Authorship, Aesthetics*, edited by

David Shepherd, Studies in Russian and European Literature, ed. Peter I. Barta and David Shepherd, 2, 141–72. Amsterdam: Harwood, 1998.

Schrier, O. J. "A Simple View of *Peripeteia*." *Mnemosyne* 33 (1980): 96–118.

Scobie, Alexander. *Aspects of the Ancient Romance and its Heritage: Essays on Apuleius, Petronius, and the Greek Romances*. Beiträge zur Klassischen Philologie, hrsg. Reinhold Merkelbach, Heft. 30. Meisenheim am Glan: Anton Hain, 1969.

Scullion, John J. "*Märchen, Sage, Legende*: Towards a Clarification of Some Literary Terms Used by Old Testament Scholars." *VT* 34 (1984): 321–36.

Seldon, Daniel L. "Genre of Genre." In *The Search for the Ancient Novel*, edited by James Tatum, 39–64. Baltimore: Johns Hopkins University Press, 1994.

Shaitanov, Igor'. "The Concept of the Generic Word: Bakhtin and the Russian Formalists." In *Face to Face: Bakhtin in Russia and the West*, edited by Carol Adlam et al., 233–53. Sheffield: Sheffield Academic Press, 1997.

Shim, Ezra S. B. "A Suggestion about the Genre or Text-type of Mark." *Scriptura* 50 (1994): 69–89.

Shiner, Whitney. "Creating Plot in Episodic Narratives: *The Life of Aesop* and the Gospel of Mark." In *Ancient Fiction and Early Christian Narrative*, edited by Ronald F. Hock, J. Bradley Chance, and Judith Perkins, SBL Symposium Series, ed. Gail R. O'Day, no. 6, 155–76. Atlanta: Scholars, 1998.

Shipley, D. R. *A Commentary on Plutarch's "Life of Agesilaos": Response to Sources in the Presentation of Character*. Oxford: Clarendon, 1997.

Shukman, Ann. "Soviet Semiotics and Literary Criticism." *New Literary History* 9 (1978): 189–97.

———. "Between Marxism and Formalism: The Stylistics of Mikhail Bakhtin." *Comparative Criticism* 2 (1980): 221–34.

———. "M. M. Bakhtin: Notes on His Philosophy of Man." In *Poetry Prose and Public Opinion: Aspects of Russia, 1850–1970*, edited by William Harrison and Avril Pyman, 241–50. Letchworth, England: Avebury, 1984.

———, ed. *Bakhtin School Papers*. Translated by Noel Owen and Joe Andrew, Russian Poetics in Translation, ed. Anne Shukman, vol. 10. Oxford: RPT Publications, 1983.

Shuler, Philip L., Jr. "The Synoptic Gospels and the Problem of Genre." Ph.D. Diss., McMaster University, 1975.

————. *A Genre for the Gospels: The Biographical Character of Matthew.* Philadelphia: Fortress, 1982.

————. "The Genre(s) of the Gospels." In *The Interrelations of the Gospels: A Symposium Led by M.-É. Boismard, W. R. Farmer, and F. Neirynck (Jerusalem 1984)*, edited by David L. Dungan, BETL, 95, 458–83. Leuven: Leuven University Press, 1990.

Smith, D. Moody. "John and the Synoptics and the Question of Gospel Genre." In *The Four Gospels 1992: Festschrift Frans Neirynck*, edited by F. Van Segbroeck et al., BETL, 100, 3:1783–97. Leuven: Leuven University Press/Peeters, 1992.

Smith, Jonathan Z. "Good News Is No News: Aretalogy and Gospel." In *Christianity, Judaism and Other Greco-Roman Cults: Studies for Morton Smith at Sixty, Part 1, New Testament*, edited by Jacob Neusner, Studies in Judaism and Late Antiquity, ed. Jacob Neusner, vol. 12, 21–38. Leiden: E. J. Brill, 1975.

Smith, Morton. "Prolegomena to a Discussion of Aretalogies, Divine Men, the Gospels and Jesus." *JBL* 90 (1971): 174–99.

————. "On the History of the 'Divine Man'." In *Paganisme, Judaïsme, Christianisme: Influences et affrontements dans le monde antique*, 335–45. Paris: Éditions E. de Boccard, 1978.

Staiger, Emil. *Basic Concepts of Poetics.* Edited by Marianne Burkhard and Luanne T. Frank, translated by Janette C. Hudson and Luanne T. Frank, with an introduction by Luanne T. Frank. University Park: Pennsylvania State University Press, 1991.

Standaert, Benoît. *L'Évangile selon Marc: Composition et genre littéraire.* Brugge: Zevenkerken, 1978. Reprint, 1984.

Stanton, G. N. "The Gospel Traditions and Early Christological Reflection." In *Christ, Faith, and History*, edited by S. W. Sykes and J. P. Clayton, 191–204. Cambridge: Cambridge University Press, 1972.

————. *Jesus of Nazareth in New Testament Preaching.* SNTSMS, ed. Matthew Black, 27. Cambridge: Cambridge University Press, 1974.

————. "Matthew: ΒΙΒΛΟΣ, ΕΥΑΓΓΕΛΙΟΝ, or ΒΙΟΣ,?" In *The Four Gospels 1992: Festschrift Frans Neirynck*, edited by F. Van Segbroeck et al., BETL, 100, 2:1187–201. Leuven: Leuven University Press/Peeters, 1992.

Stephens, Susan A., and John J. Winkler. *Ancient Greek Novels: The Fragments: Introduction, Text, Translation, and Commentary*. Princeton: Princeton University Press, 1995.

Strecker, Georg. *History of New Testament Literature*. Translated by Calvin Katter with Hans-Joachim Mollenhauer. Harrisburg, Pa.: Trinity, 1997.

Strelka, Joseph P., ed. *Theories of Literary Genre*. Yearbook of Comparative Criticism, vol. 8. University Park: Pennsylvania State University Press, 1978.

Stuart, Duane Reed. *Epochs of Greek and Roman Biography*. Sather Classical Lectures, vol. 4. Berkeley: University of California Press, 1928; Reprint, New York: Biblo and Tannen, 1967.

Stuhlmacher, Peter. "The Genre(s) of the Gospels: Response to P. L. Shuler." In *The Interrelations of the Gospels: A Symposium Led by M.-É. Boismard, W. R. Farmer, and F. Neirynck (Jerusalem 1984)*, edited by David L. Dungan, BETL, 95, 484–94. Leuven: Leuven University Press, 1990.

Stutterheim, Cornelis F. P. "Prolegomena to a Theory of the Literary Genres." *Zagadnienia Rodzajów Literackich* 6, no. 2 (11) (Lodz 1964): 5–24.

Suvin, Darko. "On Metaphoricity and Narrativity in Fiction: The Chronotope as the *Differentia Generica*." *Substance* 14, no. 3 (1986): 51–67.

Swain, Simon. "Biography and Biographic in the Literature of the Roman Empire." In *Portraits: Biographical Representation in the Greek and Latin Literature of the Roman Empire*, edited by M. J. Edwards and Simon Swain, 1–37. Oxford: Clarendon, 1997.

Swinden, Patrick. *Literature and the Philosophy of Intention*. New York: St. Martin's, 1999.

Swingewood, Alan. *Sociological Poetics and Aesthetic Theory*. New York: St. Martin's, 1987.

Talbert, Charles H. *What is a Gospel? The Genre of the Canonical Gospels*. Philadelphia: Fortress, 1977. Reprint, Macon, Ga.: Mercer University Press, 1985.

———. "Biographies of Philosophers and Rulers as Instruments of Religious Propaganda in Mediterranean Antiquity." In *ANRW* 2.16.2, hrsg. Hildegard Temporini and Wolfgang Haase, 1619–51. Berlin: Walter de Gruyter, 1978.

———. "The Gospel and the Gospels." *Int* 33 (1979): 351–62.

———. "Once Again: Gospel Genre." *Semeia* 43 (1988): 53–73.

Tannen, Deborah. "Involvement as Dialogue: Linguistic Theory and the Relation between Conversational and Literary Discourse." In *Dialogue and Critical Discourse: Language, Culture, Critical Theory*, edited by Michael Macovski, 137–57. New York: Oxford University Press, 1997.

Telford, William R. "The Interpretation of Mark: A History of Developments and Issues." In *The Interpretation of Mark*, 2nd ed., edited by William R. Telford, Studies in New Testament Interpretation, ed. Robert Morgan, 1–61. Edinburgh: T & T Clark, 1995.

———. "The Pre-Markan Tradition in Recent Research (1980–1990)." In *The Four Gospels 1992: Festschrift Frans Neirynck*, edited by F. Van Segbroeck et al., BETL, 100, 2:693–723. Leuven: Leuven University Press/Peeters, 1992.

Thatcher, Tom. "The Gospel Genre: What Are We After?" *ResQ* 36 (1994): 129–38.

Thibault, Paul. "Narrative Discourse as a Multi-Level System of Communication: Some Theoretical Proposals Concerning Bakhtin's Dialogic Principle." *Studies in Twentieth Century Literature* 9 (1984): 89–117.

Thompson, Ewa M. *Russian Formalism and Anglo-American New Criticism: A Comparative Study*. De Proprietatibus Litterarum, ed. C. H. Van Schooneveld, Series Maior, 8. Hague: Mouton, 1971.

Thomson, Clive. "Bakhtin's 'Theory' of Genre." *Studies in Twentieth Century Literature* 9 (1984): 29–40.

Tihanov, Galin. "Reification and Dialogue: Aspects of the Theory of Culture in Lukács and Bakhtin." *Bakhtin Centre Papers*. September 9, 1998. <http://www.shef.ac.uk/uni/academic/A-C/bakh/tihanov.html> (June 12, 2000).

Tiede, David L. "Religious Propaganda and the Gospel Literature of the Early Christian Mission." In *ANRW* 2.25.2, hrsg. H. Temporini and W. Haase, 1705–29. Berlin: Walter de Gruyter, 1984.

Titunik, I. R. "The Formal Method and the Sociological Method (M. M. Bakhtin, P. N. Medvedev, V. N. Voloshinov) in Russian Theory and Study of Literature." In *Marxism and the Philosophy of Language*, translated by Ladislav Matejka and I. R. Titunik, Studies in Language, ed. Michael Silverstein, vol. 1, 175–200. New York: Seminar, 1973.

———. "M. M. Baxtin (The Baxtin School) and Soviet Semiotics." *Dispositio* 1 (1976): 327–38.

———. "Bakhtin &/or Vološinov &/or Medvedev: Dialogue &/or Doubletalk?" In *Language and Literary Theory: In Honor of Ladislav Matejka*, edited by Benjamin A. Stolz, I. R. Titunik Lubomír Doležel, Papers in Slavic Philology, vol. 5, 535–64. Ann Arbor: University of Michigan, Department of Slavic Languages and Literatures, 1984.

———. "The Baxtin Problem: Concerning Katrina Clark and Michael Holquist's *Mikhail Bakhtin*." *Slavic and East European Journal* 30 (1986): 91–95.

Todorov, Tzvetan. *The Fantastic: A Structural Approach to a Literary Genre*. Translated by Richard Howard, with a forward by Robert Scholes. Ithaca: Cornell University Press, 1975.

———. "The Methodological Heritage of Formalism." In *The Poetics of Prose*, translated by Richard Howard, with a forward by Jonathan Culler, 247–67. Ithaca: Cornell University Press, 1977.

———. "Bakhtin's Theory of the Utterance." In *Semiotic Themes*, edited by Richard T. DeGeorge, University of Kansas Publications Humanistic Studies, vol. 53, 165–78. Lawrence: University of Kansas Publications, 1981.

———. *Mikhail Bakhtin: The Dialogic Principle*. Translated by Wlad Godzich, THL, ed. Wlad Godzich and Jochen Schulte-Sasse, vol. 13. Minneapolis: University of Minnesota Press, 1984.

———. *Literature and Its Theorists: A Personal View of Twentieth-Century Criticism*. Translated by Catherine Porter. Ithaca: Cornell University Press, 1987.

———. *Genres in Discourse*. Translated by Catherine Porter. Cambridge: Cambridge University Press, 1990.

Tolbert, Mary Ann. *Sowing the Gospel: Mark's World in Literary-Historical Perspective*. Minneapolis: Fortress, 1989.

———. "The Gospel in Greco-Roman Culture." In *The Book and the Text: The Bible and Literary Theory*, edited by Regina M. Schwartz, 258–75. Cambridge, Mass.: Basil Blackwell, 1990.

Tomashevsky, Boris. "Literary Genres." In *Formalism: History, Comparison, Genre*, edited by L. M. O'Toole and Ann Shukman, translated by L. M. O'Toole, 52–93.

Toporov, V. N. "Toward the Problem of Genres in Folklore." In *Semiotics and Structuralism: Readings from the Soviet Union*, edited by with an introduction by Henryk Baran, 76–86. White Plains, N.Y.: International Arts and Sciences, 1976.

Toulmin, Stephen. "The Marginal Relevance of Theory to the Humanities." *Common Knowledge* 2 (1993): 75–84.

Townend, G. B. "Suetonius and His Influence." In *Latin Biography*, edited by T. A. Dorey, Studies in Latin Literature and Its Influence, 79–111. London: Routledge & Kegan Paul, 1967.

Trenkner, Sophie. *The Greek Novella in the Classical Period*. Cambridge: Cambridge University Press, 1958.

Ugolnik, Anthony. "Textual Liturgics: Russian Orthodoxy and Recent Literary Criticism." *Religion and Literature* 22 (Summer-Autumn 1990): 133–54.

Usher, Stephen. "Greek Historiography and Biography." In *Civilization of the Ancient Mediterranean: Greece and Rome*, vol. 3, edited by Michael Grant and Rachel Kitzinger, 1525–40. New York: Charles Scribner's Sons, 1988.

Via, Dan O., Jr. *Kerygma and Comedy in the New Testament: A Structuralist Approach to Hermeneutic*. Philadelphia: Fortress, 1975.

Vice, Sue. *Introducing Bakhtin*. Manchester: Manchester University Press, 1997.

Viëtor, Karl. "Probleme der literarischen Gattungsgeschichte." *Deutsche Vierteljahrsschrift für Literaturwissenschaft und Geistesgeschichte* 9 (1931): 425–47.

Vivas, Eliseo. "Literary Classes: Some Problems." *Genre* 1 (1968): 97–105.

Vološinov, V. N. "Discourse in Life and Discourse in Art: Concerning Sociological Poetics" (1926). In *Freudianism: A Critical Sketch*, edited by I. R. Titunik in collaboration with Neal H. Bruss, translated by I. R. Titunik. Bloomington: Indiana University Press, 1987.

———. *Marxism and the Philosophy of Language* (1930). Translated by Ladislav Matejka and I. R. Titunik, Studies in Language, ed. Michael Silverstein, vol. 1. New York: Seminar, 1973.

———, [M. M. Bakhtin]. "Literary Stylistics" (1930). In *Bakhtin School Papers*, edited by Ann Shukman, translated by Noel Owen and Joe Andrew, 93–152.

Vorster, W. S. "Mark: Collector, Redactor, Author, Narrator?" *Journal of Theology for Southern Africa* 31 (1980): 46–61.

———. "Kerygma/History and the Gospel Genre." *NTS* 29 (1983): 87–95.

———. "Der Ort der Gattung Evangelium in der Literaturgeschichte." *VF* 29 (1984): 2–25.

Voßkamp, Wilhelm. "Gattungen." In *Literaturwissenschaft: Ein Grundkurs*, 4. aufl. Hrsg. Helmut Brackert, and Jörn Stückrath, Rowohlts Enzyklopädie, 253–69. Reinbek bei Hamburg: Rowohlt, 1996.

Votaw, Clyde Weber. "The Gospels and Contemporary Biographies." *AJT* 19 (1915): 45–73 and 217–49. Reprinted as *The Gospels and Contemporary Biographies in the Greco-Roman World*, FBBS, ed. John Reumann, 27. Philadelphia: Fortress, 1970.

Wallis, Bascom. *Mark's Memory of the Future: A Study in the Art of Theology*. North Richland Hills, Tex.: Bibal, 1995.

Weinstein, Marc. "Qu'est-ce Qu'un Genre Littéraire? (Propositions par-delà le Linguisticisme)." *Champs Du Signe* 3 (1992): 201–32.

Weisman, Ze'ev. *Political Satire in the Bible*. SBLSS, ed. Vincent L. Wimbush, no. 32. Atlanta: Scholars, 1998.

Wellek, René. "Genre Theory, the Lyric, and *Erlebnis*." In *Discriminations: Further Concepts of Criticism*, 223–52. New Haven: Yale University Press, 1970.

Wellek, René, and Austin Warren. *Theory of Literature*, 3rd ed. New York: Harcourt Brace Jovanovich, 1956.

White, Sidnie Ann. "In the Steps of Jael and Deborah: Judith as Heroine." In *"No One Spoke Ill of Her": Essays on Judith*, edited by James C. VanderKam, SBLEJL, ed. William Adler, no. 2, 5–16. Atlanta: Scholars, 1992.

Wilder, Amos Niven. *Early Christian Rhetoric: The Language of the Gospels*. New York: Harper & Row, 1964. Reprint, Cambridge, Mass.: Harvard University Press, 1971.

Wilamowitz-Moellendorf, U. von. "Plutarch as Biographer," translated by Juliane Kerkhecker. In *Essays on Plutarch's "Lives,"* edited by Barbara. Scardigli, 47–74. Oxford: Clarendon, 1995.

Williams, Juanita Sullivan. "Towards a Definition of Menippean Satire." Ph.D. diss., Vanderbilt University, 1966.

Wills, Lawrence M. "The Jewish Novellas." In *Greek Fiction: The Greek Novel in Context*, edited by J. R. Morgan and Richard S., 223–38. London: Routledge, 1994.

———. *The Jewish Novel in the Ancient World*. Myth and Poetics, ed. Gregory Nagy. Ithaca: Cornell University Press, 1995.

————. *The Quest of the Historical Gospel: Mark, John, and the Origins of the Gospel Genre*. London: Routledge, 1997.

————. "The Book of Judith." In *The New Interpreter's Bible*, 3.1073–183. Nashville: Abingdon, 1999.

Wimsatt, W. K., and Monroe C. Beardslee. "The Intentional Fallacy." In *The Verbal Icon: Studies in the Meaning of Poetry*, 3–18. Lexington: University of Kentucky Press, 1954.

Winkler, John J. *Auctor & Actor: A Narratological Reading of Apuleius's "The Golden Ass."* Berkeley: University of California Press, 1985.

————. "The Novel." In *Civilization of the Ancient Mediterranean: Greece and Rome*, edited by Michael Grant and Rachel Kitzinger, 3:1563–72. New York: Charles Scribner's Sons, 1988.

————. "The Invention of Romance." In *The Search for the Ancient Novel*, edited by James Tatum, 23–38. Baltimore: Johns Hopkins University Press, 1994.

Wittgenstein, Ludwig. *Philosophical Investigations*, 3rd ed. Translated by G. E. M. Anscombe. New York: Macmillan, 1958.

Wrege, Hans-Theo. *Die Gestalt des Evangeliums: Aufbau und Struktur der Synoptiker sowie der Apostelgeschichte*. BBET, hrsg. Jürgen Becker and Henning Graf Reventlow, Bd. 11. Frankfurt am Main: Lang, 1978.

Xenophon. *Xenophon*. Translated by Carleton L. Brownson et al., LCL, 7 vols. Cambridge, Mass.: Harvard University Press, 1918–68.

Zavala, Iris M. "Bakhtin and the Third: Communication as Response." *Critical Studies* 1, no. 2 (1989): 43–63.

Zhongwen, Qian. "Problems of Bakhtin's Theory about 'Polyphony'." *New Literary History* 28 (1997): 779–90.

Zima, Peter V. "Bakhtin's Young Hegelian Aesthetics." *Critical Studies* 1, no. 2 (1989): 77–94.

Index of Modern Authors

Index of Texts Cited